Winning with Data in the Business of Sports

New technologies mean that sports clubs and governing bodies are generating more data than ever to help manage their relationship with fans, their performance, and their income streams. This new edition of *Winning with Data in the Business of Sports* explains how to acquire, store, maintain, and use data in the most effective ways. The key developments are three-fold: new technology, new understanding of how to apply that technology, and the new laws informing and controlling the data that can be generated from the technology.

Important developments that have occurred since the publication of the first edition include the General Data Protection Regulations (GDPR) and the COVID-19 pandemic. With a focus on these unique challenges, coupled with the opportunities the use of data creates, this book is essential reading for professionals within the sports industry. This second edition includes:

- An introduction to new technologies, the data they generate, and the supporting processes we need to have in place to use them.
- Brand new case studies with recent examples of creative applications from clubs, teams, leagues, and governing bodies, including Arsenal, AS Roma, ICC Cricket World Cup, LA Kings, Portland Trail Blazers, and UEFA.
- The sports industry's response to tighter data legislation introduced primarily though the GDPR.
- The role of data and direct engagement during the COVID-19 pandemic.

The book provides clear guidance and knowledge that sports industry professionals need to understand the role of data for the business side of sports. It is essential reading for sports clubs, governing bodies, and those working in sports marketing, media, and communications, sponsorship, merchandise, ticketing, events, and participation development. The book will also be of interest to students of sports management.

Fiona Green has operated in the sports industry for over 30 years. Her experience has predominantly been representing rights owners in sponsorship, TV rights, and merchandise/licensing across many sports including football, athletics, cricket, sailing, rugby, Formula 1, horse racing, and tennis. Fiona specialises in the field of data-driven marketing, business intelligence, and analytics and applies her knowledge of this area to her inherent understanding of a rights owner's business model and objectives, specifically in revenue generation, participation growth, and stakeholder engagement.

Winning with Data in the Business of Sports

CRM and Analytics

Second edition

Fiona Green

Routledge
Taylor & Francis Group
LONDON AND NEW YORK

Second edition published 2021
by Routledge
2 Park Square, Milton Park, Abingdon, Oxon, OX14 4RN

and by Routledge
52 Vanderbilt Avenue, New York, NY 10017

Routledge is an imprint of the Taylor & Francis Group, an informa business

[First edition published by Routledge 2018]

British Library Cataloguing-in-Publication Data
A catalogue record for this book is available from the British Library

Library of Congress Cataloging-in-Publication Data
A catalog record for this book has been requested

ISBN: 978-0-367-61070-8 (hbk)
ISBN: 978-0-367-61195-8 (pbk)
ISBN: 978-1-003-10456-8 (ebk)

Typeset in Bembo
by Apex CoVantage, LLC

Contents

Figures

Foreword

In the short few years since *Winning with Data* was released, it went from being a 'valuable guide' to an indispensable manifesto. It's not just because this second edition contains critical new chapters and insights, but also because the world has changed dramatically. If you were the person who anticipated a global pandemic that would lead to the death of hundreds of thousands of people, or expected the biggest economic downturn since the Great Depression, or predicted that sports events around the globe would be cancelled by the thousands, please raise your hand. Right, me neither.

There are four realities that make *Winning with Data* one of the most important books that any sports business executive or student will read. First, we live in a time when the only thing we can be certain about is that the world was different yesterday and will be different tomorrow. There was a time when change evolved. It materialised over months and years. Today we live in a world where technology is winning the war against stability. The velocity of information sharing is a major catalyst for change. The half-billion tweets per day and the 4 billion users across all social media platforms worldwide are drizzling fuel on the fire of 'change'. In the past, as new ways of doing business emerged, there were early adopters and laggards, but even the latter eventually 'caught up' to run with the crowd. But now, even putting our smart phones down for a day is a terrorising thought, as we live in fear that we will fall behind forever.

The second reality is the data and information explosion are radically transforming the way we do business, as they provide deeper and more personal insights about our customers and prospective customers. Customers now *expect* you to know them on a more personal level and to cater to their interests. If your products, the medium you choose to communicate, the messaging, and even the tone of your interactions aren't tailored to their needs and preferences, then you will lose, because your competitor *will* likely be engaged in a way that connects and resonates with your customers.

The third reality is that sports fans are different from packaged-goods consumers or consumers of other goods and services. The sports 'sale' is less transactional as the relationship between athletes, clubs, and leagues and their fans has always been complicated. While price, service experience, convenience, and value are all important considerations, it's not an entirely rational relationship. The traditional factors are relevant, but they are commingled with deeper psychological and sociological issues like identity and the in-group/out-group behaviours that are associated with membership in a fan community. Unmistakably, the most productive and profitable fan relationships are built on the foundation of a deep understanding of customers' behaviours and attitudes and an ability to 'connect'. A high-performance CRM can be your secret sauce.

Finally, in order to effectively compete in this new world disorder, you need to institutionalise not only the tools and processes to compete but also build a culture that continuously adapts to change – create a learning organisation. A learning organisation is a means to acquiring antibodies that inoculate an organisation from the deadliest of all diseases – maintaining the status quo and resisting change. For most, change produces anxiety, while accelerated change can lead to mind-numbing chaos. The key is to create structure amidst the chaos and to channel processes and systems into the development of next-gen products, pricing structures, and new service models and ultimately value propositions, which employ new media and messaging. Once you've embraced these four principles, *Winning with Data* will be your playbook. It provides the foundation to creating a culture that embraces systemic change.

On a personal level, I value this book from two vantage points: as a sports business educator and as a consultant and advisor to professional sports organisations. As an educator, I delight in developing our students' critical thinking, allowing them to hone their problem-solving skills. Their ability to clearly define problems and process data and information in a way that reduces natural biases allows our students to have an immediate impact on organisations from their first day on the job. Throughout this book there are valuable lessons and case studies which facilitate this learning. From the ICC Cricket World Cup to the Portland Trailblazer's approach to retention modelling for season ticket holders, we can explore the range of applications enabled by a comprehensive CRM system. There are also illustrations of how data-driven marketing can be a difference-maker not only for large-scale professional sports organisations but also for a third-tier English football club that lacks the capability for a massive investment in technology.

Wearing my consultant's hat, I value the insights on topics like data governance, the debate as to the effectiveness of loyalty programs, Major League Soccer's approach to developing customer personas, and the hot topic of data and the law. Another important area that is changing rapidly is sponsorships. There are value-creation opportunities from targeting the optimal-fit sponsor for a sports brand or developing a leads-generation process that more directly generates revenue for sponsors. The use of data to address a crisis is another important lesson showcased through a case study of the LA Kings and the impact the coronavirus has had on their data modelling: what they thought they knew about their fans has been revamped, as the pandemic has led to changes in their fans' behaviour, feelings, and priorities.

Finally, I am most impressed with the thought-provoking final chapter, which wades into the implications of machine learning, neural networks, and blockchain on the future of CRM. From beginning to end, the perceptive insights of this timely, well-written book will provide many answers and, more importantly, will equip you to address the next generation of questions. It's time to cease our 'fiddling' with this introduction and allow you to get on with the substance of this wonderful book. After all, Rome is burning.

Vince Gennaro

Associate Dean, NYU Tisch Institute for Global Sport

Author, *Diamond Dollars: The Economics of Winning in Baseball*

Preface to the second edition

A book is rarely free from error and can often be improved, so from the minute I submitted the manuscript for the first edition I knew there were areas I would have liked to update. I spotted typos that I previously missed and references that were slightly misaligned, but more than that, my knowledge of, and exposure to, industry-use cases that I wanted to share had increased in the time between submitting the manuscript and the book's publication. I was also fortunate enough to receive lots of feedback from readers of the first edition, along with recommendations for changes and additions, should I get the opportunity.

With this knowledge, I first approached Routledge, the publishers of this book, with a proposal for a second edition in December 2019, and at that time very few of us knew the term *coronavirus*, and the name *COVID-19* had not yet been given to the disease. Yet during the time I've spent updating this book, we have seen an unparalleled amount of change around the world. Our freedom to travel, shop, and socialise; to meet with our friends and families; to mourn their passing or share in their celebrations was taken away from us during a period of 'lockdown'. At the time of writing, we still don't know what the 'new normal' will be.

Among all the industries considered the hardest hit, sport has to be up there along with the travel, retail, and food and drink industries. And while the financial loss will not have been of the same scale – purely because the sports industry is by far the smallest of these sectors – the impact of matches and competitions being cancelled or postponed has created a real threat to business continuity among many rights owners.

In my view this has only emphasised the importance of acquiring, analysing, and using data in the business of sports and through the generous contribution of many rights owners, industry professionals, and journalists to the case studies and reference points, I hope to bring this to life for you.

Throughout this book there are references to the coronavirus, COVID-19, and the global pandemic, but some other key additions in this second edition include:

- An update to the Major League Soccer case study to include its approach to personas through the 'jobs-to-be-done' framework.

- An update to the case study from Mic Conetta at Arsenal, discussing transformational business change when implementing structural reorganisation.
- The addition of case studies from AS Roma, ICC Cricket World Cup, LA Kings, Lincoln City Football Club, Portland Trail Blazers, and Team INEOS.
- The introduction of a framework for sponsorship that encourages rights owners to think and behave like digital advertisers.
- A look at the impact of increased data legislation primarily through the application of the General Data Protection Regulations (GDPR).

As before, I thank my amazing colleagues at Winners who enabled me to focus on this update while they took care of business, our clients for continuing to entrust Winners with their data, and everyone who has contributed to this book with case studies, references, or anecdotes. I also extend my grateful thanks to Vince Gennaro who generously provided the foreword to this book himself the author of one of the earliest books on the use of data in sports, *Diamond Dollars: The Economics of Winning in Baseball*, first published in 2007 – before I even knew the meaning of an algorithm.

The foreword to the first edition was provided by Paul Greenberg and is a great read in itself. You can download a copy from www.winnersfdd.com/winningwithdata-first/foreword.

One final note – the publication of this second edition has been timed to coincide with the development of an eLearning course that takes you through the principles and concepts discussed in these pages. You can find it at https://winnersfdd.com/winning-with-data/elearning.

Here's to a future rich with data.

Fiona Green
9 August 2020

Preface to the first edition

In 2011, when I first entered the world of CRM in sports, I struggled to understand the different terminology I heard and read and the different systems and processes being used. I would constantly Google 'CRM' in the hope that the next result would somehow shed light on what was a complete mystery to me at the time. Instead, I found myself trying to determine the difference between software like Microsoft Dynamics and SAP, Salesforce, and Sage and wondering why I kept reading that CRM projects fail and email marketing is dead.

My usual sense of logic was challenged when I started working with data, and I even battled with the prolific use of acronyms so common in the world of CRM. I should have been used to them. At that time I'd already been in the sports industry for 24 years, and boy, have we got our fair share of them.

These memories are what inspired me to write this book. I decided that if I could help just a few of you who are new to this game get to a position of understanding quicker than I did, then the long days and sleepless nights would have been worth it. And if, in the process of tending to the uninitiated, my words also help the more experienced of you to move further along your development, then I'll consider that a bonus. If any CRM veterans can say I validated a thought for them or provided additional insight, I'll feel like I've scored a hat trick. For England!

This book does not set out to tell you everything you need to know about CRM. You'd need quite a few books, each with a different focus, to achieve that. Instead this book aims to:

1   Dispel a common myth about the use of CRM. This is not the first time you'll hear me say that it's not just about technology. Nor is it just about the data. Having a strategy, systematic processes, and the right culture are just as important to be successful.
2   Provide a helicopter view of the way the sports industry uses data to make decisions and engage with fans, customers, and participants. This is different from how we use data for performance. There are many great books out there that cover that subject – this one is for strictly off-the-field.

3   Provide real-world examples that put the theory into perspective. Thanks to the generosity of UEFA, Mic Conetta of Arsenal FC, MLS, and Special Olympics International, to name just a few, you'll learn how these rights owners approach the unique challenges in their organisation or sport, applying the different principles discussed in this book.

Both as an individual and with Winners, the CRM, Business Intelligence and Data Analytics consultancy I set up to service sports' rights owners, I'm passionate about sharing knowledge with anyone and everyone – our clients, students, fellow professionals, even our competitors. You'll often see us out at conferences and other speaking events recording podcasts and writing blog posts for both our own website and others.

This isn't just a philanthropic leaning – it's a nod to all the people who have shared their knowledge with me along the way. In the 30 years I've been in the sports industry I've been fortunate enough to be mentored or helped along by some amazing and generous people. From Paul Fletcher, the scorer of what many believe was Burnley FC's best-ever goal, himself a published author of several sports management books who never fails to motivate and inspire, and Tony Stephens, the revered football agent who over 20 years ago first said to me, 'Don't chase the money, and it will come'. Along the way there's also been Alan Pascoe MBE, Olympic medallist and former owner of several highly successful sports agencies, who has always been generous with his time when I've requested it. There's Ilika Copeland, a business professional who has been consistent in her willingness to offer me all types of advice at any time of the day. More recently, Christine Stoffel, one of the first female CIOs in US sports and owner of SEAT, the must-attend technology, CRM, and digital conference for sports rights owners, who enabled me to network with some of the most advanced thinkers in the use of data in sports. And, of course, Paul Greenberg, who so generously provided the foreword for this book, an undisputed thought leader of CRM, best-selling author of the 'Bible' of our industry, *CRM at the Speed of Light*, and owner of the highly anticipated annual award, CRM Watchlist.

One final influencer, who is sadly no longer with us, not only set me on the path that led me to where I am today but did the same for several of my competitors. More than that, he was the visionary that first established a business to introduce the UK sports industry to CRM, but unfortunately, he passed away before he could fully make his impact. Stuart Dalrymple, founder of The Goodform Group, I salute you.

I've been a member of a team all my life, so it seems natural that in setting the scene for this book I'd highlight those that have given me immeasurable support over the years. Continuing on that theme, I'd also like to thank Winners' amazing clients for selecting us to work with them; the founding partners that helped me set the business up; our incredible team of passionate, loyal, and brilliant staff; my professional network, always there to brainstorm, help, challenge, and debate; and of course my family and friends who have had my back every step of the way.

Let's turn the page and start talking CRM.

Fiona Green
16 February 2018

Chapter 1

CRM for the digital age

CRM: an introduction

In the first edition of this book, published in 2018, my opening paragraph referred to George Orwell's words 'Big Brother is watching you'. I suggested that in referring to the authorities of a fictional totalitarian state in his acclaimed novel, *1984*, his readers must have scoffed at the thought of anyone being able to watch them constantly. I pointed out that not only was it now widely accepted that the authorities could, and indeed, were doing this, thanks to digital technology, anyone – not just the authorities – can watch anyone else. The last line of that opening paragraph was 'not only do we know what people are doing, we can predict what they may do next!'

But then the coronavirus hit, and suddenly everything we thought we knew went out the window. And far from predicting what *other* people will do next, we were searching for information that would help us just to decide what *we* would do next. Oh yes, and we were rewriting our algorithms because 'traditional' behaviours were no longer 'traditional' (more about that in the LA Kings' case study in Chapter 10).

But despite the huge impact the global pandemic has had on all of us – the natural changes enforced on the way we live, work, and act – there are still a few certainties. We will carry on loving sports, we will carry on playing sports, and at some point in time, perhaps before this book hits the shelves, we'll be back watching sports, live and in stadiums and arenas around the world.

Until then we had to consume live sports digitally – in fact, we're doing more digitally than we ever have done before, with Alexia Quadrani of JPMorgan Chase going so far as to state that 'A permanent shift has taken place across the industry from a linear platform to a digital platform' because of the coronavirus (Quadrani, 2020).

And so while the opening paragraph in this second edition has been amended to reflect the situation in July 2020, and at the time of writing we don't know what the 'new normal' will be, we do know that the theme of this book is now more relevant than ever: that in this digital world people happily tell us what they're doing (through digital and social media), we can see what they're doing (through analysis of their digital behaviour), and through these analyses we've got the closest thing we're ever going to get to a crystal ball.

With people using more digital platforms, consuming more digital content, and interacting more through digital media, this digital activity is generating more data, and it's this data that provides the cornerstone of CRM and analytics. It allows us to engage with these people at a very deep and personal level, giving us the ability to tell them what they want to hear when they need to hear it. This in turn increases the chances that these people – our customers, fans, or other stakeholders – will then do what we want them to, whether it's to spend, watch, participate, or engage.

To quote the late Peter Drucker, an industry great, 'for 50 years, information technology has focussed on the T in IT. . . . The new information revolution focuses on the I' (Drucker, 2001). Drucker was an oft-quoted international management consultant described by *Forbes* as the founder of modern management; so when he said that information, rather than technology, will be the new focus of the IT industries, we knew we should sit up and pay attention.

This is a great starting point for any book about CRM, business intelligence (BI), or business analytics (BA). It perfectly demonstrates how we've moved from an era of technological focus to one of data and insight. Drucker died in 2005, but the use of data for business is still largely in its infancy in many sports organisations. That tells us plainly how far behind we are in this area. Back in 2012, *Harvard Business Review* published an article famously titled 'Data Scientist: The Sexiest Job of the 21st Century' (Davenport and Patil, 2012), but despite this, we are still catching up. Today the need for professionals who understand data in the sports industry is rapidly growing. Indeed according to the European Union, data and analytics are at the top of the list of critical skills shortages (Publications Office of the European Union, 2020), with the European Data Market Monitoring Tool attesting that in 2018 there were 571,000 unfilled positions due to the shortage of professionals with data skills (European Data Market Monitoring Tool, 2019).

Oscar Ugaz, a leading consultant in digital strategies for the sports industry and former digital executive at Real Madrid, agrees that this is also the case in the sports industry and shared his thoughts with me in an email in May 2020:

> I think there is an 80/20 challenge between how much money you are investing in software versus how much money you are investing in brainpower to analyse all the data and analytics that you are obtaining. Today people are fascinated with data capture and want to have all these flashy products, but they are not investing in people that are capable of understanding the business, taking all that data and extracting insights out of it. [Sports] properties should be investing 80% in professionals capable of understanding the data and 20% in software and technology to extract it. Data is everywhere. What is very scarce is professionals capable of analysing it.
>
> (Ugaz, 2020)

As we look to bring CRM into the sports industry, how can we learn from the mistakes and successes of the many businesses that have gone before us in their quest to become data-driven organisations? Let's start by looking at what CRM means, and more importantly what it means for sport- rights owners.

Gartner, the leading IT research and advisory firm, defines CRM as

> a business strategy that optimises revenue and profitability while promoting customer satisfaction and loyalty. CRM technologies enable strategy and identify and manage customer relationships, in person or virtually. CRM software provides functionality to companies in four segments: sales, marketing, customer service, and digital commerce.
>
> (Gartner, 2017)

I like this definition for two key reasons:

1 It uses the word *strategy* from the start. Too often we come across sports organisations that don't have a strategy or, if the management has defined a strategy, it hasn't filtered down to the operational teams.
2 It emphasises technology as an enabler not a driver. Too often, business decisions have been driven by technology when it should be the other way around.

Ed Thompson, a Gartner analyst, discussed the definition of CRM with me via email on 15 December, 2017. He advised that I shouldn't worry so much about the accepted definition of CRM and that I should instead focus on coming up with my own. At Winners, the company I founded over seven years ago to support the sports industry in this area, we simply define CRM as 'getting the right message, to the right person, at the right time'. We don't claim ownership to that now ubiquitous phrase. I've tried to trace the origins and have identified three points of reference. In 2004, the deceased mathematician, Benoit Mandlebrot, when interviewed for the book *Candid Science IV: Conversations with Famous Physicists*, said, 'scientific creation presupposed three elements – "the right person, the right place and the right time"' (Hargittai and Hargittai, 2004). The November 2005 edition of the *Harvard Business Review* led the marketing section with an article titled 'The Perfect Message at the Perfect Moment' (Kalyanam and Zweben, 2005), and then Jerry Della Femina, the American advertising executive, observed in a *Financial Times* article in 2013 that it's now possible to target adverts 'to the right person at the right time in the right place' (Femina, 2013).

It's also not the shortest definition of CRM. That honour goes to Don Peppers, globally recognised as a leading authority on marketing and business competition, who refers to the 'accurate but concise *treating different customers differently*' (Peppers, 2014). This book builds on these ideas and will chart how you can get the right message to the right person at the right time.

But what about the right platform? In a world where the term *omnichannel* is universally used and disliked in equal measure, we don't feel the need to refer to channels or platforms individually because the world is now channel-blind. We switch from email to Facebook, Twitter to Snapchat, Instagram to Pinterest, and mobile app to desktop without a second's thought. We don't care about the channel; we just want the message, content, or interaction. If this is the way your fans, customers, and stakeholders think, it's implicit that you know what channel to use.

So, we've got the right message, the right person, the right time, and the right platform. It's now left for us to make sure these messages work to achieve our business objectives. Unlike many other industries, sports organisations need to generate revenue, but sometimes selling is not the priority. The original meaning of CRM, coined back in the early 1990s, was about business to business (B2B) software; they were programs that helped sales reps stay on top of their leads as they moved through the sales process, from initial contact to contract signed. This has led to CRM strategies and processes focussing on sales, selling larger quantities, cross-selling, selling more efficiently, and predicting how sales can increase.

Operating in the sports industry, however, we're acutely aware that the primary business objective isn't always to sell. Sometimes the focus is on increasing participation, demonstrating governance, and improving reputations. While we know each of these will indirectly bring financial reward, the approach you take to upgrade a fan who has bought a ticket, or one who might spend more for a VIP experience, can seem very different to how you would encourage a retired player to become a coach, or a parent to become a volunteer. But, despite the different end goals, these objectives utilise similar CRM processes that promote engagement in all its forms, and it's this that leads to the desired result – more revenue and more participation.

There's no doubt that the principle of a sales funnel, the concept of nurturing a prospect to a sale, and minimising attrition while maximising repeat purchases are all valid, but where we previously might have focussed purely on CRM to optimise return on investment (ROI), we now hear more about return on opportunity (ROO) and return on experience (ROE).

While working with one of Winners' clients, a major rights owner sponsored by Adidas, Colin Rattigan, VP of Consumer Engagement told me that his key performance indicators (KPIs) are not based on dollars or euros but on engagement metrics and data. When engagement is the objective, revenue is the result.

Intelligent customer engagement

In May 2016 at the CRM Evolution Conference in Washington DC, I was fortunate enough to speak about the use of the term *CRM* with Jujhar Singh, former General Manager for Microsoft Dynamics, North America. I questioned the relevance of the three-letter acronym in the digital age, and he agreed that it was outdated, adding that 'we don't call it CRM in our office – we call it intelligent customer engagement' (Singh, 2016, 24 May). Shortly afterward, when Dynamics 365 launched in November 2016, those three letters, *CRM*, had been dropped from the product name.

So, the term *CRM* is no longer just about the software that an organisation uses to manage its customers and sales processes. It's become more of a collective concept that describes an entire business approach, driven by access to unlimited data, multiple digital engagement channels, and most crucially, the age of the savvy consumer.

I'll discuss this more later, but for now, consider that while sports rights owners may aspire to Amazon, Netflix, and Spotify levels of engagement, we don't do it with an exclusive focus on the sales funnel. We must think of engagement as a primary focus that will then lead to the successful achievement of our business goals and objectives.

Why now?

The sports marketing industry has been around for many years. While the 1984 Los Angeles Olympics hold claim to being the first US event to generate broadcasting fees, the to-the-death arena fights of ancient Rome could also be considered a foundation to what is now a multibillion-dollar global business. Regardless of whether you believe the catalyst was our first formalised approach to commercialising an event or wealthy aristocrats sponsoring gladiators, why has CRM become so important to the sports world that it now deserves its own book?

The sports industry is facing a lot of challenges:

We're not turning out. In Europe our biggest sport, football, saw a net decrease in attendance of 1.5%, and across the pond, Major League Baseball (MLB) attendance was down 4% in 2018, followed by a further decrease of 1.62% in 2019 (European Leagues, 2018; Brown, 2019).

Our ability to focus is decreasing. According to a report into how the internet is changing the way our brains work, our natural inclination to use multiple digital channels simultaneously, constantly switching from one to another, decreases our ability to stay focussed and ignore incoming distractions (Firth et al., 2019).

We're participating less. In the US, participation in high school sports has declined for the first time in 2019 with the biggest declines coming in gridiron football and basketball (National Federation of State High School Associations, 2019). Over in Australia, children aged 13 to 17 stop participating in sports (Australian Sports Commission, 2017), and in the EU, the percentage of people who say they never exercise or play sports has increased from 42% in 2009 to 46% in 2018 (European Commission, 2018).

Customers want more. Thanks to the amount of information that's available to us on any one of our connected devices, we have multiple options; so when we select one, we expect it to meet our expectations. Whether you have two thousand, two hundred thousand, or two million fans, they're all individuals with different wants and needs. They expect you to know them. According to global CRM software brand, Salesforce, 63% of millennials will share their data in return for personalised offers and discounts (McGinnes, 2016). They expect tailored recommendations and offers.

We are in the midst of an unparalleled period of uncertainty. Tedros Adhanom Ghebreyesus, Director General of the World Health Organisation said, 'Six months ago, none of us could have imagined how our world – and our lives – would be thrown into turmoil by this new virus' (Ghebreyesus, 2020). At the time of writing some professional sports and teams have resumed but only behind closed doors. The ability to talk directly to our fans, with relevance and in context, is now more important than ever.

But despite these challenges, there are also many opportunities. This is where I see CRM playing a huge role in shoring up our business models, helping us secure financial sustainability and ensuring that even in these uncertain times, we don't have to rely on our performance on the field to ensure performance off it.

We have passion. Lots of it. Sports can move fans to tears of joy or sadness. While global consumer brands from Coca-Cola to Visa have to pay for media attention, conjuring up storylines when launching a new product, a club can announce a new signing, an athlete can produce a personal best, and their fans on the other side of the world will be discussing it before a web page has time to load.

We have natural loyalty. While any one of the individual companies in the FTSE 100 could purchase all the football clubs in the English Premier League, they can't buy what Arsenal, Chelsea, and Everton have in abundance: loyalty. Of course, it's not just elite football. The Worcester Warriors, Glamorgan Cricket, Team GB, the All Blacks, the Wildcats (to name just a few), all have fans that would go without food before they would go without their season tickets. Barclays and Bank of America, Marks & Spencer and Home Depot, Tesco and BestBuy, Vodafone and Sprint can only dream of that kind of allegiance.

We don't have to buy column inches, likes, retweets, and follows. Whatever your frame of reference, when a club announces a new midfielder, quarterback, pitcher, or bowler, the media have dissected the decision before the athlete has chosen a locker.

We have an abundance of content. We don't need to hire PR teams and ad agencies to conjure up stories and creative narratives. We create images that are shared at the speed of light and memories that truly last a lifetime.

The use of CRM has proven to be so powerful in building customer loyalty for companies who don't have half of what the sport industry generates so naturally, I believe that when we truly embrace the use of data, the impact will be significant. We'll win back our audiences, get more people on the field, and remain our fans' number-one choice when it comes to their money, time, and attention because we'll be giving them what they want.

Amazon's approach to CRM

When I talk about aspirational CRM, I often refer to Amazon. Even though at Winners we work with clients that range from global organisations representing our biggest sports to niche rights owners that have less than a dozen back-office staff, we talk about a business approach that's the same for everybody. It's just the scale and focus that's different.

With 150 million Prime customers (Spangler, 2020), Amazon makes it easy for you to say 'yes', no matter what the question. When you visit their website you see a simple, easy-to-use interface with one-click ordering and single-sign-on across their merchant base. They make product recommendations based on your previous browsing and order history. When you purchase a product, you receive a series of notifications that inform you about the status of your order. You know when they've received your request, processed the order, dispatched your package, what day you're going to receive it, and finally, what time you can expect it to arrive. They even tell you when a new product has arrived that you will really want, even before you knew it existed.

This approach is enabled by Amazon's CRM ecosystem that captures and analyses customer data and uses it to instantly personalise a user's digital experience. Their system deals with most customer queries before the need for human intervention, providing access to order history and an automated returns process that supports an incredible level of customer service. But crucially, it's not just the software that drives Amazon's approach. It's their culture. It's their data-driven DNA. And it's their focus on the customer.

Jeff Bezos, founder and CEO of Amazon, in a letter written in 2016 to the company's shareholders, called out the biggest advantage to taking a customer-centric approach by stating:

> Customers are always beautifully, wonderfully dissatisfied, even when they report being happy and business is great. Even when they don't yet know it, customers want something better, and your desire to delight customers will drive you to invent on their behalf.
>
> (Amazon, 2017)

Bezos calls Amazon's approach a 'true customer obsession'. Does this sound familiar? Does a reference to wonderfully dissatisfied customers wanting something better sound at all familiar when it comes to the sports industry? In a telephone interview on 10 October, 2017, with Mark Bradley of the Fan Experience Company, I asked him how far the sports industry is from delighting our customers and rewarding them for their passion and loyalty:

> Many sports fans feel that they are held at an arm's length from the object of their love. Talk to any long-term fan of any sports team and while they all might not use the same words; they will all be able to articulate what their club STANDS for – what its values are. And here's the problem. Fans may know what their teams' values are, but how many owners do? Fans want their sports teams to honour the shield or respect the badge, but most sports teams just want to fill the stadium.
>
> There's only one question that matters: Does my club/league/sport/ governing body consistently act in ways that show that it has the best interests of its fans at its heart?
>
> (Bradley, 2017, 10 Oct.)

Bradley's sentiment is the underlying theme of this book. The use of CRM, BI, and data analytics is how we'll answer his question. He goes on to say:

> Other progressive growing businesses in other sectors do that because customer engagement is so important in world where 80%+ of businesses are now in the service sector. They can only prosper if the customer feels valued.
>
> When the customer feels valued – usually when adherence to core values ensures that their experiences continually convince them that their service provider has their best interests at heart – then their resulting emotional loyalty is so strong it TRANSCENDS financial incentives, like loyalty points and 'money off'.
>
> They trust. They forgive. They defend you. They may not say it (but they quietly love you). OK, so in these days of social media sniping and faceless message board terrorists, it might not be possible to get EVERYONE on board, but wouldn't we all appreciate the opportunities a positively engaged (majority) fan community would offer?
>
> In customer-driven organisations leaders talk about it all the time. Decisions are filtered through their brand values. There are customer value KPIs. Employees matter too and there is continuous open transparent dialogue between the service provider and its customers. Employees are recruited based on their values fit and rewarded when they live those values.
>
> The irony (or possibly even the explanation) is that by nature of our love for our teams, we already have the strongest levels of emotional loyalty and so maybe deep inside we genuinely feel there's no need to build it any further. Isn't it ironic then that the thing non-sports businesses envy us for the most, we simply take for granted? But, as Mark Bradley also notes the

rewards for the sports business that genuinely embraces the values-driven approach will be immeasurable.

(Ibid.)

Mark makes a very valid point – non-sports industries vie for customers, trying to tempt them away from their competitors, plying them with a lower price or better offers, a more ethical approach to sustainability, supporting charities that they care about, and many other tactics – so the next section of this chapter looks at CRM outside the sports industry.

Top industries that use CRM software

Based on research undertaken in 2015 by Capterra, the retail industry is the biggest user of CRM, focussing on the ability to track purchase behaviour, cross-sell and up-sell, and offer loyalty programmes which provide customer rewards. The next four biggest industries using CRM all operate in an environment where the purchase process is very complex. Business services (for example accounting, legal, consulting), technology, financial services, and manufacturing traditionally use CRM not just to manage and complete a sale but also to support customer communication, help requests, manage and issue contracts and invoices, and follow-up on purchases. Most interestingly this research found that while there is a preconception that implementing CRM is a cost-heavy process, 52% of Capterra's 300 survey respondents worked at organisations with less than $10 million in annual revenue (Hollar, 2015).

There are many preconceptions, and a major one is the amount of time CRM implementations take. At Winners we see this a lot with our clients. They usually underestimate, with 6 months being the most commonly proposed timeframe. However, according to 80% of Capterra's respondents, it took them up to 18 months to be up and running (Ibid.).

In Chapter 6 we look at the use of marketing automation – a key component of a data-driven approach to communications – and while it's still a relatively new extension to CRM in the sports industry, in this 2015 survey, 44% of companies were already adding marketing automation software to their CRM software (Ibid.).

However, the most interesting element of Capterra's research for me involves the respondents' attitudes to social media functionality. A quarter of all respondents wanted more (Ibid.). I'm a huge fan of social media (who wouldn't be?) but as a CRM practitioner, until we can get more of the rich data generated by social media channels like Facebook, YouTube, and Instagram into our client's CRM databases, it will continue to represent a silo to me. I talk more about this later, in both Chapter 5 on the CRM technology stack and also in Chapter 6 on data-driven marketing; and again (as this is a second edition) I've been able to update the findings from the first edition. Having said that, with the pace at which social media channels and functionality continues to develop you can expect this to be out of date by the time this book hits the shelves!

CRM in other industries

The global CRM software market is expected to reach USD 114.4 billion by 2027, representing a compound annual growth rate of 14.2% from 2020 (Grand View Research, 2020). When you factor in the industry rule of thumb that you should expect to spend $1 on consulting related to implementation for every $1 in annual subscription costs, then you're looking at a lot of money to keep customers happy. But is it worth it? Let's take a quick look at some success stories in other industries.

Financial services

Asset management company Aegon, which manages approximately £542 billion in assets globally, is dependent on intelligent analytics to enhance sales performance and excellence. Aegon's global sales increased by more than 15% to €12 billion in 2016. According to Duncan Jarret, the UK Retail Managing Director at Aegon:

> Everyone has personalised dashboards powered by our CRM software, so they can see what business they are bringing in and how it relates to our overall goals. We can have more informed conversations about the dynamics we are seeing not only in our business but also in their businesses. This gives us a real competitive edge and helps us serve our end customers better.
>
> CRM software underpins the entire opportunity process for Aegon's distribution operation – from forecasting and pipeline management to bid co-ordination and lead conversion. More than 3,500 new opportunities are logged every month. They've been using CRM software since 2008, and it's become fundamental to how they operate and grow their business.
>
> (Aegon, 2014)

Retail

CRM has been growing as a business discipline at John Lewis, currently the UK's fifth largest retailer based on 2015/2016 sales data (Wiggenraad, 2017). According to Chris Bates, Head of Customer Marketing, it's now used as the primary vehicle for new product launches.

Bates gives the example of when their Stratford store opened in 2011; 'above-the-line' was the predominant way to announce the launch, using mass media that included conventional advertising format. But just four years later in Birmingham they used a different approach with a focus on their loyalty scheme, *my John Lewis*, launched in 2013, targeting members within the area. Direct marketing was used to spread the word, with an exclusive preview for their members two days before the store opening. This resulted in a turnout that Bates says was 'phenomenal' (Fisher, 2015).

Now with close to two million members, the *my John Lewis* programme includes an innovative app that removes the need to carry a plastic card and includes the opportunity to store receipts and product guarantees digitally, a service that was identified as a problem-solver for its customers.

The UK's sixth largest retailer, Marks & Spencer recently posted a 2.3% rise in clothing and homewares sales for the first time in two years (Wiggenraad, 2017). It's no coincidence that when their new CEO, Steve Rowe, started in 2016 he placed a lot of emphasis on analysing data to understand their customers better.

Nathan Anstell (Global Director of Loyalty, Customer Insight, and Analytics at Marks & Spencer) is responsible for making sure his colleagues have access to the right customer data to enable them to make decisions, citing the importance of being able to demonstrate a direct link between 'a brilliant customer experience and delivery of results' (Tesseras, 2017).

Now accountable for their *Sparks* loyalty card, Anstell can produce data on how often people visit their stores, the merchandise those people are interested in, and of course, what they're buying. Going further in his belief in the value of data, Anstell says:

> Good marketers in the future will need to have a thorough understanding of different data sources and how to use them in their roles – it's a critical part of a marketer's tool kit. If I were to give someone who is coming into marketing advice, I would say understanding data and analytics right from the beginning of your career will hold you in good stead.
>
> (Ibid.)

Telecommunications

Everything Everywhere (EE) went on record in 2014, publicising a 400% increase in mobile phone sales after implementing CRM with the rollout of new software to 11,000 customer agents in telesales and retail stores. They credit the initiative with helping to both triple the value of its customers and win new ones citing 4% less churn, an incremental £4 spend per customer, and a 300% increase in the value of retained customers thanks to an integration between their retail and telephone sales channels. Furthermore, EE proposed the CRM rollout helped improve customer engagement, reduce the use of more expensive outbound channels, and improve customer satisfaction (Goodwin, 2014).

EE's Head of Customer Base Management, Suzanne Woolley, said:

> Ninety per cent of offers we sell in our service transactions are from our top three recommendations. We know our decision-making is right. We are picking the right offers, picking relevant offers, and offers our customers are interested in. . . .
>
> Not only are we retaining the right customers, and we are retaining more of them, we are growing their value. And that is really important, and that is key to success of the system, and its key to the acceptance of the tool we have had internally.
>
> (Ibid.)

CRM software considers a wide range of factors – including how customers use their phone, their lifestyle, and their strategic value to EE – to automatically generate three recommended deals personalised to that customer. This allows EE to assess the contribution of a customer, their risk of leaving, and cost to serve to create tailored budget and handset recommendations for each customer.

> As conversations progress and we learn more about the customer, we go through the loop and we talk to the customer about their needs, we refine that personal recommendation. We can connect that conversation across all those channels. So regardless of which channel you go in, your browsing history is there, the offers you have had presented to you that you are thinking about are there for any other agent to pick up.
>
> (Ibid.)

Conclusion

Even before the global pandemic hit, the sports industry had its challenges driven by the greater choice we have with where we spend our time, money, and attention. But we also have tremendous opportunities that have only been emphasised by the increased use of digital channels as a result of the restrictions coronavirus has placed on us. Rights owners often take for granted what non-sports businesses work hard to generate – natural loyalty – so when we successfully implement the processes these non-sports businesses have been successfully using for many years, we will achieve more. And we'll achieve it with more efficiency and effectiveness. We'll increase our revenue streams, get more people participating, and we'll keep them wanting more.

Case study: 2019 International Cricket Council (ICC) Cricket World Cup

The fundamentals of CRM in the digital age can sound relatively simple: getting the right message to the right person at the right time. But for sports organisations, the media revolution that has enabled a vast and rapid extension of their visibility, popularity, and reach has also made this task an increasingly challenging one to accomplish.

In the first edition of this book, we interviewed UEFA to discuss the thought processes they had to go through when adopting their own approach to CRM – you can download a copy of that case study from www.winnners-fdd.com/winningwithdata-first/ch1casestudy.

For this second edition I turned to Adrian Wells, currently Chief Marketing Officer of Harlequins, a rugby union team that plays in the top level of English rugby, who was Director of Marketing, Communications, and Ticketing when England hosted the ICC Cricket World Cup in 2019.

Adrian joined the Local Organising Committee (LOC) in October 2017 with a remit to build an internal team and network of suppliers that would help them deliver a primary goal of selling £40-million worth of ticketing and hospitality, a record for a Cricket World Cup, while growing the game for new generations of fans. I interviewed Adrian during the COVID-19 lockdown in April 2020 to understand the role CRM and data had in his strategy for what the ICC considers the as the third most-watched global sporting event based on broadcast numbers.

> Sponsorship and broadcast were both sold by the ICC out of Dubai, which meant the LOC's commercial objective was to maximise revenue by ensuring a sell-out tournament across 48 matches. So, for me the starting point was to work backwards – look at how many tickets we had to sell across the tournament and what capacity we needed to achieve for each match to hit our goal. From there we had to work out how many people we needed to reach, how many we needed to engage with, and ultimately how many we needed to convert into customers. Data and insights were the cornerstone of the whole plan.

With this approach Adrian demonstrated one of the key principles of a data-led strategy: using data to help him with decisions. He worked backwards, starting with what he needed to achieve and then looking at what he would have to do to achieve that. But to be able to do this, you must have data to start with, so I asked Adrian what sort of information he had:

> We inherited a database of 155,000 records and that was made up of people who had attended other global cricket events in this country, for example the ICC Champions Trophy events in 2013 and 2017, which are like a mini World Cup, plus we'd had the ICC Women's World Cup

in 2017. We also had some of the Rugby World Cup 2015 data that had been shared with other governing bodies. In the end we created a data warehouse of what we called 'global event attendees'.

Adrian was able to use this data for two purposes – looking at behaviours to understand purchase propensity, and to consider how likely their interest would be in cricket, particularly among the South-Asian audience segments.

The database was cleansed, specifically removing old email addresses that were no longer valid and ensuring all had been opted-in for marketing communications. The next step was a strategy planning meeting with Two Circles, his data and insights partner agency.

We started off with some very rough KPIs in terms of reach, engagement, and monetisation, based on our expectations of the interest and size of the market. We made estimates of demand from different countries, and of national versus international interest, all based on facts from previous [cricket] events. Interestingly, post-event we found that the Men's Cricket World Cup added an extra 30% to everything in terms of demand and interest – compared to all of our numbers on Champions Trophy and Women's World Cup we drove 30% more engagement and 30% higher interest.

This initial session led to the development of the whole marcomms and ticketing strategy, which was based on a fundamental need to build our database. To maximise the growth of it we devised a ballot-led approach to ticket sales. This involved a series of ticket ballots, a 'cricket family ballot', with a priority access window for anybody who had previously bought a cricket ticket – that gave them the first priority to buy a certain percentage of tickets to every match. And then we created a 'public ballot' for anybody to buy a ticket to any match, with follow-up ballots of the last remaining tickets for the venues, or the last few tickets for every team. This approach co-developed with Two Circles, our ticketing partner and media partner, enabled us to drive huge spikes in interest and maximise registration of that data.

It is important to start with a strategy, but what about resources? Most sports rights owners operate as quite lean organisations, so we asked Adrian what resources he had to call on when it came to bringing his strategy to life:

We used Two Circles to help us manage our single customer view (SCV), to help us develop the strategy, and to reach, engage, and ultimately monetise our fanbase around the world, specifically by helping us send and analyse our email campaigns. We did a lot of the campaign building internally, specifically pulling the content together from across the business, and as each campaign was sent, we'd analyse the results and slowly become more effective. I acted as an internal data champion across the organisation, leading our approach to GDPR and the relationship with Two Circles, then we had one email and one Digital Marketing Executive. In terms of other people, we had a Communications team and a Marketing team who leveraged email and data as a service, so we held regular workshops with them, presenting some of the insights and the things we learned. We also had a Spectator Services team, so we regularly provided them with insights that we'd gained from our audiences, for example, where our fans were coming from, their travel plans, and how long they're going to be staying in host cities. Understanding things like this through email and surveys allowed us to better understand our supporters and their plans, and then adapt our communications to them as a result.

As you will read in Chapter 2, the use of technology is a tremendous enabler of a CRM strategy, but the point I always make clear is that it should never be a driver. Having identified Two Circles as the LOC's agency of choice to help devise the strategy, the LOC made the decision to also use the different software that made up their technology stack. DotDigital was used as the email campaign platform, a SQL database was built by Two Circles and used to host all incoming data including ticketing before opt-ins and segmented audiences were then pushed into DotDigital. Data visualisation was supported through an array of graphs and charts displayed in an Insight Portal linked to the SQL database and Google Analytics, specifically Google Data Studio to provide web statistics alongside campaign metrics, ticket sales information, and customer data.

I talk more about a CRM technology stack in Chapter 5 but suffice it to say that through this stack, Adrian had the key functionality needed to implement CRM – a data warehouse, campaign platform, analytics capability, and data visualisation.

One misrepresentation in the world of data is that 'bigger is better' – the more data you have, the better position you're in – but while having a large database might be a good thing, it's the quality of the data that can often be more important. I addressed this point with Adrian to hear his thoughts:

That's an interesting story. We started with 155,000 records and we targeted growth to 330,000 but then GDPR arrived and [because of the cleansing processes we implemented] we lost 50% of our records. This took us down to 70,000 but then because of the huge demand and interest in tickets through our ballot strategy, people desperately wanted to stay in touch, so we built it back up to over 400,000 records with nearly 85% opted-in for marketing.

When it comes to hosting major sporting events, legacy has always been an important consideration, raising questions such as how the country, the sport, and the community will benefit from hosting a global event. In addition to an increase in the profile of the country, the economic impact from jobs created and tourism, along with the groundswell of enthusiasm for a sport that usually translates into an increase in participation, we now have a database legacy to consider. Adrian talked us through their end-of-event process for ensuring that the rich and valuable database they produced did not go to waste.

We did a 'closure campaign' with all our databases – everyone from ticket buyers who attended the event to our tournament followers around the world – in which we formally closed the World Cup. We had a wrap-up video, some of our best sponsor content, cricket highlights content, and we said 'Thank you, we hope you've loved being part of this and we hope that you'd like to stay involved in cricket'. At this point the fans had three options to select how to stay engaged with the sport. If they selected to stay in touch with cricket in their area they would tick the England and Wales Cricket Board (ECB) opt-in box that enabled us to share their contact details data with the counties as well as the ECB, to engage people with England tickets as well as participation programmes.

We also had a 'stay in touch with cricket and global tournaments' option which was, in effect, an opt-in for the ICC, and then we had a third box which was for partners of the ICC, so a traditional sponsor/partner opt-in.

Adrian and his team oversaw the process of transferring this data to these cricket stakeholders and event partners, ensuring GDPR compliance at all times and guiding the use of 'welcome campaigns' so that the World Cup customers and fans would understand why they were now hearing from other parties. The transfer of data also came with an agreement that it would not be used for overt commercialisation and would instead focus on growing the sport. These various ground rules ensured the legacy database would be used in a controlled manner and fans would not feel bombarded with post-World Cup communications.

Maintaining and growing participation in sport is a huge focus for rights owners and cricket is no different, so we asked Adrian to tell us more about the legacy data opportunity.

The majority of data went to the ECB, and they were able to use this to encourage World Cup fans to get involved in cricket in their local area through playing, coaching, or volunteering. We also went out to the [18 first-class] counties and provided them with the records of people that registered to hear about local cricket and lived within 30 to 40 miles of their ground. Finally, we went to the ten World Cup Host Cities and said, 'if you have cricket-related activities and want to communicate with these fans who are local to your area, and they've opted-in to hear about cricket, you can contact them as well'.

Through these multiple opt-ins and processes, over two-thirds of our database was used to keep our fans and customers informed of cricket in the future.

Developing a CRM strategy for a one-off event is always going to be different from a strategy for an ever-present entity, such as a governing body, team, or league, but we asked Adrian what he would do differently if he could turn back the clock.

We used a lot of segmentation based on the geography of our fans and the teams they were following, but we didn't do anything language-specific – multilingual emails would have been brilliant, but whether or not they would have improved our engagement metrics is unknown. Having said that, we were getting open rates of over 80% from fans in Pakistan and India. Also, we evolved the database legacy plan over the course of the two years, so it wasn't really put into place until the beginning of the tournament itself. I think, in hindsight, we would have started working on it with the end in mind and would have prioritised the ECB, and 'staying in touch with cricket in your area' as the first opt-in tick box because you can really see the drop-off [from the first box to the last] when you use three.

Despite Adrian's desire to have approached language in email and legacy planning a bit differently, he's really pleased with two specific tournament successes – the ticketing strategy that focussed on a ballot to drive maximum demand and generate significant quantities of data, and the huge number of people who were introduced to the sport through targeting 'big eventers' and people who had not previously been to a cricket match. The diversification of customers within the ticketing database bore testament to this with 130,000 tickets taken by fans under 16 years old and 150,000 taken by females, and 40% of all tickets going to fans who were new to cricket.

Our final question for Adrian centred around his current role as Chief Marketing Officer for Harlequins and specifically, the learnings he has taken from the 2019 ICC Cricket World Cup into his new environment.

> The top three things I've taken into Quins are the requirement of an SCV, the development of an annual plan based on engagement across the club (including commercial partners), and the integration of email as well as various other digital channels to produce one consolidated plan rather than communication in silos.
>
> (Source: Wells, 2020)

Key chapter ideas

1   CRM is not just about software – leading definitions of CRM prioritise strategy over technology.
2   The sports industry is adopting CRM at a fast pace – if this is not yet on your radar, start to investigate what you need to know.
3   Significant changes in customer behaviour have led to a greater need to fulfil customer expectations than ever before.
4   CRM is not just an implementation – it's a way of doing business; it needs time and commitment, but it produces results.
5   We need to put our fans and other stakeholders at the centre of the way we operate – we need to emulate Amazon's approach to customer service but frame it for the size of our opportunities.

References

Aegon. (2014). *Aegon's 2014 review: Creating and sharing value*. The Hague: Aegon [online]. Available at: www.aegon.com/globalassets/corporate-2018/sitewide/reports-and-other-publications/annual-reviews/2014/aegon-2014-review-en.pdf.

Amazon. (2017). *About Amazon – 2016 letter to shareholders* [online]. Available at: www.amazon.com/p/feature/z6o9g6sysxur57t.

Australian Sports Commission. (2017). *Addressing the decline in sport participation in secondary schools* [online]. Available at: www.sportaus.gov.au/__data/assets/pdf_file/0006/678687/34896_Youth_participation_project-full_report_acc2.pdf.

Bradley, M. (2017). Telephone interview, 10 Oct.

Brown, M. (2019). From terrible teams to rising costs: Why MLB attendance is down over 7% since 2015. *Forbes.com* [online]. Available at: www.forbes.com/sites/maurybrown/2019/10/04/from-terrible-teams-to-rising-costs-and-more-why-mlb-attendance-has-been-down-over-7-since-2015/#1fff6f831a8d.

Davenport, T. and Patil, D. (2012). Data scientist: The sexiest job of the 21st century. *Harvard Business Review* [online]. Available at: https://hbr.org/2012/10/data-scientist-the-sexiest-job-of-the-21st-century.

Drucker, P. (2001). *Management challenges for the 21st century.* New York: HarperBusiness, p. 104.

European Commission. (2018). *New eurobarometer on sport and physical activity* [online]. Available at: https://ec.europa.eu/sport/news/2018/new-eurobarometer-sport-and-physical-activity_en.

European Data Market Monitoring Tool. (2019). *Data as the engine of Europe's digital future* [online]. Available at: http://datalandscape.eu/sites/default/files/report/EDM_D2.5_Second_Report_on_Policy_Conclusions_final_13.06.2019.pdf.

European Leagues. (2018). *European leagues presents its new fan attendance report* [online]. Available at: https://europeanleagues.com/epfl-presents-new-fan-attendance-report/.

Femina, J. (2013). A glimpse into the second golden age of advertising. *Financial Times* [online]. Available at: www.ft.com/content/4877d0e4-f911-11e2-a6ef-00144feabdc0.

Firth, J., Torous, J., Stubbs, B., et al. (2019). The 'online brain': How the Internet may be changing our cognition. *Official Journal of the World Psychiatry Association*, June [online]. Available at: www.wpanet.org/english.

Fisher, L. (2015). How CRM is becoming the 'new advertising'. *Marketing Week* [online]. Available at: www.marketingweek.com/2015/11/09/how-crm-is-becoming-the-new-advertising/.

Gartner. (2017). *Customer relationship management (CRM)* [online]. Available at: www.gartner.com/it-glossary/customer-relationship-management-crm/.

Ghebreyesus, T. A. (2020). After 500,000 deaths, WHO warns worst of coronavirus pandemic is 'yet to come'. *CBS News* [online]. Available at: www.cbsnews.com/amp/news/coronavirus-pandemic-world-health-organization-worst-yet-to-come/?__twitter_impression=true#app.

Goodwin, B. (2014). EE drives mobile phone deals with CRM software implementation. *Computer Weekly* [online]. Available at: www.computerweekly.com/news/2240222345/EE-drives-mobile-phone-deals-with-CRM-software-implementation.

Grand View Research. (2020). *Customer relationship management market worth $114.4 billion by 2027* [online]. Available at: www.grandviewresearch.com/press-release/global-customer-relationship-management-crm-market.

Hargittai, I. and Hargittai, M. (2004). *Candid science IV: Conversations with famous physicists.* London: Imperial College Press, p. 505.

Hollar, K. (2015). CRM industry user research report. *Capterra* [online]. Available at: www.capterra.com/customer-relationship-management-software/user-research.

Kalyanam, K. and Zweben, M. (2005). The perfect message at the perfect moment. *Harvard Business Review* [online]. Available at: https://hbr.org/2005/11/the-perfect-message-at-the-perfect-moment.

McGinnes, D. (2016). Please take my data: Why consumers want more personalized marketing. *Salesforce Blog* [online]. Available at: www.salesforce.com/blog/2016/12/consumers-want-more-personalized-marketing.html.

National Federation of State High School Associations. (2019). *2018–19 high school athletics participation survey* [online]. Available at: www.nfhs.org/sports-resource-content/high-school-participation-survey-archive/.

Peppers, D. (2014). Treating different customers differently. *LinkedIn* [online]. Available at: www.linkedin.com/pulse/20140909180730-17102372-treating-different-customers-differently/.

Publications Office of the European Union. (2020). Communication from the commission to the european parliament, the council, the european economic and social committee and the committee of the regions. *A European Strategy for Data* [online]. Available at: https://ec.europa.eu/info/sites/info/files/communication-european-strategy-data-19feb2020_en.pdf.

Quadrani, A. (2020). *Media consumption in the age of COVID-19* [online]. Available at: www.jpmorgan.com/global/research/media-consumption.

Singh, J. (2016). Personal interview, 24 May.

Spangler, T. (2020). *Amazon prime tops 150 million members* [online]. Available at: https://variety.com/2020/digital/news/amazon-150-million-prime-members-1203487355/.

Tesseras, L. (2017). M&S's Nathan Ansell on proving the value of customer experience. *Marketing Week* [online]. Available at: www.marketingweek.com/2017/02/10/ms-proving-value-customer-experience/.

Ugaz, O. (2020). Personal interview, May.

Wells, A. (2020). Chief Marketing Officer, interview by phone, 17 May.

Wiggenraad, P. (2017). Data: Top 50 retailers by sales during 2015/16 financial year. *Retail Week* [online]. Available at: www.retail-week.com/data/data-top-50-retailers-by-sales-during-2015/16-financial-year/7018511.article.

Chapter 2

The principles of CRM

I've worked in the sports industry for over 30 years, starting when my approach to CRM consisted of a landline, a Rolodex, and a desk diary. The closest I could get to the 'right message to the right person at the right time' back then was asking my match sponsor if he wanted to support the next leg in the Littlewoods Challenge Cup and taking a punt that the combination of a 2–0 win and an afternoon of executive box hospitality would create the right mix for him to say yes. Fast forward to 2020 and things are quite different, and I don't just mean that it's now called the Carabao Cup.

In Chapter 1 we addressed why the sports industry needs to use CRM as a way of doing business. Now we'll start to look at how we go about it, breaking down what we, at Winners, consider the different elements to implementing a CRM approach. It's not just about technology. I'll look at the perfect circle, the CRM pyramid, SCV, and then end with a glimpse at customer personas.

CRM's perfect circle

Winners' approach to CRM is based on the principle of the perfect circle. This principle consists of five key elements, all five weighted with equal importance. If you place less emphasis on one element over another, the circle collapses (see Figure 2.1).

Ironically, there's a suggestion that outside the world of pure mathematics there's no such thing as a 'perfect circle' (Payne, 2019), and I'm quite happy to accept this as truth. While we use the term quite liberally among our rights owner clients, we also know how incredibly hard it is to achieve, and when Google throws up nearly 200 million search results (most of them suggesting that CRM is just about software), it's easy to understand why there's such a challenge in our industry.

One of the purposes of this book is to dispel that software myth and redress the balance. I want sports organisations that are looking to start their own CRM journey, or those who are already making headway, to understand that software isn't a magic bullet. Indeed, when you go into developing your own approach to CRM believing that buying the right software will make sure it

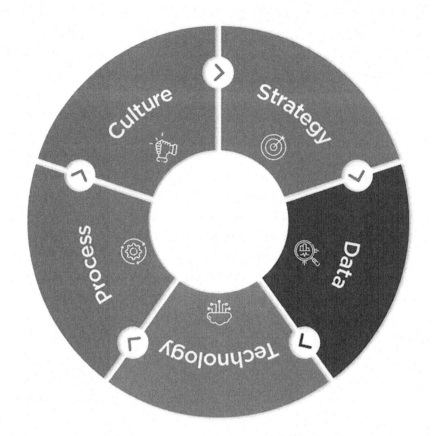

Figure 2.1 Winners' CRM perfect circle (source: Winners FDD Ltd)

happens, you can be confident yours will be one of the 60% of projects that reportedly fail (Gould, 2015).

So, let's look at these five key elements of the CRM perfect circle and understand what they mean in the real world of our day-to-day business.

Strategy

We all need to have a strategy for the way we work, to make sense of our operational delivery and ensure that across the organisation we're all heading in the same direction. With the implementation of CRM as a business approach it's no different. We need to know the goals we want to achieve, align them with our business objectives, determine what resources we have to achieve them, and establish a timeline so we know when we want to have achieved them by.

I've already referred to the 'CRM journey' and will reiterate it here. The implementation of CRM is not a destination that you arrive at, nor a project that you complete. It's a journey. CRM is a way of doing business, and once it's embedded, its role within an organisation continues to evolve. As we use CRM to make decisions and deliver results, driven by the continuing development of our digital world and the masses of data it produces, we'll continue to progress because technology, the quantity of data we have access to, and our drive for success are also progressing. Once we've successfully moved from A to B, we'll then want to move to C and, once we've started moving in the direction of C, you can bet your life someone's thinking about how you start moving to D.

When it comes to your strategy, it doesn't have to be a long document supported with dozens of spreadsheets. It can be easily summarised in one page. As with so many concepts, it really is about quality over quantity. I believe that a CRM strategy can be created in just three steps:

Identify your main goals, such as increased revenue, participation, and insight, and understand why you want to achieve them. What difference will they make to your business? How will they support the overall business objectives?

Understand your current situation, for example, the extent of your customer data, tools, and other available resources. Audit your staff capabilities so you know what gaps you have when it comes to operational delivery and review your customer journeys. What experience do your fans have when they engage with you?

Roadmap the journey or the milestones that will help you to get from where you are now to where you want to be. Itemise the steps that will get you there. Within this, I always recommend you identify a leader or sponsor, ideally at the highest level of management possible, who will champion what you're trying to achieve. For example, selling your approach to the board, lobbying for more support, or managing the messaging when things have gone slightly off plan.

What's really key to your CRM strategy is that you support it with quick wins. We're looking for marginal gains that keep your management and team members motivated and excited as you push forward with your delivery. So, make sure you've included a few of these aims in your roadmap. They should show an increase in revenue, engagement, or any other KPI that has been identified as important to your business.

Data

We must have data, but it's not any old data, and it's definitely not 'big data'. In 2018 there were 33 zettabytes of data in the world (Press, 2020). And in case you've not heard that reference before, a zettabyte is one trillion gigabytes.

But just seven years later, in 2025, it's estimated that 463 exabytes of data will be created *each day* globally – that's the equivalent of 212,765,957 DVDs, or 90 times all the words ever spoken by the human race! Some of the daily activities contributing to this include 500 million tweets, 294 billion emails, 5 billion internet searches, and 65 billion WhatsApp messages (Desjardins, 2019).

Big data gives us huge amounts of information, but by its very nature it can be overwhelming. So, what we need instead of data quantity is data that's relevant to our strategy, the data that will help us achieve our business objectives. Data can help us do two things. It can provide us with the foundation on which we make decisions, and it can enable the use of personalised and highly targeted communication, whether marketing-specific or content-related.

Most crucially, it's not just about quantity but also about quality. As we think about our utopian scenario in CRM (the SCV, single version of truth, golden record, or any other term you use for all the information you have about your stakeholders in one place), we must remember that we need all our databases to merge into one. This task is made immeasurably easier when we use consistency in our approach to gathering that data (we will look at data normalisation and standardisation later in the book).

On top of that, it's about the way we use data within our CRM approach – how we collect, store, manage, and protect it. This is even more important in the EU, where we must conform to GDPR. This imposes a standard set of data protection laws across the 27 countries of the EU, but it is also applied in the UK, as well as the European Economic Area Countries of Iceland, Lichtenstein, and Norway. We will examine data legislation in more detail in Chapter 9.

Finally, we need to think about the way we maintain our data, how we keep it clean, continually improving and enhancing it, and how we ensure our data will continue to deliver our objectives that in turn ensure we support our overall strategy.

Technology

The role of technology is to act as an enabler in the use of CRM. I consider the CRM technology stack in more detail in Chapter 5, but there are two main points here:

First, we don't start with technology, and the technology department doesn't lead on CRM. For those rights owners without an IT department this will be a relief because it is the CEOs and Marketing Directors who should be the drivers of your CRM implementation. We lead with business needs, not technology.

Second, at Winners, we don't talk about CRM systems. We refer to CRM ecosystems. There isn't one piece of software, technology, or platform that can deliver everything you need to get the right message to the right person.

We use several of them, each playing its own role within its niche sector or perhaps multiple roles to bring together a few tasks and disciplines. But all these individual components are interacting and interconnected.

While it is undeniable that the right software and hardware can make things work more efficiently, the best technology in the world is unable to deliver CRM in isolation. It's one of the five principles. Consequently, a technology-led CRM approach could lead to you being one of those failing 60% we discussed earlier and, most importantly, cost you both time and money: something that most rights owners have in short supply.

This is a great place for one of my favourite Bill Gates quotes – 36 words that perfectly sum up this point:

> The first rule of any technology used in a business is that automation applied to an efficient operation will magnify the efficiency. The second is that automation applied to an inefficient operation will magnify the inefficiency.
>
> (Gates, 1996)

When Gates wrote those words nearly 25 years ago, the world didn't have the technology we have today. Moore's Law implies that technology will 'dramatically increase in power and decrease in relative cost, at an exponential pace' (Futurism, 2018). If so, then technology will be just as disruptive in the next two decades as it has been in the past two. As Baroness Martha Lane Fox put it, when speaking at the CIPD Annual Conference and Exhibition in Manchester on 9 November, 2017, 'today technology is developing at the slowest rate it will ever develop in the future' (Fox, 2017). I had to think about that one for a while before realising the absolute truth in it.

Process

The definition of *process* is 'a series of actions that you take in order to achieve a result', according to Cambridge Dictionary (Cambridge University Press, 2020). While that certainly applies here, I'd like to expand just a little. In our world, where 'data is the new oil' (Humby, 2006), we should be taking the data output from previous processes and analysing it before we apply the next process, using that data to inform appropriate decisions. A further, key aspect of our processes is that we must repeat them, do them consistently and with the same approach as before and, where appropriate, add improvements along the way.

We'll be looking at some of these processes later in areas such as data collection, digital campaign management, and campaign reporting. These are the day-to-day things that we do, the tasks and actions that make up our working day in a data-driven organisation. When you apply best-practice CRM you're given the opportunity to streamline these processes across your organisation's departments, with workflows or automation that will increase efficiencies, effectiveness, and speed up manual tasks.

Jeff Bezos, founder and CEO of Amazon, warned in his 2016 letter to shareholders of the danger that processes can do the opposite of what was originally intended. They can lead to downfalls, not improvements:

> A common example is process as proxy. Good process serves you, so you can serve customers. But if you're not watchful, the process can become the thing. This can happen very easily in large organisations. The process becomes the proxy for the result you want. You stop looking at outcomes and just make sure you're doing the process right. It's not that rare to hear a junior leader defend a bad outcome with something like, 'well, we followed the process'.
>
> (Bezos, 2017)

So, the tempered message is that while we need processes (and we need to be constantly improving them), we must also be aware that we don't do things by rote, that while following processes, we must continue to learn.

Culture

Perhaps the element that is most likely to hold up progress in the development of any CRM strategy is culture, or more importantly, cultural silos. Cultural silos are natural divides that occur within organisations and minimise collaboration.

Even if every element of the perfect circle is in place and running smoothly, if your business is unable to function as a cohesive whole, all forward momentum can stall at this point. Having the right business culture can be the most difficult part in the implementation of any new strategy. It requires interdepartmental trust and teamwork to be managed effectively. But natural silos, or department-centric attitudes, aren't unique to implementing CRM. These silos have been in the workplace long before we were introduced to databases. So, why do we see so many rights owners specifically struggling in this area?

While silos may indeed have existed, they haven't caused many issues up to this point because very few business functions are cross-organisational. Finance and IT often work together; after all, no one puts up a barrier when it comes to being paid or getting their laptops fixed. Yet when it comes to the sharing of data, production of content, and agreement of priorities, there can be a clear lack of co-operation, intentional or otherwise. We will talk more about this later. Look for Chapter 8 on business change.

Gartner's eight building blocks

This is a perfect moment to introduce readers to what Gartner, one of the world's leading information technology research and advisory companies, proposes as the eight building blocks for the successful implementation of CRM. They align with my use of the perfect circle, but were first introduced in 1996, long before intelligent customer engagement was a concept:

Vision: The board must take leadership in creating a CRM vision for the enterprise. The CRM vision should be used as the guide to the creation of a CRM strategy.

Strategy: The CRM strategy is all about how to build and develop a valuable asset: the customer base. It must set objectives and metrics for attaining that goal. It directs the objectives of other operational strategies and the CRM implementation strategy.

Customer experience: The customer experience must be designed in line with the CRM vision and must be constantly refined, based on actively sought customer feedback.

Organisational collaboration: Changes to organisational structures, processes, metrics, incentives, skills, and even the enterprise culture must be made to deliver the required external customer experience. Ongoing change management will be key.

Process: Successful customer process reengineering should create processes that not only meet customers' expectations and support the customer value proposal, but also provide competitive differentiation and contribute to a designed customer experience.

Information and insight: Consistent and accurate customer information and insight are the foundation of CRM. Strong customer information management strategies enable application leaders to deliver on the business goals of their CRM strategy.

Technology: CRM technologies form a fundamental part of any enterprise's application portfolio and architecture. CRM application needs should be considered as the provision of integrated functionality that supports seamless customer–centric processes across all areas of the enterprise and its partners.

Metrics: Enterprises must set measurable CRM objectives and monitor all levels of CRM indicators to turn customers into assets. Without performance management, a CRM implementation will fail. (Thompson, 2019)

Gartner's approach emphasises the importance of breaking down CRM in this manner. Whether it's five principles or eight building blocks, the key message is that CRM is not just about technology. I urge you to follow either framework, devise your own, or even research others.

The CRM pyramid

Another foundation that we build on at Winners is what we refer to as the CRM pyramid. For any reader who has worked in sales, this is the equivalent of a sales funnel but turned on its head, building from the base up as opposed to the top down (see Figure 2.2).

At the base of the pyramid you have your passive fans, those who have a passing interest in your team or your sport but with whom there's little or no engagement. They're unknown to you. They may perhaps class themselves as fans, but they have none of the interaction or communication that would typically come with the term.

In the next level up, you have the digitally engaged. They follow you on social media, they watch what's happening on Facebook, you feature in their Twitter feed, but they don't actually interact with you. At this stage they're still anonymous because they use your website without leaving their details. However, they could be identified through their IP address, Facebook ID, or Twitter handle.

Next we have casual fans; they'll come to a match maybe once or twice a season, buy from your online store at Christmas, and watch the occasional TV broadcast. You'll have their details because they interacted with you directly and, thanks to your data collection processes, you secured enough information to identify them as individuals.

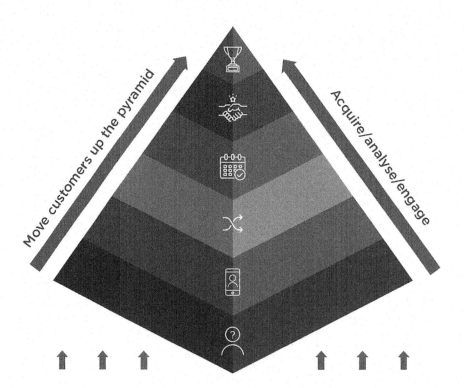

Figure 2.2 Winners' CRM pyramid (source: Winners FDD Ltd)

Moving up the pyramid we have frequent fans – they do the same thing as casual fans, but more often – followed by your loyal fans – if you cut their arm off they'd bleed the colours of your logo. And then finally at the very top, you have your advocates. These are the fans who do your job for you – they tell their family, friends, and followers to support you; they ask them to join them at the match, check out your website, and follow your social channels.

This is your CRM objective – to get as many loyal fans and advocates as possible. We aim to move our fans from their passive status to digitally engaged, from casually involved to frequently involved and then ultimately, to loyal advocates at the top of the pyramid. The way we do that is by acquiring data about them, analysing that data, and then engaging in a way that's relevant, all while aiming to increase the size of our pyramid, getting more fans into the base.

The single customer view

An SCV is exactly that – a single, unified view of each of your customers allowing you to see what relationships they have with your organisation. Imagine the value of seeing how your ticket buyers, members, store buyers, players, referees, and volunteers overlap, representing more than one relationship with you. A SCV is a key element of your approach to using data, but it can be challenging to achieve – according to Forrester's CustomerThink survey of 2015, a key challenge for 47% of organisations implementing CRM is the creation of an SCV (Leggett, 2015).

To create an SCV you need all your customer data in one database, but crucially it's not *all* the data you have about these individuals that we're after; it's just the data that supports your CRM strategy, the information that you need to support your targeted marketing campaigns and to help you make decisions. I talk more about the different types of data in your SCV in the next chapter.

From an SCV to DMP and CDP

We touched on an SCV, but we also have two further data management systems to introduce at this point: a customer data platform (CDP) and data management platform (DMP). So, what are the key differences?

As we discussed previously, your SCV presents the information you have about an individual, including contact data. This means you know who they are and, subject to their opt-in status, can communicate with them directly. They're known to you.

A CDP is commonly used to refer to the database environment that allows you to store both known and anonymous data together. This approach ensures that you retain the rich behavioural history of your anonymous fans (and you will have many of them – your website visitors and social followers) so that when they do become known to you (once they buy a ticket, register to use your site, or subscribe to a newsletter), you can link all the relevant information you have into one single record. You then have an SCV!

A DMP manages the data of your customers who are a little lower in the CRM pyramid, your fans who engage with you digitally, who can be targeted on an individual basis but using non-personally identifiable information. In other words, you can identify them but they're anonymous to you. This includes IP address, mobile identifiers, and cookie IDs. These are specifically used by advertisers and agencies who use the data to improve ad targeting, but often they will work alongside CDPs to target both known and unknown customers through the same advertising campaign.

Admittedly, at the point of writing, I'm only aware of a few rights owners who have their own DMP –you can read about one of them in the case study at the end of this chapter – but many of the elite level rights owners already have a CDP. However, there are many more that are still challenged by the notion of an SCV. Chapter 5 is dedicated to technology stacks so you can read more about this area.

Customer personas

Having looked at the five elements of CRM, the CRM pyramid, and the SCV, we now come to what, for me, is the natural conclusion or rationale for these precursors: creating customer personas. This is the cosmetic manufacturing of your ideal customers based on the data you have in your SCV or CDP. However some organisations may not use digitally generated data – some create them based on market research and then find a way to match them back to their database.

The creation of customer personas is becoming increasingly common in the sports industry as we further evolve in our use of data and CRM; in fact you can read a great case study around personas from the MLS at the end of this chapter. While they are to be addressed at quite an advanced stage, it's natural and indeed expected that you do include them in your strategy as they are incredibly important. They enable you to determine where to focus your time and how to use your budget and can be used cross-organisationally for ease of reference and help you track and measure your key business metrics, including ROI.

In the words of Tony Zambito, the founder and authority in personas:

> Buyer personas are research-based archetypal (modeled) representations of who buyers are, what they are trying to accomplish, what goals drive their behaviour, how they think, how they buy, and why they make buying decisions.
>
> (Zambito, 2013)

Customer personas are specific to you and your organisation. You create them based on the data you hold, the goals you set, and the approaches you apply to develop your business. They'll be different from those of your competitors and even your peers. That's a point that evaded Ron Johnson, a formerly acclaimed retail maverick who famously pioneered Apple's high street stores and Genius bars. Unfortunately, he went on to acute failure at JC Penney, one of America's oldest stores, when he implemented a complete rebrand in 2012 that cost the company $1 billion in lost sales. Johnson admits that his failure at JC Penney came down to three factors: he didn't know what his customers wanted; he didn't know who they were; and he didn't test his ideas on them. In short, he didn't use customer personas (Tuttle, 2013).

Customer journeys

Now you have your customer personas, based on the data you have about them in your SCV, so the final step in the principles of CRM is to develop your customer journeys. These are the maps you create for each of your personas to understand how your customers 'travel' through their relationship with you – for example, how they evolve from first hearing about your team, club, sport, or governing body to buying something from you or how they go from buying one ticket from you to becoming a season ticket holder.

When it comes to your digital customer journeys, look at your website and social data, using the rich analytics they provide to understand how these customers behave and what they're thinking – you can also increase the richness of this data through the use of customer surveys.

As I mentioned earlier in this chapter, the key point to me about the use of customer journeys is that while they should be focussed on helping you achieve the objectives you mapped out in your CRM strategy, we ensure they deliver 'quick wins' along the way. We delve even deeper into this in Chapter 8 on business change.

Case Study: Major League Soccer (MLS)

MLS represents the sport at the highest level in both the United States and Canada. It was founded in 1993 as part of a successful bid to host the 1994 FIFA World Cup and, despite a rocky start, now has 26 teams including a franchise in Miami owned in part by David Beckham, with future expansion teams in Austin, St. Louis, Sacramento, and Charlotte.

Charlie Sung Shin is the Vice President of Data Strategy and Analytics at MLS. He is the business lead when it comes to cross-organisational adoption of CRM, responsible for devising the strategy and implementation across the whole league, not just within MLS offices. Charlie worked with me to provide a case study in the first edition of this book and then helped me update it through a telephone interview on 17 July 2020.

The MLS has a centralised approach to CRM that is quite unique among rights owners. While others, particularly in North America, may emulate this approach, it's not at the same level of integration and governance, and certainly not something we see in the major sports across Europe. This can, in part, be attributed to the relatively recent formation of the League, along with its unique business structure that makes league-wide implementation logical. Each club 'owner' is in fact an investor in the League as a whole – it holds team contracts centrally, and revenues are shared across the board. Each investor-operator therefore has a stake in the profitability of the whole organisation.

Our ownership had the foresight to appreciate the importance of CRM and made an investment at a very early stage, also recognising that if we do this at an individual club level, we're never going to get the best results. It's been a journey in building this out, but we can now see the value of this in many areas.

With our business model, the club owners get the operational rights to manage one of the clubs in their market. They'll have their own P&L [profit and loss] and then revenue share from tickets, sponsorship, and media rights. So, there are two revenue opportunities for our owners: revenue that can be generated from their local operation, then another at the League level as part of their ownership of MLS.

In this respect, while the clubs are individual legal entities, they are essentially operating on behalf of MLS for their individual markets. While this might sound similar to the way the English Premier League, Premiership Rugby, or indeed the ECB operate as centralised bodies that distribute revenues across their member teams, they don't have the same centralised approach to data governance and technology.

MLS' strategy has two main objectives: to grow its sport's fan base and drive value for its enterprise. To achieve this, Shin realised early on that one of his primary aims should be to unify fan data across the whole league, which would then support business decisions at a strategic and operational level.

Our data strategy is an enabler for the overall enterprise strategy. It aligns with what we're trying to do as a company. We have a five-year plan that we develop and execute at the league level, and the data strategy is a reflection of that. Building the right infrastructure was as important as thinking about collecting the right data to execute our overall enterprise strategy.

Echoing the Amazon approach discussed in Chapter 1, MLS is constantly thinking about how it can become a more fan-centric organisation. It's not just data for data's sake but to support the way MLS engages with and services its fans. The more data the organisation gets, the more it understands the fans and what drives them. Fans are at the centre of all its business goals, and the right data helps it to build better fan relationships, which in turn enables it to achieve these goals.

One of the cornerstones of the MLS' approach to technology is to have a centralised fan database that provides a full view of engagement and transactions across the whole League.

> MLS is a single entity, so I think the structure of the organisation made it much easier for us to centralise a lot of the technology stack. The biggest benefit of having the data centralised, as well as the technology that supports the data infrastructure, is really the efficiency, as well as ensuring that we are collecting, and have visibility into, the data. We now have this not just at the league level, but also across all our clubs, which gives us a full, holistic view of all our customers.

While a key objective was always the creation of a centralised database, the overall CRM vision for MLS extended beyond just the technology and looked at establishing an internal capability that could serve the fans in the best way possible.

> What we realised was our fans are fans of the clubs, and not the league. Therefore, the areas that we needed to focus on weren't really at the League's consumer touch point: we needed to look at an infrastructure that could support our clubs, who should then establish those engagements in each of their local markets.

As a result, MLS divided its strategy into three key areas: data, customer analytics, and D2C (direct to customer). In this respect, MLS treats CRM as a B2B2C (business to business to customer) strategy: from the League to the clubs to the fans.

MLS uses its customer data to understand how fans are actively engaging, and then it chooses the best channels to communicate certain messages. At the moment it uses emails and push notifications, with a great deal of digital retargeting through Facebook and Google. It's investing in technologies that will take its data to the next level of efficiency, help get the most out of paid media advertising, and get more creative in targeting new audiences based on additional insights.

The MLS' data warehouse is central to all of this. Here different technologies allow for different processes, as well as custom data models provided by third-party partners. All of the data, no matter which technology has collected it, is connected to the data warehouse, ranging from ticketing, merchandising, digital subscriptions, website registrations, and even international event ticket sales. On top of this, MLS has implemented an analytics solution that offers a visual dashboard, allowing the entire organisation to easily see and conceptualise its data.

Central to MLS' technology stack is a data warehouse that stores league and club-level data, operating as an SCV and built-in SQL. Shin expanded on how MLS uses this resource:

> The SQL data warehouse is the centre of everything, but there's different technology that goes into it. We use SAS [software] for our ETL [extract, transform, load] process with a custom data model. It houses all our data – ticketing, merchandise, digital subscriptions such as fantasy, website registration, and international event data. We also get data from our strategic partnership with EA Sports, of their customers who play with our affiliated clubs. Our third-party data [from an external provider] is also integrated into the data warehouse.
>
> We then use an identity management solution within SAS to create our golden ID [unique identifier] by applying different logic, using the name, email address, birthday, zip code, phone number, and other information that can help us identify that multiple records belong to the same person.

Achieving an SCV, or a golden ID, is still a distant objective for many rights owners but, as Shin has already achieved this, he's now looking at how he can progress his data warehouse with thoughts of a CDP:

> The three key features that I consider in a really good CDP would be identity resolution, audience segmentation, and the activation. Right now, we're not using any out-of-the-box technology solutions because when we first started this, there wasn't a true CDP platform out there. You had some solutions that could help with identity, you had solutions that would focus on the activation, and some would focus on audience segmentation. As there wasn't a product that we felt would provide all three of them at once, we took our own steps to building that out.

So, on the identity recognition side we've reached the point where we have our own golden ID which allows us to identify different customers and different fans coming in from different places using different IDs. We then deduplicate and merge these. We also do a little bit of managing their attributions to a certain extent, but not at the level we want to; so what I've now realised is that the custom work we're doing [in SQL] can't keep up with the speed of the products being developed out there. I'm finding there are now solutions that provide all three features, and they're really good. So admittedly, I have a dilemma – do I now evaluate these solutions or continue with our homegrown product? I'm leaning towards the out-of-the-box solutions just because they're so much better than what we would be able to do in-house; they're more affordable, and they're already there.

As well as the central data warehouse, Shin explains that MLS has also built a central resource bank, which saves individual clubs having to make costly investments on analytics. This allows Shin to build data models that can be implemented in one or two clubs as a pilot, before scaling out across all clubs, because they use the same data set.

Our analytics solution sits on top of our data warehouse, which is SAS again. We use their visual analytics module, which is more of a BI dashboard and is very easy to use, and then we use our enterprise data mining tools for more of the advanced analytics that we work on. We also have Tableau [data visualisation software] that we use to visualise a lot of the third-party aggregated data.

I asked Shin about the different roles played by SAS' visual analytics and their Tableau dashboard, and it came down to individual data versus aggregate data: SAS is used at an individual record level, with Tableau used for Google Analytics and social data, replacing the way PowerPoint was previously used to present graphs and charts.

In addition to their data warehouse, analytics, and data visualisation software, MLS uses Salesforce Marketing Cloud for marketing campaigns and have invested in a Salesforce Audience Platform (DMP), along with Salesforce's Audience Studio. This ecosystem enables Shin to work with both his known and unknown audience when it comes to their media buying/paid media approach with a direct pipeline from his DMP to Facebook, Google, and YouTube.

MLS supports the clubs centrally by designing and managing the technology, infrastructure, and processes relevant to the role of data from collection, cleansing, and normalising through to storing, interrogating, and transferring to the clubs for their local market use. This approach provides the clubs with everything they need to support fact-based decision-making and data-driven marketing: it enables the use of CRM, analytics, and marketing across the League to provide a standardised approach. But to re-enforce its direct-to-fan strategy for individual clubs, they each have autonomy to decide the right marketing approach to engage with their fans.

Instead of mandating the use of certain tools across the league, MLS opted to show value in the tools it recommends with the ultimate decision resting with the clubs. With a structure that has every club owner personally invested in the profitability of the league, it was Shin's job to ensure they all understood the benefit of a uniform set of marketing and CRM tools. By taking this approach to achieving buy-in and support, Shin found that the utilisation was much better than if MLS had simply forced all league members to come on board. You can read more about this type of approach in Chapter 8 on business change.

The resources MLS offers are the same for all their clubs. They include marketing software for email, SMS, web advertising, and social media tools. However, as an acknowledgement that the League has a very different relationship with soccer fans than it does with the clubs, its sales automation solutions are chosen individually based on the club's needs and resources, along with any extra technology it uses to support the ticket sales process. According to Shin, this approach enables the clubs to take advantage of the knowledge they have of their own markets and their own fans and to optimise the vital direct engagement data that the league does not necessarily have access to.

> [The clubs] are really at the frontline where the rubber meets the road, and our clubs understand their market and their fans the best. We didn't want to dictate how sales prospects should be managed or even standardise how that engagement should be with our local clubs and their local markets. So that's where the local clubs have made investments on how they acquire fans and how they engage. And what we try to do from the back is to provide the necessary data and analytic support that's really going to help them enhance that relationship.

MLS has a number of centralised revenue streams from ticketing and sponsorship through to broadcasting and media rights. Clubs are able to exploit data to drive and increase the value they derive from ticket sales, but there's a huge opportunity in that data for increased sponsorship and media value. By consolidating the data, MLS has an in-depth understanding of its fans and how they engage with the sport. This in turn supports its sponsorship strategy.

We've built what we call a two-product 'offering' for our sponsors. One provides access to an audience segment via our DMP, for example, access to an avid soccer fan or someone who is interested in X, Y, Z, or using the taxonomy within our websites to come up with creative segmentations, and then layering on third-party data to put some more demographics onto it. The DMP then passes on that segmentation to any of the third parties that our sponsors are working with to buy media, or if they're on the same DMP, we can use a data exchange for them to access our audience. The other offering we have for sponsors is a data append service where we're mapping our first-party data to their records and providing a service like we have here from Acxiom.

You can read more about this approach to sponsorship leverage in Chapter 7 as well as the use of data appending services in Chapter 3.

We've just discussed how MLS' business structure allowed for the building of this centralised resource and how it's being used to support individual clubs to drive their fandom and build relationships with fans to grow the customer base. Now let's look at the technology behind this centralised approach.

MLS developed a unique approach to customer segmenting. Instead of using the more traditional approach of fan demographics, it focussed on fans' needs and what they hope to get out of MLS.

We tended to look at demographics in the past, but we moved away from just looking at our fans from this standpoint and started looking at them for their needs and the reason behind their consumption of soccer. We started looking at demographic data, but it's so limited in terms of how you segment and navigate – you could be looking at different demographics but still see the same needs or reason for why they're consuming certain brands or certain products. For this reason, we went beyond using demographics and looked more at a needs base to understand our fans.

Based on the needs it's seen, MLS identified two key segments to align with its strategy by improving and delivering on the needs of those segments. The two needs segments they identified are:

1 **Soccer Enthusiasts:** Fans who consider soccer to be their primary sport and who have a positive perception of MLS.
2 **Sports Fans:** They consume soccer as one of a mix of sports but not as their primary sport. They also have a positive perception of MLS but tend to have a positive perception of many different leagues.

When MLS looked at these two segments, there were certain characteristics unique to each. Soccer enthusiasts were interested in on-field performance and team rivalries, whereas sports fans were more interested in the atmosphere of the stadium experience and the social aspect of watching a game. These needs transcend demographics, so MLS focussed on trying to pinpoint opportunities in those segments in order to increase its share of the market.

However, having worked with these segments for a while, Shin recognises the need for more granular details to make it more actionable, this time using a framework developed by Clayton Christensen, a former academic and business consultant who in 1997 developed the theory of disruptive innovation, a principle that's been labelled the most influential business idea of the early 21st century. Unfortunately, Christensen passed away in early 2020, but one of his most recent works was to develop the framework of 'jobs-to-be-done': the need to understand what progress a customer is trying to make when they consider your product or service and what the customer hopes to accomplish with the purchase. It's this approach that Shin is now applying to the MLS:

We continue to use our two segments of soccer enthusiasts and sports fans, but we've been hearing from our clubs and the League staff that it's quite difficult to act against them. They've been incredibly useful in helping us understand what the market looks like, but when someone wants to act against those segments we've realised it's still too broad – it makes it really difficult at the operational level to execute campaigns because it's still too vague from a marketing and customisation standpoint. So, we asked ourselves 'How do we bring this down? How do we create something that could help us provide our clubs with a little bit more granular segmentation?' And we said, 'Let's create some personas to help us have a little more granular understanding of the audience below the soccer enthusiast and the sports fans'. With this objective we looked at the concept of jobs-to-be-done, a personalisation model that's widely used across other industries.

So, the basic concept is that there's a reason people hire a certain product; if someone purchases a product there is a reason; and Christensen uses the analogy of someone hiring or buying the product to a job. There is a certain job they're trying to get done by purchasing that product.

So if you're going to a restaurant, your basic functional role is to satisfy your hunger, but what Christensen is saying is it's not just about taking care of your hunger. There's also an emotional role and a social role that takes place – when someone goes to a restaurant, the job that they're doing certainly touches on the functional, but the person might go to a 3-Michelin-star restaurant because he wants to satisfy his social job which is 'I want to look like I'm a high-flyer' or 'I'm a food guy who goes to really well-known restaurants'. That's the job he's trying to satisfy by going to the high-end restaurants – the job-to-be-done isn't the food but more about what people see when they look at him.

Shin explains that when considering why people follow MLS they've been focussing on the team and player performances, the quality of plays, and players; but when considering jobs-to-be-done you can see these are functional features. As they review their segmentation work, they realized that this wasn't the only reason; so they started with focus group interviews to identify which of the two segments the participating fans were part of and then conducted very detailed interviews with both the soccer enthusiasts and sports fans across three key markets to understand the 'jobs' that their fans were hiring MLS to do.

Based on the response to our interviews, we were able to identify about six different jobs that became the foundation for our persona segmentation. Each persona had a combination of different jobs because we found that there were five primary jobs-to-be-done, but then when using different combinations, we found a sixth persona. These personas were the peak fan, the kind of 'addict' who's at the top, at the peak in terms of how they're engaging as part of the team. Then there's mostly constrained-personas – these are people who have competing priorities. They love soccer but you know what, 'I also have to live my life'; they have a lot of things to be done. Then we have the solo-fandom – they're a person who is enjoying soccer on their own – compared to the seeking-social persona who represented people who seek out the games, not because of the sport but because of the social component. The fifth persona is share-with-kids, and the last one is business-connects.

I asked Shin to go a little deeper into this approach to provide more insight into what jobs-to-be-done they identified within the six personas:

For peak fandom, these are people with three primary jobs, one of which is 'participate' – they're coming to MLS or following MLS to try to participate, being part of a community, to help build something, and that's the motivation behind it. The other one is 'connect' – they're using this sport to share quality time with their fellow fans and connecting with the club as their twelfth man. And the final one is 'identity' – they want to represent their city; they're kind of showing off and expressing who they are through the sport.

The share-with-kids, family persona, also has the primary job to 'connect', but with their connecting job they're spending quality time with their kids, sharing their favourite sports with their kids, and connecting through shared family memories.

This demonstrates how the jobs can overlap between the personas – they're not exclusive to a specific persona, and they change based on circumstance. 'Connect' for the peak fandom persona represents one thing, and then for the share-with-kids/family persona it represents the same thing but slightly adapted to their situation.

The other primary job that this family group has is 'inspire' – they're inspiring their kids, teaching them about the game, and also teaching them about life throughout the games. The other job is to 'entertain' – keeping the kids occupied, spending quality time together, and having fun as a family.

Now these two personas – peak fan and family – come with certain constraints. The circumstance for the family is that one of their kids is interested in soccer, but they have a huge time constraint because of the kid's schedule. So, schedules are really important for them, and that's one of the constraints that they have. For the peak fandom persona, their circumstance is that they have a little bit more time when looking for activities, but they have a constrained budget because they're a younger demographic.

Now, across all of the personas that we identified, there were seven common barriers that we found by asking them 'What is preventing you from engaging with this kind of sport?' The point is, if we're able to understand those barriers and if we could help them to remove those barriers, then they're able to consume more or engage more with us. So now we've identified these seven key barriers that cut across each of these personas but to a different degree for each one.

The different barriers Shin identified included budget, stadium convenience/ease of access (how easy it is to get to the stadium), broadcast access (ability to see the games on a regular basis on TV), knowledge of the sport (understanding the rules), time (available time to consume the sport), routines (having a routine that didn't allow for a relationship with the sport), and awareness (how well they knew the clubs, or whether they even knew their town had a club).

When rights owners, or indeed any business, creates personas in this manner – using focus groups and performing qualitative research – the next task can often be to map them back to their database, to identify which of their fans in their database fit into which of their personas. I asked Shin how he intended to deal with this, but again, MLS has taken a different approach:

> Our personas are based on very qualitative information, which means mapping them back is going to be quite a challenge, so rather than focus on the persona itself, we're going to focus on the barriers. Since there are common barriers that we're able to identify, since we know why our fans aren't consuming MLS, we decided that if we can identify those restrictions and then remove them, we'll have a better chance at getting them engaged with us. We did build the model to map out our data against the segmentation – there are about eight questions that can be used to help with this – but it can't be done at scale: so we could do it for our season ticket holders because they're more active and engaged, but there's no way the general market would answer those questions. So, now that we have some parameters to know what the characteristics are, we can use this information to look at segments and kind of treat them like those personas, but as I mentioned, we found that a persona could change overnight if someone's circumstances changed. So, we're taking what we know of our personas but focussing on the barriers to understand what needs to be addressed.

Having completed the jobs-to-be-done work and having understood the types of personas and their primary jobs, Shin now understands the barriers that are preventing greater consumption of, or engagement with, MLS. What's the next step in this approach to understanding their fans? I asked Shin how this information can be used for segmentation:

> We've started to build out what we call a 'fan score' to help us segment and use with qualitative targeting around the personas. This is a quantitative approach to scoring people based on what we call an 'MLS fan score' – it consists of a fan value score and a fan opportunity score. The fan value score addresses your current contribution to MLS – this is broken out by current level of spending and current level of engagement, so it's not just from a financial standpoint. The fan opportunity score looks at the potential contribution and is broken down into an affinity score – the likeliness of a level of affinity to MLS – and then a friction score which measures the likeliness of a barrier to consumption of the MLS.

> The friction score then links back to our jobs-to-be-done personas and the seven barriers we identified.

To wrap up this examination of MLS' approach to personas we asked Shin to explain how they're analysing the seven barriers they identified in the jobs-to-be-done work and creating an appropriate friction score. He looked at the barriers of budget and time to provide further detail:

> When we're looking at budget it's quite straightforward – we're using our third-party data source to look at their discretionary income. This allows us to determine their level of budget [within our framework]. But, for time barrier this is a bit more complex. In the qualitative interviews we asked, 'What takes time away from you?' and the common responses were that they didn't have time when they got married, just had a baby, or just changed jobs. So again, we went to our third party and looked for the external data points that would help us identify those moments – data that shows anyone with a kid under the age of 1, someone who has just changed jobs, or someone who just got married. What we're doing is looking for proxies that help us identify these moments in time, these barriers to consumption, and then turning that into a score.

Legal compliance is another major topic for Shin, and MLS is taking a very pragmatic approach, watching what's happening in the EU with GDPR while conforming to legislation in their own markets, led by the California Consumer Privacy Act and Canada's Personal Information Protection and Electronic Documents Act (PIPEDA):

> We don't market to or target fans outside of the US. There could be people in our database that are coming from the EU, but we are not proactively targeting people in the UK for instance, so we're OK from that perspective. But, the way I'm viewing this more stringent approach to data protection is that it's a trend we're going to see across the world. We've seen it in Canada and how they've improved their policies; we've seen it in the EU, and in California with the CCPA, so it's just going to be a matter of time until the remaining states take on some of these strict policies.

We've been very focussed on compliance, which involved a ton of work – we've been making sure our policies are updated, and we've updated our internal procedures – but it's still ongoing; there's more to do.

Privacy has been emphasised across so many different industries; it's not just sports – it's across any business where data is growing in importance, and it's been highlighted by public advocacy. You can see it with the social media companies that are being pressured to answer how their data's being captured and what logic is being used. So, I think it's just a matter of time before we have a major incident and our legislation is updated and looks more like the GDPR across all our states.

And where does Shin see the next step when it comes to using their Golden ID, their CDP and DMP, in addition to their understanding of barriers to engagement and consumption?

We're trying to get to a place where we could execute a seamless marketing automation across our key channels – our website, our emails, and our mobile app. We want to execute fan journeys and automate them to deliver that cross-channel experience for our fans. And right now, we don't have the level of customer behaviour data that could be used for targeting, segmentation, or other ways for us to create different journeys.

Our data warehouses have been focussed on just profiles and basic transactional data – we haven't got to capturing behavioural data. So, that's why I think I'm looking at platforms that do a really good job of understanding behavioural activity, using it to create a target, and then activating from it. Because right now, although we're using Salesforce Marketing Cloud, our activations are limited to certain channels that don't synchronise with each other. I want to use our CDP as a cockpit – a central link where we could co-ordinate the activities of different audiences and have that single understanding from where everything is put in place.

At the end of the interview, I asked Shin to tell us about his work with customer lifetime values, and again he has a different perspective to many CRM practitioners – he provides a viewpoint that demonstrates the somewhat unique situation we have in the sports industry:

I think customer lifetime value in sports is a tricky one. Everyone's trying to do it, but I don't think there's anyone who's actually doing a true customer lifetime value because in sports there are different ways the revenues are being generated. Just because someone's not buying tickets or merchandise doesn't mean you don't have a value against that customer – because if that customer is exposed to sponsorships or watches your broadcast, they're going to be valuable – as valuable as people who are actually spending directly.

So, if we accept that as fact, then the question comes back to 'How do you measure those exposures, and how do you measure those values that come from a fan viewing those sponsorships and broadcasts?'

To answer your question, yes we do it, but only from the value of ticketing, and our fans deliver a lot more value than just through ticketing.

(Shin, 2020)

Key chapter ideas

1   Strategy, data, technology, process, and culture each play an equal role in implementing CRM – each area must be given focus and consideration to enable a data-driven environment.

2   A CRM pyramid represents your most passive fans at the base and fans who advocate for you at the top – the objective of CRM is to move these stakeholders up the pyramid, constantly adding more into the base. This is achieved through acquiring data about those in the pyramid, analysing that data, then using that analysis to determine how to increasingly engage with those stakeholders.

3   The holy grail of data management is the creation of a centralised database that holds *all* the data you have about your stakeholders – known and unknown. It will include who they are, how they behave, their interests, and their needs.

4   Once you have your centralised database you can create customer personas. These are manufactured representations of the different groups of stakeholders based on the information you have in your database. Customer personas will help you plan, market, and communicate more effectively and efficiently and are tailored specifically to your organisation and its aims.

References

Bezos, J. (2017). About Amazon – 2016 letter to shareholders. *Amazon.com* [online]. Available at: www.amazon.com/p/feature/z6o9g6sysxur57t.

Cambridge University Press. (2020). *Cambridge dictionary* [online]. Available at: https://dictionary.cambridge.org/dictionary/english/process.

Desjardins, J. (2019). How much data is generated each day? *World Economic Forum* [online]. Available at: www.weforum.org/agenda/2019/04/how-much-data-is-generated-each-day-cf4bddf29f/.

Fox, M. (2017). *CIPD annual conference and exhibition.* Available at: https://www.personneltoday.com/hr/cipd-annual-conference-exhibition/.

Futurism. (2018). Moore's law. *Futurism* [online]. Available at: https://futurism.com/new-discovery-breaks-the-boundaries-of-moores-law.

Gates, B. (1996). *The road ahead.* Rockland, MA: Wheeler Pub.

Gould, L. (2015). Characteristics of a failing CRM project. *C5 Insight* [online]. Available at: www.c5insight.com/Resources/Blog/tabid/148/entryid/605/characteristics-of-a-failing-crm-project.aspx.

Humby, C. (2006). Data is the new oil. *ANA senior marketer's summit* [online]. Available at: https://ana.blogs.com/maestros/2006/11/data_is_the_new.html.

Leggett, K. (2015). CRM success is simple if you avoid these common pitfalls. *Customer Think* [online]. Available at: http://customerthink.com/crm-success-is-simple-if-you-avoid-these-common-pitfalls.

Payne, E. (2019). *Do perfect circles exist? Maybe.* Mellon College of Science [online]. Available at: www.cmu.edu/mcs/news-events/2019/0314_pi-day-perfect-circles.html.

Press, G. (2020). 6 predictions about data in 2020 and the coming decade. *Forbes.com* [online]. Available at: www.forbes.com/sites/gilpress/2020/01/06/6-predictions-about-data-in-2020-and-the-coming-decade/#5892aae74fc3.

Shin, C. (2020). Marketing, Data, and Technology Strategist, interview by phone, 17 July.

Thompson, E. (2019). The eight building blocks of CRM: Overview. *Gartner* [online]. Available at: www.gartner.com/en/documents/3913640/the-eight-building-blocks-of-crm-overview.

Tuttle, B. (2013). The 5 big mistakes that led to Ron Johnson's Ouster at JC Penney. *Time* [online]. Available at: http://business.time.com/2013/04/09/the-5-big-mistakes-that-led-to-ron-johnsons-ouster-at-jc-penney.

Zambito, T. (2013). *What is a buyer persona? Why the original definition still matters to B2B.* [online]. Available at: http://tonyzambito.com/buyer-persona-original-definition-matters.

Chapter 3

The importance of data

Previously, I quoted Clive Humby's proclamation that 'Data is the new oil' (Humby, 2006), but in this chapter I look a little deeper at the role of data and quote an even more ambitious sentiment: that 'Data is the new soil' (McCandless, 2010). I add detail to this with McKinseys' statement that 'Data is now a critical corporate asset . . . and its value is tied to its ultimate use. While data itself will become increasingly commoditized, value is likely to accrue to players that aggregate data in unique ways, and especially to providers of valuable analytics' (McKinsey Global Institute, 2016).

Within the sports industry we have an incredible amount of data at our disposal, and digitisation is producing even more. Rights owners who want to stay ahead are now becoming data-driven businesses. We use data to derive insight that informs decisions and ensures we know who our current and future customers are, where and how they live, what they like, what they don't like, what they want from us and, most importantly, what they'll do for us.

Where we used to go on gut instinct and intuition, we now use data, actionable insights extracted from analyses, and modelling to ensure we make fact-based decisions. And we're not the only industry sector doing this. Retailers combine data on their customers and the weather to predict sales, banks use predictive analytics to determine if they should approve consumer loans and which of their customers are most likely to repay them, and Barack Obama's 2012 rise to the White House was touted as 'The First Big Data Election' (Hellweg, 2012). Of course, the data-led tactics used by Donald Trump's team in 2016 to support his US presidential election overshadowed any activities of Obama and his election team, and there are suggestions that the UK's decision in 2016 to leave the EU was also influenced by the clever use of data.

However, it's important to accept that while data has immense power, we must also combine this with what we already know about our fans and the way they behave. In a telephone interview on 11 January 2018, I asked Amie Becton Ray, the National Hockey League (NHL)'s Director of Database Marketing and Strategy, her view of the way we use data:

> The thing about sports is it's a very emotional business. Our fans are passionate about their team; they really care about them so if their team is

doing well then everything is great, the website works wonderfully, the emails they receive are fabulous. But if their team loses, then there's less satisfaction with the brand as a whole. So, while I agree that data is extremely important in decision-making, we still always have to factor in emotion.

A great example is our All-Star Fan Vote. Every year we step back and look at the program's analytics and metrics and think about how to improve the experience and engage fans. One year we allowed fans to vote 30 times a day, but the data showed us most people voted just once. So, the next year we implemented a ten-vote limit and most people voted ten times on each day they voted.

It is important to use a combination of what we know about our fans, and what we are continually learning from the data in order to formulate the programs that make the most sense, that we think will be the most effective. And then we test and learn, and tweak things as we go.

(Ray, 2018, 11 Jan.)

Another version of this sentiment is provided by Jo Brown, Lincoln City Football Club's Ticket Office Manager, in a discussion I had with her in June 2020. Jo had to supervise a project to provide fans with refunds for season tickets when their football season ended prematurely because of the coronavirus (you can read more about that from the club's CEO, Liam Scully, in Chapter 6). A process was developed that ensured fans received a personalised email and form allowing them to quickly and efficiently select their preferred refund method. Unfortunately, an error in the ticketing system at the start of the season meant not all the data could be handled in the same manner, so Jo explains how she had to go through a quantity of records manually:

The email and form worked really well for about 98% of our season ticket holders. Their details were perfectly listed and accurately represented their situation but for the remaining 2% we had to perform some manual cross-checking across different source files.

We also had individual fans that we knew had a different set of circumstances than those evidenced in their record – a change in personal circumstances, contact details, seat swaps, and various other situations. These had not been captured in our ticketing system accurately but, thanks to our personal awareness of these individual issues, we could easily amend the appropriate records.

While it was a bit time consuming to have to check these records manually, it was a small price to pay to ensure we gave the right fans the right opportunity in the refund programme. And we only had to do it for a small number of fans.

(Brown, 2020, 26 June)

Both of these use cases demonstrate that while we need data to tell us things about our fans, the processes we use are just as important, and we must be prepared to apply our personal knowledge, gut instincts, and years of experience when required.

I can't imagine there are many rights owners out there who still need convincing that data is important to their future. In reality, *data* is really just another word for information, and undervaluing the need for information in a business would be reminiscent of the film companies who underestimated the threat from digital photography and the video rental companies who initially ignored growing interest in online streaming services. However, I suspect there are many who still haven't taken charge of their data, so this chapter is dedicated to you in an attempt to simplify the subject, help you understand some of the key areas of importance, and provide a way to navigate the many points for consideration.

Data as a corporate asset

The data that you have about your customers is almost as important to a rights owner as the sport or event itself and should be treated as a valuable asset. Just like your logos, images, and media rights, it should be nurtured, protected, and maximised.

I was first asked about the value of a rights owner's database in 2012 by a contact who often found himself advising buyers and, in this case, sellers of English football clubs. He posed the question of how much a fan database adds to the asset value of a club. We discussed the types of analyses that would provide him with the answer, Customer Lifetime Value (CLTV) and propensity modelling being the most relevant and easy to formulate. We'll talk more about these in the next chapter.

When calculating the value of your database, while you can model your fans' spending power by analysing historic transactional data, a further question that needs to be answered to provide an accurate evaluation is how many fans it takes to generate *a specific value* in sales for the sponsor. Taking this one step further we should also identify how many of our fans are contributing to our media rights negotiations – what impact does their viewership have on the fees we end up securing from intermediaries? Modelling these factors and applying them to your database will add a further dimension to your CLTV, increasing its asset value.

Despite our growing ability to apply a value to the individual customers in our database, the world isn't quite ready for this to be listed as a company asset and is perhaps one of the reasons many businesses still do not have a more dedicated focus on their data. We'll take a cursory look at this in the last chapter of this book.

Data-driven decisions in sports performance

This book isn't about the use of data in sports performance, that is, the winning or losing of a game, performing a personal best, or winning a championship. It's about the impact data has on the business of sports, to support targeted marketing and decision-making to increase revenue, participation, and engagement. But it's impossible to write a chapter on the importance of data in sports without making some sort of reference to *Moneyball*, the 2003 book about the Oakland Athletics baseball team and their approach to using data to become the 2002 league champions. Billy Beane, the Oakland A's manager at the time, used data to assess a player's value during the recruitment process, taking on a failing team and operating with a limited budget. Despite these odds, Beane's team went on to secure a record of 20 consecutive wins (Lewis, 2003).

I have another favourite example of the use of data to inform sports performance: Lewis Hamilton's debut F1 title win for McLaren in 2008. At the Brazilian Grand Prix, Hamilton needed to finish in the top five and was sitting pretty with a few laps to go. But he had a challenger behind him, Sebastian Vettel, who, desperate to pass, could have put them on a collision course had Hamilton decided to fight for his position. McLaren's CEO instructed Hamilton to let Vettel pass rather than risk a crash because the data predicted Hamilton would take fifth place at some point during the last lap. The data was right. He did, but not until the very last corner.

However, my favourite example of data impacting a performance result is the recent INEOS 1:59 Challenge. For those of you who missed it, on 11 October 2019 Eliud Kipchoge, the Kenyan athlete, achieved a world record running a marathon in under two hours. The usual analyses were applied to ensure Eliud's training; his pacemakers, the event venue, and course format would support ultimate success, and while marathon runners are used to considering weather as an influencing factor, it was so paramount to this event that the team worked on three different forecasts at various stages of preparation (INEOS 1:59 Challenge, 2019).

To me, these examples are equivalent to using predictive analytics when trying to sell a product, for example, a new VIP hospitality package, season ticket, or even a piece of merchandise. If the data tells you how much your customers might pay for a product, how many of them could afford to do so, over what period of time and with what frequency, you'll have all the information to need to launch it with confidence. Scale this approach up, and, as an example, rights owners could more accurately predict how many seats their new stadium should have, as opposed to constructing something that's oversized or, conversely, not providing enough capacity for growth. Apply this to the way our development teams grow our sports and we can fight the negative trend of sports participation we highlighted in Chapter 1. And when it comes to the weather, this is our favourite external data point to help understand and predict attendance: if you know attendance goes down when it rains and who would normally attend but chooses to stay away when it rains, and the forecast tells you to expect a shower, you can tailor your messaging – and your offers – accordingly.

Data management strategy

As you sit and consider how to become a data-driven organisation, you need to think about your data management strategy – that is, all the processes you put in place to manage the data you use in your organisation; how you acquire, manage, store, use and improve it.

Below are the key considerations and questions you should ask when creating your data management strategy. As you read through, see how many answers you already have. You might be surprised to discover you could already be halfway there:

1   **What data do you need to achieve your business objectives?** For example, when considering the data from your ticketing systems, do you need credit card numbers and expiry dates or do you just need to know who bought what, when, for how much, and how often? If you're working with your registered athlete database, do you need their height, weight, and medical status or just the date they registered, the last time they played, and their performance record?

2   **Where are you getting your data?** What is the source system – what database is hosting that information, and how can you get it? Continuing the previous example, you may be using a third-party ticketing provider, so you need to get your data from their system to yours. Conversely, your athlete registration database may be housed by your sports development team, although this may again be supported by a third party or could be internally managed.

3   **Is your data accurate?** You need to understand how accurate your information is and how you can improve on that level of accuracy. It makes sense that if your data isn't accurate then, whatever you do with it – whether you're making decisions or setting up targeted campaigns – won't be accurate either. If you address a casual ticket buyer as though they're a season ticket holder or a referee as though they're a coach, your message will lose its impact and won't achieve its objective. If you're analysing ticket-buying behaviour to assist with a pricing or loyalty strategy, your plans will be flawed if your ticketing data isn't accurate. Inevitably this will lead to less-than-predicted success in your offering.

4   **How can this data be used, and how can those users access it efficiently?** At an early stage of your CRM progress, the number of people that have direct access to your data might be limited to just one individual or department, or when you're more advanced you might have the resources for a dedicated CRM and data department that services the whole business. But whatever your internal procedures, and whether one person or multiple people need to access and use your data, we need to have processes to ensure data can be accessed, shared, and distributed by the business to support its different uses – whether for targeted messaging or to support decision-making.

5   **Does your data management strategy include your KPIs and metrics?** What does success look like for you? Clearly defining this will enable you to ensure your data management strategy stays on track. You'll know when you need to make adjustments, and you'll stay abreast of your timing. Examples of this could be:

- Reduction in your email marketing bounce rate (those email addresses that are no longer valid), demonstrating that your customers' email addresses are being used before they've had chance to decay and that they're being updated.
- The amount of time your data governance committee meetings take and the frequency of these. You can imagine that at the start of your data management strategy, you'll have several issues that need to be discussed regularly and take up more time, so taking less time in these discussions can be considered a success metric.
- Percentage completion of data attributes: the amount of information you have about your customers in your database. You may have set a goal of understanding their favourite players in your team, adding their date of birth or gender, knowing where they live, their occupation, etc.
- Reduction in the number of incidences where data issues have been identified, for example, incorrect format of data fields that are supposed to merge.

6   **Within your data management strategy, do you have a set of rules and processes that collectively make up your data governance?** It's common, and indeed recommended, to set up a data governance body or committee that takes responsibility for the implementation of these rules and processes, is accountable for the progress, and ensures the approach is maintained. With a sports right's owner, this committee might be made up of representatives from your commercial/sales team, marketing, ICT, and legal departments, ensuring that all key areas of the business are represented. If you're a national governing body or international federation with responsibility to grow the sport, you would also include your sports or development department within this committee.

Once you have documented your data management strategy in an easy-to-use format – perhaps a one-page summary for your management backed up by a more comprehensive document – it's important to maintain its relevance. Your approach to data management is not a one-off project but an ongoing set of initiatives that support both long-term goals and short-term wins. Hence your strategy will need to undergo constant review and measurement as your business objectives change and evolve, year to year, season to season.

Data to focus on

The data you should focus on is that which aligns with your business objectives, enables you to make decisions quickly, and will help you achieve your goals. It's not 'big data' or data for data's sake. Going back to the first consideration of your data management strategy, when I talk with clients about the type of data they ought to be collecting, I refer to four key categories:

1   **IDENTITY DATA** is the collective name given to data that can identify an individual and includes the following types:
    Contact information – With your likely CRM objective being to get the right message to the right person at the right time, then securing email addresses of your customers is highly recommended. Email marketing remains one of the most cost effective and measurable methods of keeping your customers informed. Adding mobile phone numbers to your customer records will allow you to use SMS marketing – another channel for fast, efficient, and targeted delivery of your messages. This approach is particularly useful for in-stadium promotions where there may be no Wi-Fi and limited 3G/4G bandwidth. It can also be a preferred channel for last-minute sales messages. However, while SMS marketing can play a valuable role in your CRM strategy, the costs are significantly higher than those of email marketing, so it is only recommended for highly targeted marketing. We discuss this further in Chapter 6 on data-driven marketing.
    Address data – Knowing where your fans live has multiple uses. These include sending personalised and relevant messages, demonstrating relevance to your sponsors/partners, informing event-related decisions such as parking and traffic requirements, and purchasing data appendages from third parties such as Experian and Acxiom. You can read more about these later in this chapter.
    Note: address data is often confused with location data, but these are very different. Location data is commonly defined as information collected by a network or service about where a user's mobile, laptop, or other digital device is or was located. In other words, it's generated automatically and through the use of technology.
2   **QUANTITATIVE DATA**, in a CRM context, tends to refer to how your customers have behaved in their relationship with you, both offline at your events and online through your digital channels. The types of data include:
    Demographics – the data points that are common for all of us. Gender, age, marital and family status, household income, location, education level, and employment status can all be considered within this category.
    Fan engagement/behavioural – the way your customer digitally interacts with you: their usage pattern on your websites, mobile applications, online games, and even how they respond to your email campaigns and text messages.

Transactional – this is purchase data from ticketing, corporate hospitality, merchandise, and even content is of significant value as it's usually the most accurate and richest of all your data categories. For example, asking someone for their postcode because you want to know where they live could result in false information, but asking for it so you can send them something they've purchased significantly increases the chances of you receiving something accurate.

Participation – your registered participants who play, coach, referee, and volunteer in your sport or who enter a competition/promotion, attend your events, or watch on TV/online may all be forms of participation data.

Communication preferences – the consent or permissions that your customers have given you to send them direct messages. Depending on your communication channels, approach to content, and use of segmentation, your preferences centre might include channel preferences (email, SMS, mobile app push, and web) and content (newsletter, shop news, ticketing alerts, etc.).

3   **DESCRIPTIVE DATA** is the information that allows you to understand a bit more about customers. This includes the location data I refer to earlier as well as lifestyle data. This refers to anything related to your customers' interests beyond their relationship with you. This could include the other sports they follow, their favourite newspaper, the type of car they drive, their holiday choice, and hobbies.

4   **QUALITATIVE DATA** is our fourth category, and you may already have heard this reference if you've studied or worked with market research. Generally, this includes information that tells us about our customers' attitudes, emotions, opinions, motivation, and most importantly, their needs. If we know what our customers need from us, then we can more easily deliver it, ensuring their attention, loyalty, and revenue. Qualitative data is actually the most difficult to measure precisely and to analyse. This is because much of it will be in the form of descriptive words, so the ability to examine it for patterns or comparisons through automation can be a challenge without advanced algorithms. Using questionnaires and forms that include standardised wording and phrases as a choice selection supports this – but you may risk forcing a fan into selecting an option that doesn't quite fit their state of mind.

Data sources and collection

Inevitably you will get your customer data from a variety of places. Your ticketing system secures transactional data, your athlete management system will secure your participation data, the various other forms that you produce will collect demographic data, and through the use of surveys you can supplement any data you already have with additional information, including attitudinal and needs data. When I talk about the way we collect that data, I refer to three main methods:

1 **Ask for it.** You can ask for data through the use of registration or purchase forms, data-collection landing pages (perhaps for competitions or a newsletter sign up), or the use of surveys. Asking someone directly to give you their information will result in the most accurate data. But don't forget, it's a value exchange. Some of your fans will just give it to you, but some will need to know why. They'll want the hook, for example they can access unique and exclusive content on your website, and you'll send them news and information; others will want an incentive such as the chance to win a competition or receive a discount code for your online store.

   On this point, creating an online registration form and inviting new customers to give you their details in return for receiving news and updates from you is an efficient and cost-effective method of increasing the size of your database. Once the form has been created, you can use your website, social channels, and other modes of communication to encourage fans or followers of your sport to sign up. Most importantly, the form does not have to be dynamically integrated into your centralised database or SCV. You can manually export and import your customer data with whatever frequency you decide.

2 **Look out for it.** This is specifically true of behavioural data in the digital space. Tracking the content areas of your website that your fans visit and the links they click in your email campaigns helps you know more about their areas of interest, what they like about your sport, their favourite athlete, whether they're considering attending a match, or are a potential volunteer.

3 **Buy it.** You can buy data from aggregators, and while I would never advise a rights owner client to buy contact data like email addresses or mobile phone numbers, I do consider the act of enhancing your existing records in this manner a reasonable proposition. For example, you could buy demographic and lifestyle data. However, it's important to use a company with a good reputation, as you do risk the information being inaccurate, old, and perhaps unethically sourced. I refer to this earlier in this chapter and reference Experian and Acxiom, two of the largest global suppliers of enhancement data, also known as appendages.

Different data types

There are currently three different data types. I say currently because, with the pace at which this field is developing, there will undoubtedly be more discovered before long. The current types are as follows:

1 **First-party data.** This is *your* data. The data that you collected and own, as we discussed earlier in this chapter, is one of your most valuable assets, even if you don't know it yet. In a 2015 survey by Econsultancy, almost three-quarters of marketers surveyed said first-party data provides the greatest insight into their customers (Econsultancy, 2015), and Sir Martin Sorrell referred to 2020 as 'the year of first-party data' (Sorrell, 2019).

2 **Second-party data.** This is especially prevalent in the sports industry, although this term can be confusing, given the source of this data. It traditionally comes from customers of your partners – such as sponsors or ticketing and merchandise agents – who have ticked the 'third-party opt-in' box. It's the first-party data of your ticketing agents or your sponsors whose customers have said that their data can be shared with you.

3 **Third-party data**. This is the data that you can buy from companies specialising in data collection and aggregation. As noted previously, these data sets can be purchased 'off the shelf' so, by definition, they're not unique and their quality can vary widely.

While your first-party data is of the most value and your second-party data from a credible source can add quantity, third-party data can often get you to your desired state far quicker than the others. This is because the source of this data is usually one of the global data aggregators such as the aforementioned Experian or Acxiom.

One of the forms of third-party data that I particularly enjoy using is consumer marketing classifications created by socioeconomic and geodemographic profiles of neighbourhoods. This level of data enhancement is usually at a postcode or postal address level and can then be added to each of your individual customer records.

In 2015, I demonstrated the power of this third-party data to a sports client, but his response wasn't quite what I expected. I applied socioeconomic profiles to his database and showed that it contained a higher index of affluent singles and couples than the country average and that his sport had a much lower propensity to attract former council tenants and poorer singles. I added that this suggested his fan base might have a higher disposable income, enabling him to approach TAG Heuer or Mercedes for sponsorship, and that he might possibly consider increasing his ticket prices (see Figure 3.1).

I thought this would be great news for my client, but it was actually the opposite. It turned out that his eleventh strategic objective was to use the sport to engage with their inner cities. The results I was showing him demonstrated they weren't achieving this objective. While this may seem a bad message to receive, it is better to know about it than to continue down the wrong path while thinking it's the right one. Knowledge is power, and what the data shows can help you readjust your strategies.

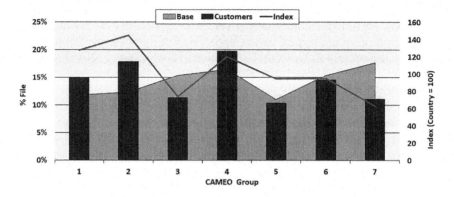

Figure 3.1 Socioeconomic profile overview (source: Winners FDD Ltd)

Data standardisation

To support the third consideration of your data management strategy, the accuracy of your data, I'd like to talk about data standardisation. As we discussed, sports rights owners will have different data sources, some internal and some external, so your data is being collected in different ways and in different formats. The principle of data standardisation is that a layer of processing can be added that ensures all your data ends up in a common format. This processing can be manual or automated, but the quote from Gates I mentioned in Chapter 2, relating to efficiency and inefficiency, is especially relevant here. Once processed, the data can then be aggregated and transformed into an SCV that, in turn, can be used across your organisation for decision-making and communication.

Data standardisation is an incredibly important part of your data strategy. It involves keeping your data clean, in the correct format, and verified before you do anything with it. Imagine how important it is to have the correct email address for a fan before sending out any campaigns, or the right data points before you try and find your actionable insights. If you ever want to merge your databases together in an SCV (or any other type of data warehouse) the relevant data fields must match up. They must use the same pattern.

Here are some easy examples that clearly demonstrate the principle, with some tactics to help minimise the occurrence of incorrect formatting:

1   **Date of birth.** In Europe and many other regions of the world, the format dd/mm/yyyy is used, but (as you'll be aware) in the US the date and month fields are reversed to mm/dd/yyyy. If you're not paying attention to the input format of the date of birth field in the different data collection forms around your business, you may be collecting records

in different formats. Imagine that one of your customers was born on 2 November 1966 and registers on your website to be a volunteer through a form that uses the dd/mm/yyyy format but then enters one of your competitions via an independently hosted landing page where your developer used mm/dd/yyyy. If you're using an SCV, or even if you just use an email campaign platform that houses all your email marketing data, depending on how you import your records and the business rules you set, you could end up sending that customer a birthday card on 11 February. Here's another point to consider: if you ask for a customer's date of birth and allow users to free type instead of using a calendar format for the input, you could end up with 2 November 1966, 2 Nov 66, 2 Nov 1966, or any one of a number of spellings and formats.

The value in a correct date of birth field can't be understated. First, there are digital birthday cards – a great tool for fan engagement that only need to be set up once a year and will then provide you with 12 months of activity. If you include a discount coupon for your online store or a sponsor offering, these could help with your commercial objectives. Second, if you want to pitch to, say, Heineken for a sponsorship, they'll inevitably want to know how many adults aged 18 to 25 you have in your database, as that information aligns with their target demographic.

2   **Gender.** Another data area which is incredibly important to your business, but prone to errors, is your gender field. Options for a customer to choose often include M or F, male or female, boy or girl, but the way in which a database may interpret this could also include a 0 and 1, or 1 and 2. If this isn't standardised when the individual data sources merge, you'll end up with a 'dirty' gender field using multiple versions of these examples when you really want completely usable information. It's interesting to note that many organisations now use a broader gender definition than male or female. Whether you do this or not should be a decision of the entire business, not decided at an individual 'form' level.

3   **Country of residence.** I always recommend, when using a country of residence field in your data collection forms, that you use a drop-down menu which enables the customer to select a specific country. If you don't, can you imagine how many different spellings of any individual country you might get? Consider someone who lives in London. Their self-type options could be *UK* or *United Kingdom*, *GB* or *Great Britain*, or indeed they could write England. If they mistype or have a problem with spelling you could end up with *Unidet Kindom*, *Grate Britain*, or *England*.

You can see from just these three simple examples that if you don't pay attention to your data standards, you could end up with a database that contains a lot of unusable information. This will skew your statistics and result in incorrect messaging sent to your fans. Creating a data dictionary that lists each data cell in each of your data sources, its format, and purpose will help you stay on top of this. You can read more about this in Chapter 5.

Using drop downs, tick boxes, and auto-populating from an external data source will help maintain your data hygiene. When it comes to your email addresses, most commercial email marketing platforms will auto-cleanse your list of any bounced records as well as those of customers who have unsubscribed, but if your campaigns have a high bounce rate it could affect your sending reputation and result in your platform blocking you from using them.

Case study: INEOS Grenadiers

In the first edition of this book, we used a case study provided by Special Olympics International, where the focus was very much on collecting data in a standard format over many years. You can download a copy of that case study from www.winnersfdd.com/winningwithdata-first/ch3casestudy.

For this edition we interviewed Dave Callan, Head of Partnerships and Business Development at INEOS Grenadiers, who gave me an overview of his approach to using CRM and data in a telephone interview in June 2020.

Team INEOS is the most successful cycling team in the world, having won seven of the last eight editions of the Tour de France. With the UK still in coronavirus lockdown at the time of writing, the team last participated in a real race three months earlier at the beginning of March – although as you'll go on to read, it wasn't long before their fans around the world could again experience the thrill of cycling through virtual eRacing. We started the interview by asking Dave about his team's general manager, Sir Dave Brailsford, who is globally renowned for his belief in the doctrine of 'marginal gains', the principle of small incremental improvements in any process adding up to a significant improvement when they are added together, and how that compares to his own approach to CRM.

> [Sir] Dave is a big believer that the marginal gains approach is one that can be applied in other environments, and it's certainly mirrored in the way we've looked at CRM in the business side of Team INEOS. We've always used the data in our social channels and website to tell us how well we're doing and what our fans like; but when it comes to individual fan data, we only really started down that path in early 2017. That might sound quite late for a sport that's won or lost on decimal points; but don't forget our team was only formed in 2010.
>
> On the bike we've always been obsessed with making the best-informed decisions. The application and use of data has always played a crucial role within this, and now we take the same approach to the way

we engage with our fans. The use of testing what we do to see how our fans respond is a major part of that. For example, when we're running a digital competition that has a data collection element, we typically run a minimum of three different versions to make sure we get it right. We look at the conversion rates and choose what to drop, amend, or change accordingly. It's interesting that what we've learned from doing this isn't just really valuable, but it often tells us the opposite of what we thought we knew. Fans will answer questions if you give them reason to. These answers then help us plan content, engage partners, and continue to build the trust between the Team INEOS brand and our fans around the world.

When it comes to CRM, our starting point was a pretty sizeable database of fans we'd collected over the previous years, so we asked ourselves how could we engage with them, how could we talk directly to these thousands of fans who, at some point over the years, had engaged with us?

We did quite a bit of research to understand more about systems and their different functionality, and in the end we decided to start our own CRM development with email marketing. That would take care of our first priority and give us the opportunity to learn more about this area before investing any further.

Dave and his team selected Mailchimp as their email platform, joining the reported 11 million other customers who together send campaigns to over 4 billion customers (Lunden, 2019). In Chapters 5 and 6 we talk more about the different technologies available to rights owners, but when it comes to a platform for advanced email marketing, Mailchimp is a market leader with 60% of the industry, so a good choice for Dave. We asked how Team INEOS used email marketing to achieve his first objective – engaging with his database of fans.

Email is a great platform for us – it really compliments our website and social activity because it allows us to send messages directly to our fans without waiting for them to come to us. And we can add a level of personalisation, using the information we have in the Mailchimp database to create segments.

We use a number of different tactics to ensure that we stay engaged with our fans. We have our regular newsletter that goes out to all our marketing opt-ins. It generally includes a round-up of different news we want to share, but we also use it to encourage some interaction with surveys and votes. And we use it to promote our online store, highlighting special offers and new items added to the range.

We also use email for specific one-off announcements – we don't take it for granted that our fans will visit our website when we want them to, or catch our social postings, so doubling our efforts with email ensures we get as much coverage as possible.

With our online store being our second revenue generator, behind sponsorship, we regularly send dedicated store emails where the focus is purely on the products we sell – both for cyclists and fans. Added to this, we have a few automations set up for new fans who enter our database, and these will be sent to different people depending on which form they filled in, how they entered our database, and how much information we have about them.

We're also slowly adding some CRM activities into our sponsorship department – starting with the traditional solus emails but also progressing to more creative data-led digital activations. We're just in the process of launching a birthday email and looking at the use of dynamic content to personalise the messaging depending on who's receiving it – we could tailor the message based on where they are in the world, their age, what products we have in our store, what products they've already bought from our store, etc. We've got quite a few ideas we're working on.

Dave joined Team INEOS in April 2016 from Manchester United, universally considered a leader in the use of fan data across European rights owners, with a database of over 36 million (Manchester United, 2019). While only a percentage of these will be ticketing customers, Manchester United will have benefited from the millions of fans around the world who will have tried, both unsuccessfully and successfully, to buy a ticket.

This is an opportunity Team INEOS doesn't have because, unlike many rights owners, it doesn't sell tickets. On top of this, as a road racing team, all the 60+ races it competes in from January to October are in the 'open air', not in venues. This means there's no form of access control to watch these races; so while it's estimated that 10 to 12 million spectators line the streets, roads, and mountains for the Tour de France, no one knows who they are – they're as anonymous as website visitors who don't register or Facebook followers who don't use your landing pages. This presents quite a problem for Team INEOS' ambitions for database growth, as ticketing systems tend to be one of the biggest generators of clean and rich fan data. I asked Dave where his database growth comes from and how he sees that developing even further:

We have two primary sources for collecting new fan data: our online store, which has sold to customers in over 85 countries around the world, and our website, where we collect subscribers for our newsletters through a pop-up and a sign-up form. We also have a microsite for competitions, and during a normal season we will use it for joint sponsor and merchandise promotions. Between these three, we've seen our database grow by 260%, and out of all the fans we have in our database, 75% have opted-in to hear from us.

The last two years have been quite a learning curve for us – we now know what data collection means; we know what to do with the data when we get it, so one of our focusses moving forward will be to get better at collecting data. We're really good at creating digital news and experiences, and we get a tremendous level of engagement, so we now need to ensure we consider how that activity helps us grow our database.

A great example of that ability to create engaging experiences came about as a direct result of the coronavirus, which called an immediate halt to nearly all professional sports around the world. This meant Team INEOS' event calendar was postponed, and while we now know the team will once again be on their Pinarello bikes at the Vuelta a Burgos, Spain's multi-day stage race that forms part of the Union Cycliste Internationale (UCI) Europe Tour, earlier this year there was no sight of a return to racing. So, Team INEOS did what many of the most innovative rights owners around the world have done and entered the world of virtual sports, combining it with another pandemic-inspired trend: at-home participation.

I asked Dave to describe the principle behind Team INEOS' first eRide and eRace and share some of the data benefits that came out of it:

We partnered with Zwift (the online training platform for cycling and running that combines gameplay with community) to create a two-tiered event. The first stage was a group ride with any Zwift user, and it set a record for the platform with 8,340 people simultaneously taking part in the first wave. This was followed up by two further waves and a total of 15,530 riders. Can you imagine that – over 15,000 people around the world all cycling in their homes at the same time but doing it as part of Team INEOS? We even had ex-England cricketer Kevin Pietersen signed up for the group ride.

That was followed by the main show – an intra-squad eRace that was broadcast live across our channels. All our 30 riders were involved, and they really took it seriously, dialling in from 11 countries with current World Time Trial Champion, Australian Rohan Dennis, taking the flag.

We wanted our fans to get as much out of this as possible – to feel as close as they could to a real race – so we used leading sports TV production company, Sunset+Vine, to ensure a quality level of production. We had live commentary from Eurosport's Rob Hatch and got the chance to try some novel in-race features like the use of power data and interviews with our riders. And, as with all sporting contests, there was some uncertainty around the outcome to keep the audience engaged and allow for a compelling product to market. I think that's a key point to why our intra-squad race was so engaging – nobody really knew what was going to happen, even us.

The results were incredible. We set another Zwift record with a live audience of 273,000 across YouTube and Facebook, and the non-live stream got 624,000 views, with a total recorded reach of 6.1 million on our channels.

You can read more about other digital-first activities throughout the book, but in terms of cycling, Team INEOS has joined a trend that is showing signs of longevity. The Tour of Flanders, usually held in Belgium in the spring and now diarised for 18 October 2020, held the first virtual UCI World Tour event two weeks before Team INEOS and drew 613,486 viewers, just in Flanders. This was followed by international broadcaster, Eleven Sports, acquiring broadcast rights to the Tour de Suisse-backed 'Digital Swiss 5' e-cycling event in six countries, Swiss public-service broadcaster SRG SSR securing rights for the next two years, followed by similar deals with France's L'Équipe, Germany's ZDF, Japan's J Sports, and FloSports in the US (Ajuonuma, 2020).

I asked Dave how his first eRide and eRace will form part of his CRM strategy moving forward, and he was quite clear about future opportunities:

We have a huge global following, 42 million fans around the world, and we are always looking for ways to bridge the gap between them and our team. We know that the majority of them can't get to our races, so digital and content are always at the heart of our engagement strategies.

Our CRM approach places a lot of focus on knowing who these 42 million fans are, what they want from us, and of course, getting as many of them as we can into our database. Next time we run an eRide and eRace with Zwift, we'll place more emphasis on collecting the data of fans who engaged as it could open us up to fans we didn't know we had. For example, Canada was in the top five participating countries, but the number of Canadians in our database is just 2% of the number of British and 17% of the number of Americans. And thanks to Egan Bernal (the first Latin American cyclist to ever win the Tour de France), Columbians are the third most populous nationality in our database, yet their presence was not highlighted in our eRide stats. This suggests that Zwift was helping us reach a new audience, introducing our brand, our team, and our values to their customers.

Dave makes a really valid point here: when rights owners partner with other organisations, such as their sponsors or media partners, to implement digital promotions or activity where the delivery is on the partners' channels, they open the sport up to a different audience. You can read more about the opportunities this brings in Chapter 7, which explores the role of CRM and data in sponsorship.

As a final note, I asked Dave to share the way Team INEOS tracks and reports on its activities and achievements, and how the information is used within the business:

Starting with our email campaigns, we look at the results of these in the same way we look at our Google Analytics and the native analytics in Facebook, Instagram, YouTube, and Twitter. Of course, the difference is we're looking at how individuals are responding – whether they're opening, whether they're interested in our stories, and whether they're going on to purchase from our online store because of what they read. Our fans seem to really love our emails – we've got an average open rate of just over 40% and an average click-through rate (CTR) of over 5.4%. We also track merchandise sales directly from our emails – both in Mailchimp and Google Analytics – so we have a great understanding of our CRM ROI.

We use Tableau (market leading data visualisation software) for centralised reporting – our email, online store, and web data is in there; 11 dashboards that auto-update so we can see where we are at any given time. It's a great motivator to see things like our database grow or the most popular item in our online store. Before the pandemic, when we worked from our offices, we had the dashboards displayed on a big-screen TV so everyone in the marketing department could see our numbers.

Thinking about what's next, we've got more work to do on our dashboards and the way we use the information we take from them.

In addition to growing our database, we want to push our use of customer segments and start to consider how we extend our CRM channels beyond email. We've already started looking at our customer personas and plan to develop them further. This will enable us to share them with our sponsors and plan how they can be used to support their promotional plans.

(Source: Callan, 2020)

Key chapter ideas

1   Your data should be viewed as a business asset with its own value and should be protected, nurtured, and utilised in the same way you monetise your logos, trademarks, images, and media rights.
2   You need a data management strategy to guide you through key considerations, as you become a data-driven organisation. These include understanding what data you need, where you'll find it, securing and maintaining its accuracy, applying specific rules and processes to the way you manage it and, finally, identifying your KPIs so you know when you're on track to achieving your data-related business objectives.
3   The right data governance practices will need to be determined, and new roles may need to be created to accommodate this issue.
4   Your data will only deliver its true potential to your organisation if it's in a format that ensures it can be readily used across the business. Implementing a process of standardisation that's applied to every individual data source will enable you to merge all your data and produce an SCV.
5   Collecting participation data in sports has a tremendous value for the development of the sport, but adding personal data at an individual contact level will add greater value – enabling you to track participants' performance to ensure progress and to communicate directly with the individual.

References

Ajuonuma, R. (2020). *Eleven sports lands digital swiss 5 virtual cycling rights in six territories* [online]. Available at: www.sportbusiness.com/news/eleven-sports-lands-digital-swiss-5-virtual-cycling-rights-in-six-territories/.
Brown, J. (2020). Telephone interview, 26 June.
Callan, D. (2020). Head of Partnerships and Business Development, telephone interview, 4 June.
Econsultancy. (2015). *The promise of first-party data.* London: Econsultancy.
Hellweg, E. (2012). 2012: The first big data election. *Harvard Business Review* [online]. Available at: https://hbr.org/2012/11/2012-the-first-big-data-electi.

Humby, C. (2006). Data is the new oil. *ANA Senior Marketer's Summit* [online]. Available at: https://ana.blogs.com/maestros/2006/11/data_is_the_new.html.

INEOS 1:59 Challenge. (2019). *Getting the weather right* [online]. Available at: www.ineos159challenge.com/news/getting-the-weather-right/.

Lewis, M. (2003). *Moneyball.* New York: W.W. Norton.

Lunden, I. (2019). *Mailchimp expands from email to full marketing platform, says it will make $700M in 2019* [online]. Available at: https://techcrunch.com/2019/05/13/mailchimp-expands-from-email-to-full-marketing-platform-says-it-will-make-700m-in-2019/.

Manchester United. (2019). *About Manchester united* [online]. Available at: https://ir.manutd.com/company-information/about-manchester-united.aspx.

McCandless, D. (2010). *The beauty of data visualization* [video]. Available at: www.ted.com/talks/david_mccandless_the_beauty_of_data_visualization.

McKinsey Global Institute. (2016). *The age of analytics: Competing in a data-driven world* [online]. Available at: www.mckinsey.com/business-functions/mckinsey-analytics/our-insights/the-age-of-analytics-competing-in-a-data-driven-world#.

Ray, A. B. (2018). Telephone interview, 11 Jan.

Sorrell, M. (2019). *The year of first-party data: Sir Martin Sorrell lays out 4 lessons for marketers to succeed in a new era of advertising* [online]. Available at: www.thinkwithgoogle.com/intl/en-apac/trends-and-insights/year-first-party-data-sir-martin-sorrell-lays-out-4-lessons-marketers-succeed-new-era-advertising/.

Chapter 4

Business intelligence and data analytics

In this book I've referred to Amazon as being aspirational, but it's important to remember that most rights owners – in fact, probably all rights owners – won't have the same data-related requirements as the leading pure plays. Tech companies such as Google, Netflix, and Spotify aren't just generating rows and columns; they're in the business of big data. They're already leading the way in Analytics 2.0 while we're still trying to make Analytics 1.0 work for us. There is so much that can be written about the use of BI and data analytics in sport, its challenges, and the opportunities, that the intention of this chapter is to provide a helicopter view of the subject and highlight directions for further exploration. It cannot hope to deliver everything you would need or want to know.

This emphasis on the use of data and creating data-driven strategies, all focussed on helping you make decisions and engage with fans on a more personalised basis, has become more important over the last two decades as we've realised that the principle of 'if you build it, they will come' no longer applies. When your season's going well and you're winning, or you've secured the services of superstar athletes, it can be like Christmas: your tickets sell themselves, merchandise flies off your shelves, and sponsors come to you looking for an association. But we, the business folk, can't control what happens on the field of play and have no impact on the decisions made in that area. We need to focus on what we can do and what we can affect; and that's the way we use data to fend off the competition for our fans' time, attention, and money: to compete in what Michael H. Goldhaber referred to as 'the scarcity of attention, the lynchpin of the Attention Economy' (Goldhaber, 1997). Restaurants, theatres, and the cinema are just a few of our competitors, and we need to learn how to keep our fans engaged and keep their attention – because if we don't, someone else will.

BI and analytics: what's the difference?

In the same way the growth in the use of data has been exponential, so too has the proliferation of new, and often confusing, terminology related to the use of data. Googling 'what is BI' gives you 683 million results in 0.47 seconds. Do the same for data analytics and you will find a further 1.1 billion results in 0.72 of a second.

If the analysis of data generally means the way you look at the information you hold to help you understand more about your business and to make decisions based on that data, then how do we define the difference between analytics and BI? This is my favourite definition, reported in BetterBuys and provided by Mark van Rijmenam, CEO of Datafloq:

> Business intelligence is looking in the rear-view mirror and using historical data from one minute ago to many years ago. Business analytics is looking in front of you to see what is going to happen. This will help you anticipate what's coming, while BI will tell you what happened. This is a very important distinction as both will provide you with different, not less, insights. BI is important to improve your decision-making based on past results, while business analytics will help you move forward and understand what might be going to happen.
>
> (Heinze, 2016)

The key thing for me, and my team at Winners, is that any form of analysis, whether backward- or forward-looking, should provide actionable insights. We refer to the importance of ensuring that when we present our analysis we're not asked, 'so what?' This is the area that seems to be confounding most organisations. A study undertaken by Gartner in 2016 suggested that while 74% of firms say they want to be 'data-driven', only 29% say they are good at connecting analytics to action (Hopkins, 2016). But that's where the value is: being able to convert your findings to your next steps. Without this, it's just data for data's sake.

In the following pages, I will take you through some of my favourite types of analysis and how you could apply them as a rights owner. There are many being used by sports and non-sports organisations around the world, but if you're one who hasn't yet started to use data, or is seeking ideas for further analyses, you might like to begin with these.

Email campaign analysis

Many organisations run email campaigns, but without proper analysis their effectiveness is limited.

> It can be argued that it doesn't really matter how optimized your emails are if you are unable to see the results of your efforts and cannot measure that performance against set targets.
>
> (Kolowich, 2016)

Your email campaign performance data (the 'so what?') tells you two important things: first, how you can plan your next campaign better because you know what worked and what didn't, and second, the interests of your recipients as you'll be able to track their engagement with the different content areas in your campaign. If they click on a content piece about your next home match but haven't yet bought a ticket, you can identify them as a prospect. If they read a piece about playing your sport but aren't in your athlete registration system, maybe they're interested in having a go.

As with everything we've discussed thus far, setting KPIs is important within your email campaign planning, as they provide you with success and failure barometers. However, these KPIs need to be aligned with the most valuable metrics for this channel. Depending on whether your objective is reach, awareness, engagement, or even direct sales, they could be:

- **Delivery rates:** displayed as a percentage of the number of emails that were received after sending. This demonstrates how clean your list is. A low delivery rate suggests too many old addresses that have resulted in a bounced email.
- **Open rates (OR):** displayed as a percentage of the number of emails opened after being received. Your subject line and even your preview text have the biggest impact on whether your email will be opened. In Chapter 6 we look at the use of multivariate testing to improve this metric.
- **Click-through rates (CTR):** displayed as a percentage of links clicked in your campaigns after being received. This metric demonstrates how relevant and interesting your content is to the recipient. At Winners, we also like to report on the click-to-open rate (CTOR), something that is presented in some email campaign platforms but not in others. We find it more relevant than the CTR because it looks at the percentage of people who clicked on a link having first opened it, as it's not possible for recipients to click on a link if they haven't first opened a campaign. We believe a more apt analysis is to look at those who opened the campaign to discover what percentage found the content of interest and relevant.
- **Unsubscribe rates:** displayed as a percentage of recipients who opened the campaign and then went on to unsubscribe. This informs you that they no longer wish to receive your emails. This is an important metric, as it demonstrates how well or poor a job you're doing and, most importantly, whether you need to improve.
- **Your campaign conversion rate:** the percentage of people who completed your desired action or campaign goal after opening it – for example, bought tickets or merchandise, signed up for a coaching course, or bought a stadium tour. This is another statistic you can report on, but it is not limited just to email marketing. The advent of technology has ensured this measurement is the *de facto* metric of our marketing efforts across all digital channels.

As with all of these metrics, or any others you choose to focus on within your email marketing campaigns, the key is to watch them over time, looking for a positive trend line to demonstrate that you're continuously improving and, if you see a downward trajectory, take remedial action, looking at what you've been doing and test an alternative approach.

Population mapping

Putting the location of your fans and customers onto a map using their postal codes enables you to see in a clear, visual manner where they live in relation to your activity or need. A visual map is easier to understand and is therefore more effective than searching rows and columns in a spreadsheet for postcodes and street addresses. If you haven't taken this step for any of your datasets, I would highly recommend it. The impact of geographic relevance can be quite immediate when you see how far your fans travel to get to your stadium or their distance to other locations, such as your grassroots clubs or sponsors' retail outlets (an example of this is included in Chapter 7 on the role of CRM and data in sponsorship).

Case study: the Polish Football Federation

At a workshop with the Polski Związek Piłki Nożnej (PZPN) on 7 September, 2013, we produced two separate maps. One showed the location of its former membership data, Klub Kibica; the other focussed on its participation data: the players, coaches, referees, and other volunteers. The results are shown in Figures 4.1 and 4.2.

Membership of Klub Kibica provided guaranteed access to tickets for the men's national team matches, so the map in Figure 4.1 clearly shows regions of the country where individuals with a strong interest in professional football live in greater or fewer numbers.

The map in Figure 4.2 shows the location of the areas that have the greatest interest in participating in football at the grassroots level around the country.

The two maps already provided value as they were. PZPN management could see at a glance where they should focus their marketing efforts, increase the number of grassroots coaches or clubs, and where to stage events for maximum attendance. However, by overlaying the two sets of data, something of even greater value was shown, as you can see in Figure 4.3.

Interpreting the different shaded dots suggest that:

The Gdansk (1) and Legnica (2) regions may provide opportunities for increased participation through the development of more coaches and the establishment of football clubs.

Figure 4.1 Location of Klub Kibica members (source: Winners FDD Ltd)

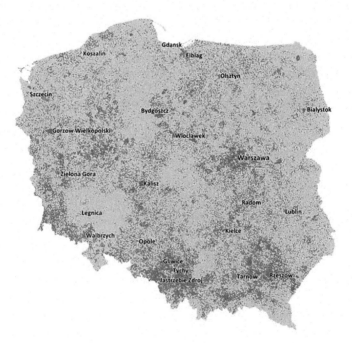

Figure 4.2 Location of grassroots football players (source: Winners FDD Ltd)

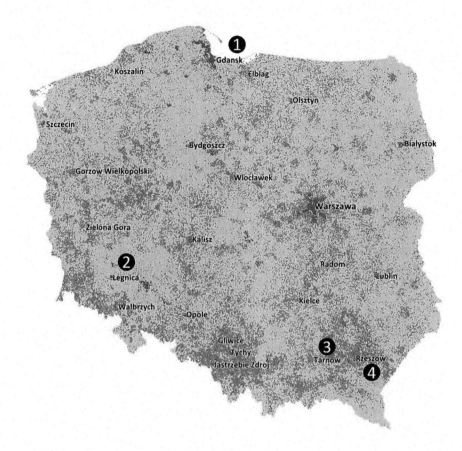

Figure 4.3 Overlaying both sets of data (source: Winners FDD Ltd)

The Tarnow (3) and Rzeszow (4) regions may be prime target areas for sales of Klub Kibica membership (and other PZPN products), as there are high levels of participation in these areas.

(Source: Bury, 2017)

The patches of light also point to areas where the PZPN might choose to focus its future development activities, as there are small numbers of both members and participants.

Bartosz Bury from the PZPN's marketing department had the following to say:

This map helped us to understand the huge potential our database has and how easy and helpful segmentation is. Mapping our data allows us to identify and select the information we need for a particular purpose. It also shows us what region has the most growth potential, so we can focus our sales and marketing efforts, and it will help us plan the location of future events.

(Bury, 2017)

Ticket sales timeline

One of my favourite forms of analysis in the sports industry is the use of a ticket sales timeline, as it supports several opportunities (see Figure 4.4).

If you have enough historic ticketing data, knowing the purchase pattern of your fans will enable you to predict when they're likely to buy for the next match. This can help in a multitude of ways:

- **Cashflow:** if you're a rights owner working within a tight cash flow, the insight you can get from analysing the pattern of your historic ticket sales will be invaluable to your planning.
- **ROI tracking:** when you plan your ticket sales marketing campaign, knowing which tactics work and which don't can save you money and increase your efficiency. Tracking peaks and troughs in your sales figures against your activity such as social posts, website advertising, flyer distribution, email campaigns, etc, enables you to hold these activities to account.
- **Performance tracking:** knowing your target number of sales at any given time before an event and comparing this to the progress you're making will enable you to understand whether you're likely to hit your target. If you're not, then you can go back to your ROI tracking and invest more in those tactics that have been identified as working for you.
- **Understanding ticket-buying behaviour:** when, why, and how much is also useful for the implementation of dynamic ticket pricing (the practice of setting ticket prices based on real-time market demand and other datasets). While in Europe we're used to seeing this with airline and train tickets, we haven't yet adopted it in sports. In the US, 25% of National Football League (NFL) teams now use this approach to provide prices that 'reflect the fair market value' (Young, 2017). This type of real-time pricing strategy relies on the ability to understand historic ticket purchase data along with future forecasts to help develop the logic that's applied to the pricing and buying process. Ticketing behaviour at an individual customer level is also needed for recency, frequency, and value (RFV) analysis – you can read more about that later in this chapter.

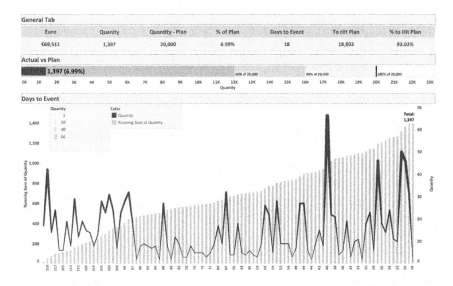

Figure 4.4 Ticket sales timeline (source: Winners FDD Ltd)

Customer churn and retention

Working with data in the sports industry, I find that I'm constantly checking myself: do I use the terms *customers* or *fans*? Sometimes I even consider *stakeholders*, although that can sound a little too corporate to represent someone with so much passion, and the term *data subjects* is just far too sterile. Many of our fans don't like to be considered 'customers', but at the same time a rights owner's customers include more than just the fans. This is particularly true for a national governing body that includes players, referees, coaches, and volunteers among its most valuable group of customers. I find myself using the words interchangeably, depending on the context and the audience. But when it comes to the discussion of churn, we can't refer to fans because they don't churn. Or do they?

Customer churn is the calculation of the percentage of customers who stopped using your company's product or service in a given period. In a sports context this could be your email newsletter subscribers, ticket buyers, grassroots players, coaches, or volunteers during a particular season. The two metrics we care about are the number of customers lost and the percentage that they represent of your initial total. This is referred to as your churn rate.

To be able to calculate churn you need to know two dates: when the customer first became a customer and when they stopped being one. But do fans ever really abandon their team if they really are a fan? Can consecutive relegation ever really cause a football fan to abandon their team? Does a Mariners fan ever get despondent enough to walk away in search of a team that will one day appear in the World Series?

In this case, *churn* can be applied to a fan but only when it refers to a specific action, such as the purchase of tickets or merchandise, but not the state of fandom itself.

But why is churn analysis such an important topic for rights owners? We've all heard that acquiring a new customer is more difficult than retaining an existing one and can be anywhere from 5 to 25 times more expensive depending on which report you read. Bain & Co., one of the biggest management consultancies in the world, also suggests that a 5% increase in customer retention produces more than a 25% increase in profit (Reichheld, n.d.).

We have a number of tactics at our disposal to reduce customer churn, but the key principle I subscribe to is that rights owners should proactively and consistently communicate with their fans and customers, respond to their responses, create and maintain that all-important engagement:

- When you've lost a match or a game, the temptation might be to ignore the result and look to the next event; but consider whether a better idea is to address the fact in a well-worded email to your ticket buyers, thanking them for their support, apologising for your lack of performance, and asking them to return to help you push through your losing streak.

- When a coach has secured a Level 1 badge, you could consider informing how they can progress to Level 2, perhaps setting up a series of digital interactions that over a period of time, perhaps six months, lead them to the relevant registration page on your website.

- When one of your grassroots players reaches 18, the change in their lifestyle as they move to university or enter the workplace could cause them to forget about registering to play again for the following season. A timely email reminding them of their performance record last season, where their club finished in the league thanks to their goals, assists, or saves, would remind them why they love playing your sport, resulting in a repeat registration.

Customer retention is what you do when you reduce your customer churn – it's your ability to retain your customers over a specified period. And again, I highlight the difference between a customer retaining their love and adoration of their favourite club or sport and retaining their interest in spending money, attention, or time with that club or sport.

When it comes to churn, we're looking to reduce our churn rate, and when it comes to retention, we're looking to increase our customer retention.

The customer life cycle

The *customer life cycle* (CLC) is a term used to describe a series of steps that a customer goes through when considering, purchasing, using, and maintaining loyalty to a product or service. It includes the journey that customers take as they lose interest in you, move away, and then come back to you later.

When discussing this with colleagues or clients, I like to refer to the Sterne and Cutler Loyalty Model (see Figure 4.5), as it throws up all sorts of contradictions when it comes to sports fandom (Cutler and Sterne, 2000).

How can we position loyalty as the end game, especially as most fans of a sports team are inherently loyal, having been 'born into' a particular allegiance? As discussed earlier, do sports fans ever really walk away? Do they ever actually abandon their teams?

Generally, not, but this isn't to say that a fan's purchasing habits won't be affected, because they will. As the economy hits a rough patch, their personal circumstances change or their choice of leisure activity is dictated by factors

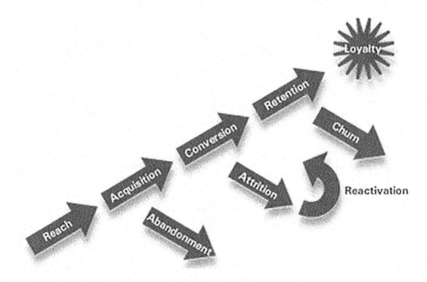

Figure 4.5 Sterne and Cutler loyalty model (source: NetGenesis Corporation)

other than their fandom, their habits might change. When this happens, while their inclination to stay with you may be very high, you will need to use your targeted engagement activities, aligned with their position in the CLC to retain them as loyal customers, not just loyal fans.

In this instance, the Sterne and Cutler loyalty model dictates that by providing excellent customer service, communicating with them in a way that is relevant to their needs and understanding their stage in the CLC their interest and your chances of retaining them will increase. This is specifically relevant for Europe, where many of our sports clubs are over a century old; so the parallel with the US industry, where teams can be moved from one state to another, requiring fans to switch their allegiance without breaking a stride, deserves to be explored as a separate dynamic that may affect the way the CLC is defined.

Customer lifetime value

Building on knowing where a customer is in the CLC and their CLTV, you can look at different customer groups and determine a value for the group as a whole. Understanding the CLTV of different customer groups helps to decide where and how to focus your marketing. By combining CLC with CLTV, you can identify the customers who are of the most value to your organisation – your most profitable customers – and communicate with them in an appropriate way.

The Football Association of Finland initiated CLTV analysis in May 2019, focussing on the value of its grassroots registered players who also purchased tickets and merchandise (group A). Their findings were that the average lifespan and CLTV of such a customer was significantly higher than those registered players who had just bought merchandise (group B) – they remained customers for 30% longer and spent more than double if they also purchased tickets. They also looked at the difference in customers who bought tickets and merchandise but didn't play (group C), and this group had the shortest lifespan and spent the least – both the lifespan and the CLTV reduced to less than half of group A. When looking at registered players who bought tickets but no merchandise (group D) they found that while the metrics were a lot higher than group B, their lifespan was still 10% shorter than group A, and the CLTV was 35% lower. This analysis clearly demonstrated the value of their registered participants.

In an email discussion in July 2020, we asked Mikko Varis, the Federation's sales and marketing director, how it would use this information:

> As the national governing body of football in Finland, one of our roles is to help grow the sport so we have to place as much emphasis on playing, coaching, refereeing, and volunteering as our professional clubs place on selling tickets and merchandise. We've always known how important our registered participants are to the sport, and this is why we have such a vast infrastructure in place to ensure we can support the football landscape – we

want everyone to be able to join a club, regardless of their ability, age or location, we want to support our coaches as they progress through their different qualifications, and we want to support our referees who play a crucial role in maintaining and enforcing our playing standards. But our CLTV analysis demonstrated that not only are our participants crucial to the continued development of our sport – they're also incredibly important to our financial future. Armed with this insight, we know how much to invest in their recruitment. We can also use this information to ensure we have a focussed objective of more cross-selling and up-selling but conversely we should also be asking our ticketing and online store customers if they want to have a go at playing the game.

You can read more about the crossover between fans who play football and their propensity to spend money on tickets and merchandise further along in this chapter under the heading of 'Regression analysis'.

As a next step, identifying the most common characteristics of your most profitable customers will help you to identify which of the other customers within your database share some, but not all, of those characteristics. These can be considered your next most valuable customers and, after identifying them, you can communicate with them in a way that will encourage them to respond in the way you want them to. For example, if you've been able to identify that your season ticket holders are predominantly males aged 28 to 35 who attended 12 matches per season immediately before buying a season ticket, you can look for other 28- to 35-year-old males in your database who have attended 10, 11, or 12 matches.

In participation, it's important to know the age at which your athletes stop playing. If you determine that males stop playing when they reach 18 (as they discover other interests) and girls stop at 16 (as they decide it's no longer 'cool'), you can set up a process to ensure that 17-year-old boys and 15-year-old girls receive encouraging messages and reasons to continue in the weeks or months leading up to their birthdays.

A well-designed email sent at the right time in your season could induce them to consider also becoming a season ticket holder for the following season.

Recency, frequency, and value analysis

Recency, frequency, and value (RFV) analysis (also known as RFM: recency, frequency, monetary) is used to determine, in quantitative terms, which customers are your most valuable. It looks at how recently a customer has purchased (recency), how often they purchase (frequency), and how much money the customer spends (value). The outcome of RFV analysis usually confirms Pareto's principle that 80% of your business comes from 20% of your customers (Ultsch, 2002).

RFV allows you to identify your best customers, not just on the basis of the quantity or value of sales, but on the basis of a combination of 'how often', 'how many', and 'how much'. Sometimes your highest-value customers only come once a year and spend a lot or come often and buy in small amounts. RFV analysis enables an understanding of this and could result in the creation of ticketing customer segments for single-visit customers, occasional attendance, regular attendance, and avid attendees.

Other applications of RFV for a rights owner could include:

- Identifying the customers who would be most likely to upgrade their match ticket to a VIP hospitality product.
- Predicting the quantity of a limited edition, high-value piece of souvenir merchandise that you could reasonably expect to sell.
- Predicting how many of your customers might be interested in hearing about your sponsor's goods and services.

RFV analysis, and the segments you create as a result, can also form the basis of your loyalty programmes as you consider what behaviour you will reward and what you can give in return for those behaviours, as well as the use of all sorts of predictive analytics models.

Predictive analytics

When we use predictive analytics, we're looking at current and historical data to make predictions about the future. For this reason, predictive analytics is considered the closest thing we have to a crystal ball. We look at what happened in the past and understand why it happened. We then look at what is happening now, applying it to the model, and from this can predict what's going to happen in the future.

For rights owners, this could include understanding how to price match tickets to ensure maximum take-up, how many special events to stage, and what quantity of merchandise to make available for sale. Rights owners who run a membership or fan club can also use predictive models to identify when a customer is likely to terminate their membership and take proactive steps to prevent this from happening. It can also be used to determine the quantity of memberships that you are reasonably likely to sell at a certain price point within a specific time frame. This leads to a greater conversion rate and lower marketing costs.

The level of accuracy in predictive analytics is dictated by the quantity and accuracy of the data available, but as we take things even further and apply machine learning and artificial intelligence, the process will become more time-efficient and even more accurate.

Correlation and regression analysis

Correlation analysis is used when you need to understand the strength of a relationship between two variables. For rights owners this could be the projected calculation of a match attendance based on a combination of the ticket price and the weather, or a team's standing in the league relative to that of the visiting team. Regression analysis is used to understand which variables have the most impact on a given result.

At Winners we were asked to use correlation and regression analysis to quantify the link between participation and consumption in European football – that is, how much more money a grassroots player spends following and supporting football versus a fan who has never played or who used to play in the past. We were also asked to look at what factors affect the value of that relationship. In the study, we looked at the frequency of match attendance, the amount spent on match tickets, the last time players attended a match or played football, how much they spent on televised football or channel subscriptions, and how much they spent on football merchandise.

The purpose of this analysis was to demonstrate that a deeper understanding of a participant's spending behaviour could help sports organisations better target marketing communications, more accurately predict future revenues, provide an ROI model for participation development programmes, and help rights owners make commercially focussed decisions relating to marketing investment.

Methodology

Over 5,800 survey participants across six different countries answered a set of multiple-choice, rating-scale, and open-ended questions. These questions ranged from basic identifications such as age, gender, occupation, and annual household income to such questions as 'How much do you spend when you attend a live professional match?', 'Which sports do you play?', and 'Which of these sports have you played in the past?'

The question 'How much of a football fan are you?' was also asked, and participants ranked their interest on a 1 to 7 scale, with 7 being a 'huge football fan' and 1 being 'entirely uninterested'.

The data was translated into a common format and, after conducting a preliminary inspection of each variable to pinpoint correlations and relationships, all compiled data was analysed using simple and multivariate regression testing.

Overall, the general statistics based on the six representative sample countries were as follows: people who currently play football spend 6.3 times more money than people who never played and 2.2 times more on match tickets than people who used to play. Regarding the purchase of merchandise and licensed products, people who currently play spend five times more than people who never played, and double that of former players. When it comes to the amount spent on TV football channels, people who play spend three times more than people who never played, and 1.2 times more than people who used to play (see Figure 4.6).

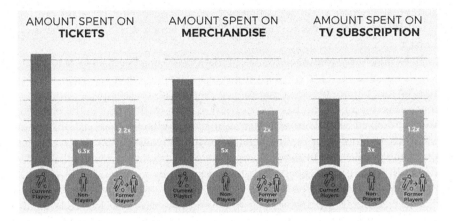

Figure 4.6 Quantifying the link between participation and consumption (source: Winners FDD Ltd)

In addition, by using single and multivariate regression analysis to identify the relationship between the variables, it was found that:

1   Participants who played football recreationally attended five more games per season on average than those who didn't play recreationally.
2   There is a relationship between frequency of match attendance, spend on football, and 'fandom' rating assigned by the participant. For every unit increase in fandom (on a scale of 1 to 7), it is expected the participant will attend one additional match per season, spend an additional €2.50 on tickets, €4 on merchandise, and €2.60 in TV content.
3   Among football participants, an increase of €13 on tickets, €22 on merchandise, and €10 on TV content is evident.
4   Football participants spend an additional €13 on a match ticket, €22 on merchandise, and €10 on TV content than a non-player.

Additional findings to note involved the gender and locale of football's biggest spenders. Specifically, men attended one to two more games than women, while urban residents attended one extra game per season than those in rural regions. Somewhat surprisingly, we found no correlation between age and income to a fan's interest or match attendance frequency. This suggests that attendance and spend have little to do with someone's income bracket or age.

How can the sports industry use this insight?

As I've previously discussed, with tighter wallets and more choice, consumers are now more selective about how they spend their money and their time.

The rise of eSports demonstrates that younger fans frequently favour video games over spectator or team sports – a marked contrast to the generations of their parents and grandparents, who grew up on the field and in the stands.

Where and how sports development and marketing budgets are allocated has become more important than ever. This type of analysis offers valuable insight that rights owners can exploit to grow revenue regardless of the changing economic and consumer landscape. Sports development teams that need justification to secure a bigger budget can point to this data, which clearly demonstrates that having more people playing results in more revenue coming directly into the sport.

Combining predictive and regression analytics

One of our rights owner clients at Winners wanted to understand how far it would be from its 2020 participation growth targets if nothing changed in the way it managed the development of its sport, i.e. if it continued to attract new registrations and lose current ones at the same pace as it had experienced since 2007. Using simple time series analysis, it was easy enough to plot the trend to demonstrate this. However, in order to provide additional context, we added the natural movement of population within that country over the same period using data provided by the World Bank. This can be seen in Figure 4.7.

We had already identified a strong positive or negative correlation with the annual revenue of the rights owner, so we overlaid this data on the time series line to see what impact this had (see Figure 4.8).

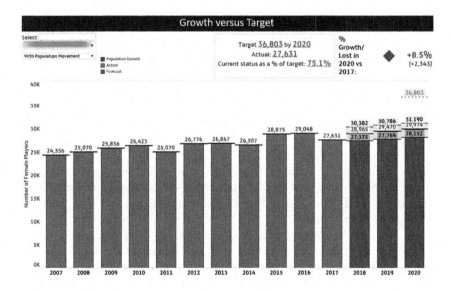

Figure 4.7 Growth based on time series analysis (source: Winners FDD Ltd)

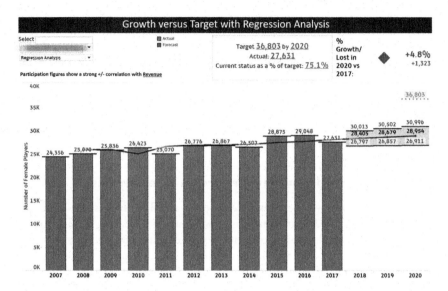

Figure 4.8 Time series with regression and correlation analysis (source: Winners FDD Ltd)

Unfortunately for this client, in both instances its natural growth pattern would leave it short by nearly 15% or 25%, depending on the worst-case or best-case scenario. But as the client had control over their revenue, unlike the impact caused by population movement, they could put strategies in place to manage this. Considerations could include either amending their targets to be in line with their projected revenue movement or planning to increase their revenues by the relevant value necessary to hit its pre-determined target.

Propensity modelling

Propensity modelling is the form of predictive analytics that tells us what actions certain customers or fans are likely to take. Applying this to sports, it can tell us which customers are most likely to buy tickets, merchandise, digital content, or our sponsors' products, and, in the case of National Governing Bodies (NGBs) and International Federations (IFs), which are most likely to play or become a referee, coach, or volunteer.

My favourite example of how powerful this can be is the case of Netflix and *House of Cards*, an online-only, multiple Emmy-award-winning television series. The decision-makers at the online streaming service committed a reported $100 million investment without seeing a pilot episode of the show thanks to their use of propensity modelling. They combined the data available for viewers of the original *House of Cards* series from 1990, viewers of movies with Kevin Spacey (the show's then-golden star), and (finally) viewers of other movies directed by David Fincher (the show's executive producer). The intersection of the Venn diagram they produced was sufficient for them to believe the show would be a hit and to commit to the requested nine-figure investment (Petraetis, 2017).

Consider how this can be used by a rights owner when addressing season ticket sales. They could start by creating the different segments of their customers based on combined demographic data, including their distance from the stadium, with RFV analysis formed from ticketing data. They could then classify these customer groups based on how likely they think they are to become season ticket purchasers. For example, a fan who has purchased tickets for 70% of your home matches and lives less than 20 km away is more likely to purchase a season ticket than someone who has been to 20% of your matches and lives 70 km away.

When segmenting customers in this way, you could create marketing plans for each of the different groups, measuring the applicable ROI. As the first segment in this example represents 'hot leads', you can expect to use less effort to convert those customers into becoming season ticket holders. The second example, your 'cool leads', will need more effort. Perhaps a series of automated marketing messages set up to nurture the recipient to a purchase will be sufficient for the hot group, but the cool group may also need a follow-up phone call.

In Chapter 6 on data-driven marketing, I look at the different communication channels we use, how we combine them with the different analyses, and the insights they generate to create a customer journey that results in a conversion or a sale.

Customer loyalty

Building on the question of churn in sports – and if we accept that when it comes to fandom, we don't really lose fans; we lose their interest in acting on their own fans' fandom – we need to look at the subject of loyalty and what it means to you. That's the starting point for this discussion: that loyalty means something different for every team, club, governing body, or international federation, and it's defined across a host of different variables.

In many cases, loyalty may not be financially driven, nor based on how many matches or events a fan may have attended. This is even more the case if you're a global sports brand with a fan base that exceeds the capacity of your stadium. In today's digital world loyalty can include metrics such as the length of time a fan stays on our websites, the frequency with which they visit, their interactions in our social channels, their frequency of opening our email campaigns and clicking on the links, the number of times they visit our sponsors' websites, or how often they watch our broadcast partners' digital streams. This can be added to more traditional metrics such as number of matches attended, quantity of merchandise purchased, and (from a participation standpoint) number of training sessions attended or matches they've played in.

In addition to choosing attributes that represent loyalty, the calculation of that loyalty can also be done in several ways. I've already referred to RFV analysis: scoring the three individual factors, or the total scoring across all three, could be used as a straightforward loyalty calculation. Another method is looking at the multiple relationships you have with an individual, i.e. how many different source databases they sit in or which other departments also have a relationship with that individual. Are they a home *and* away fan? Do they buy merchandise as well as play your sport? Do they follow you on Facebook and open your emails? The more relationships an individual has with your organisation, the more you could consider them 'loyal' to you and your sport.

At Winners we introduced the concept of a Super Fan to a group of clients who shared a common business model within the same sport. The Super Fan was a simple loyalty analysis identified on a monthly basis throughout a season, using whatever metrics the client had access to. Generally, it included:

- Number of matches they attended.
- Number of tickets they purchased.
- Total value of ticketing spend.
- Any other purchases made: merchandise, stadium tours, summer schools, etc.
- Number of emails they opened.
- Number of times they clicked on email content.
- Social media following status. (Did they or didn't they retweet, like, or share?)

The intention behind the monthly Super Fan was that, in addition to introducing the client to a simple form of loyalty analysis, the output could be used in a variety of ways from directly rewarding the fans to producing content for their digital channels. The concept could even encourage other fans to change their behaviour with the aim of becoming the next month's Super Fan themselves.

We performed this exercise at least 20 times in one year with 20 different rights owners; my most memorable moment was when we presented one client as the Super Fan of August 2016. He was the best friend of one of the client's team members who was in the room. The team member immediately sent a message to that friend to tell him his face was displayed on a large screen in their stadium boardroom. His pleasure was palpable!

Fan/customer loyalty programmes

The key point I want to make about loyalty at this point is that understanding the loyalty you have among your customer or fan base is not the same as building a loyalty programme. Conversely, a loyalty programme is not something that you launch to generate loyalty.

Earlier in the chapter I discussed the cost of acquiring a new customer as a comparison to the cost of retaining an existing one. This results in a clear understanding that, notwithstanding the natural fan loyalty we've also looked at, we should do what we can to keep our customers coming back to us. In this regard, a loyalty programme should be a vehicle you use to reward that behaviour and extend it.

It's important to consider that any loyalty programme you launch should be grounded in analysis. Your starting point must be to understand current behaviour so you know what will work. It's the reason this section has come at the end of this chapter, to emphasise my earlier point: that the launch of a loyalty programme should come after you've performed the aforementioned analysis, not before.

One reason this is important is because according to The Loyalty Report 2019, North America's largest loyalty study, the average consumer has registered for 14.8 loyalty programmes but is only actively engaged with 6.8 of them (Bond Brand Loyalty, 2019). If you don't understand what your fans or customers want from a loyalty programme, your chances of becoming one of those 50% who aren't used beyond registration are very high. This will mean wasted resources (budget and time), loss of reputation (who wants to spearhead a programme that has failed to deliver?), and possibly, fatigue and future lack of interest from your fans (they'll ask themselves how much you actually care or know about them).

An effective loyalty programme uses various tactics to drive the customer behaviour that you desire. The collection and analysis of relevant data as outlined in this chapter will provide you with the knowledge needed to identify the right tactics to use in your loyalty programme. To reiterate, while a loyalty programme should not be considered your answer to revenue growth, it is a useful tool to reward existing customers and generate new ones, and it should be considered at an appropriate stage of your data-driven development.

Case study: Portland Trail Blazers

In the first edition of this book, I interviewed Noel Mooney of UEFA to discuss their approach to supporting 55 member associations to use data to support decision-making and targeted marketing, specifically focussing on the role of data to grow football participation. You can download that case study from www.winnnersfdd.com/winningwithdata-first/ch4casestudy.

For this second edition, we talk to the Portland Trail Blazers to bring to life the churn analysis and customer retention that we refer to earlier in this chapter.

The Portland Trail Blazers (the Blazers) is an American professional basketball team based in Portland, Oregon – they compete in the National Basketball

Association (NBA) as a member of the league's Western Conference North-west Division.

Mike Schumacher is their Director of Business Analytics and provided us with this case study through an email interview conducted throughout May 2020. We selected the Blazers to provide an insight into the application of data among those rights owners who have focussed on developing some important customer-centric capabilities: indeed the Blazers already position their customers as the centre of all their conversations, and they ensure the customer is the driving factor in all decision-making. Immediately I can imagine some readers recoiling after that sentence because we are again using the term *customers* instead of *fans*, but as we have already discussed in the book, I for one, welcome this approach. Viewing fans as customers is something that will mini-mise the natural inclination for rights owners to take their fans for granted, to ensure they deliver a great customer experience, and (referring back to Mark Bradley's words in Chapter 1) a rights owner 'can only prosper if the customer feels valued'.

So on the basis that the Blazers do treat their fans as customers, we asked Mike to tell us about their approach to customer retention using the principles we looked at earlier in the chapter to retain customers over a specific period, minimising their propensity to churn.

> As a starting point, we're already using extremely targeted email cam-paigns and digital marketing, with lead-scoring and cart-abandonment tactics. Customer retention is a big focus, so we have a year-round reten-tion model that we apply to our season ticket holders, where our aim is to reduce the amount of effort it takes to understand fan churn risk.
>
> We create one score per customer that continuously identifies how likely they would be to renew their season tickets for the next season and allows our service reps to be alerted and intervene early on with their accounts.

Mike makes an interesting point here – a year-round focus on season ticket retention is probably different to many rights owners who may, instead, choose to focus on just the natural renewal period. But if your retention model is focussed on a specific timeframe, your actions might be based on the insight that is available to you at that time, and with so many data points contributing to the model, a potential churn trigger could be missed. Mike expands on this point for us:

> This is a huge development compared to in the past where we would run one model each year right before our renewal campaign to try and

understand how likely customers would be to renew their season tickets for the next season. While that process was useful, it wasn't as proactive as we would like to be – this new retention model is a real-time look at how likely a season ticket holder is to renew their tickets at any time in the year. We also have a detailed breakdown of why the model predicts the likelihood for each customer, and with this information available to all our service managers, they can see where the customer stands when talking to them. It also lets us proactively reach out to customers long in advance of us asking for renewals, when it can be too late to remedy issues.

Ensuring this information is readily accessible to the Blazers' representatives is a key part of their programme – it's not just used to create personalised digital conversations/journeys. Outbound call centres for season ticket purchases, and a proactive approach to renewals, are less prevalent in sports across Europe but are a cornerstone of a US clubs' sales activity. We asked Mike to tell us how his service and sales team use the programme outcome:

The retention-model scores are made available in our CDP provided by StellarAlgo, but they are also available directly in CRM on the customer record. Our service managers are nurturing their client relationships and use the model results to guide those conversations. Within CRM there is a history of the retention-model score and how it has changed over time. There is also a list of reasons and attributes that have caused the score to change over time.

We discussed earlier in this chapter that to create a retention model we need certain metrics. Here Mike tells us about their approach to sifting through the vast quantities of data to identify what's needed:

We take all our customers' purchase history – which Blazer games and concerts they've purchased tickets for, the form of payment they've used, and their contact information. We also have hundreds of demographic and psychographic data points that are made available by Ticketmaster and Acxiom, plus our sales agents and service managers also collect several additional data points. Each customer profile also includes how long they've been a ticket holder, how many games they've attended, how well they utilise the

> tickets they purchased, whether they share their tickets, and whether they try and resell them. And, in addition to all of this, we have our customer interactions – email campaign responses, online chat interactions, and notes added from our customer service phone calls.

To maintain the Blazers' retention model most data points are refreshed daily, and while the additional data points Mike refers to add more accuracy to their formulas, it's transactional data that's the most critical. This makes your ticketing partner, and their willingness to provide you with comprehensive and timely access to your customer data, crucial to the success of your retention strategies for ticketing customers – demographic and behavioural data alone will not provide you with the information you need. This is an important point because 99.9% of rights owners use a third party for ticketing systems, so you need their co-operation and their agreement that this data should come to you in order to ensure you have access.

So how does Mike use all this information – what does he do with these data points, his customer profiles, and the output from his segmentation model?

> Our digital marketing efforts are quite advanced, and we closely monitor and adjust the performance of our campaigns and audiences through metrics like return-on-advertising-spend (ROAS), cost-per-acquisition (CPA), cost-per-thousand (CPM), and purchase frequency. Automation remains an ongoing challenge for us, even though StellarAlgo helps us more easily segment and activate our audiences through dynamic lists. When we put the effort in to carefully segment and then create an audience in Facebook, we want to maximise the value of our campaigns by adjusting the Facebook audience to remove recent buyers or add new people who meet the audience criteria automatically. For example, if in our universe we have concert prospects for a Rose Quarter event (a 30-acre area in Portland that comprises the Moda Center, home of the Blazers, a second arena and a theatre), our system will automatically pull them into our campaigns and target them on Facebook. It will then also tell us how our Facebook audience is performing and remove concert prospects who have bought so we don't spend money on continuing to advertise to them or oversaturate them with ads.

Like many modern marketers, the Blazers use cross-channel digital marketing – this is the use of multiple channels that provide customers with a consistent experience across your digital estate, mapped into customer journeys for each segment or persona. Mike expands on his multichannel approach here:

We use multiple platforms for channel activation. For single game sales and awareness campaigns we use a JavaScript pixel from our marketing campaign platform, Marketo, to pull cart abandoners into our data warehouse and retarget them via email. We also use social sign-on information and our CDP to build custom audiences that we push into Facebook. We then track our activation efforts from here as well as manage audience suppression when they're getting saturated (with our messages) or when they have already bought. For search, we use Google's ad platform, but there is very little in terms of targeted campaigns there, nor do we do any tracking of referral from search at an individual customer level.

In terms of our retention activity, there's no automated personalised content for those at risk of churn for any product but automated; this is something we are looking at. Leveraging a CDP like StellarAlgo certainly provides a foundational element to support personalised content via predictive scoring and analysing web behaviour.

In Chapter 5 we talk about the use of dashboards to provide a quick and easy overview of current business performance using charts and graphs. The use of dashboards in this case highlights trends that can be measured in order to assess the efficiency of a retention model, and as you might expect, the Blazers also have this area covered:

We have our own internal reporting suite that utilises Tableau, but there are a number of useful reports in the StellarAlgo platform that we utilise. The one I use the most is the customer journey dashboard – it shows the customers purchasing path from year to year. For example, if a single-game buyer later went on to purchase a package and become a season ticket holder, you can see that visually and at an aggregate level. We also leverage the platform's segment tool to build no-code access to segments to help our (internal) stakeholders outside of the analytics team service themselves instead of relying on us to run SQL queries.

As the development of a retention strategy might still be a far-off option for many rights owners, we asked Mike what advice he'd share with his peers:

I think it depends on where you are at as an organisation. If you haven't stepped into this area yet, I would recommend speaking to someone like

StellarAlgo about industry best practices and capabilities rather than trying to reinvent the wheel. Our yearly retention model was useful, but had this technology been available to me earlier on, I would have pursued the more real-time models. I am proud of the static-retention models we used in the past – they were able to predict the overall renewal expectation within 1% on most years, but they did not give us the confidence and actionability that a real-time model did. It was always a big guess at the end of the year, which felt risky. At one point we had contemplated creating our own real-time retention model but didn't have the internal resources to pull it off. The StellarAlgo real-time retention-model scoring is great, and if I could go back and do anything differently, I would have prioritised this project earlier and brought them in earlier on.

While Mike and the Blazers may be advanced compared to the majority of rights owners, they're not sitting still – indeed in Chapter 2 we talk about the implementation of CRM as a journey, not a destination or a project.

We are constantly tweaking our formulas and data models. Some require more attention than others, but in general we are always assessing their accuracy, adding more data points where applicable, and reimplementing. You never know where a new data point will come from either. With all the recent happenings with COVID-19, we are even looking at how this could impact our models as the coming season may not fit the normal patterns.

We discuss the impact of COVID-19 in Chapter 10, how the global pandemic that was first identified as a virus in December 2019 has impacted the world of sports; but as Mike's insightful last comment highlights, it also wreaked havoc with our fan-behaviour models! (Schumacher, 2020).

Key chapter ideas

1   BI and data analytics refers to two different forms of analysis – the former looks at historic data to understand why things happened; the latter uses historic data to predict what will happen next.
2   The purpose of analysis is to produce actionable insights and not leave you asking, 'so what?'.
3   Analysing your email campaign performance is important to ensure you consistently improve your processes.

4   There are many forms of analysis that can be performed on data. Most popular for rights owners are population mapping, ticket sales timelines, RFV analysis, CLV, and customer lifecycle.

References

Bond Brand Loyalty. (2017). *The loyalty report* [ebook]. Available at: https://info.bondbrand-loyalty.com/loyalty-report-2019.

Bury, B. (2017). Personal interview, 7 Sept.

Cutler, M. and Sterne, J. (2000). E-metrics: Business metrics for the new economy. *NetGenesis* [ebook]. Available at: www.targeting.com/wp-content/uploads/2010/12/emetrics-business-metrics-new-economy.pdf.

Goldhaber, M. H. (1997). *The value of openness in an attention economy* [online]. Available at: https://journals.uic.edu/ojs/index.php/fm/article/view/1334/1254.

Heinze, J. (2016). Business intelligence vs. business analytics: What's the difference? *Better Buys* [online]. Available at: www.betterbuys.com/bi/business-intelligence-vs-business-analytics/.

Hopkins, B. (2016). Think you want to be 'data-driven'? Insight is the new data. *Forrester* [online]. Available at: https://go.forrester.com/blogs/16-03-09-think_you_want_to_be_data_driven_insight_is_the_new_data/.

Kolowich, L. (2016). Email analytics: The 8 email marketing metrics & KPIs you should be tracking. *HubSpot* [online]. Available at: https://blog.hubspot.com/marketing/metrics-email-marketers-should-be-tracking.

Petraetis, G. (2017). How Netflix built a house of cards with big data. *CIO* [online]. Available at: www.cio.com/article/3207670/big-data/how-netflix-built-a-house-of-cards-with-big-data.html.

Reichheld, F. (n.d.). *Prescription for cutting costs* [ebook]. Boston: Bain & Company. Available at: www.bain.com/Images/BB_Prescription_cutting_costs.pdf.

Schumacher, M. (2020). Director of Business Analytics, telephone interview, 3 Aug.

Ultsch, A. (2002). *Proof of Pareto's 80/20 law and precise limits for ABC-analysis* [online]. Available at: www.uni-marburg.de/fb12/arbeitsgruppen/datenbionik/pdf/pubs/2002/ultsch02proof.

Young, J. (2017). Dynamic ticket pricing use takes off, and teams hope it'll lure fans back into sports stadiums. *CNBC* [online]. Available at: www.cnbc.com/2017/12/01/dynamic-ticket-pricing-use-takes-off-and-teams-hope-itll-lure-fans-back-into-sports-stadiums.html.

Chapter 5

CRM technology stack

The theme of this book has been to address the more evolved definition of CRM that, unlike its origins in contact management software to track sales activity, is not just about technology. Many consider CRM a philosophy; it can incorporate and impact strategy, process, and organisational culture. This means that implementing CRM or addressing digital transformation, of which CRM has an inherent role, should not be led by your IT department but by your business requirements. We shouldn't think about technology first. While it is undeniable that the right software can make things work more efficiently, without the other elements of the perfect circle, the right culture and stream-lined processes, clean data, and a clear strategy, the best technology in the world will be unable to deliver what we set out to achieve. Consequently, it will become a costly mistake and an expensive lesson. However, it is also a truism that the more you advance in the development and delivery of your strategy, the more your need for technology will grow. Therefore, there is without a doubt, a role for technology as an enabler.

This chapter will look at the different supporting technologies that are relevant to the business model of a sports rights owner. We'll focus on an SCV, data–driven digital marketing, data analytics, and data visualisation. Sales force automation, customer service, and business process management have not been included in this book.

At the end of this chapter the NBA's San Antonio Spurs provide us with an insight into their technology stack.

A CRM ecosystem

In Chapter 2 I referred to the approach we take at Winners where we talk about CRM *ecosystems*: the technical environment you need to enable data-driven marketing and address digital transformation, composed of multiple pieces of software, platforms, or channels that work together. While they will all have distinct roles (and sometimes the same product will have several roles) your objective should be that, between them, they enable targeted market-ing, customer journeys, and interactions across the multiple channels that our fans and customers now use. They should also produce actionable insights that can be implemented to ensure you make progress and achieve your business objectives.

Specifically, your technology stack should enable:

1   **A customer–centric approach to marketing and service.** We want to put your fans and stakeholders first, and to do this we need to know more about them.
2   **A customer experience that encourages your fans to come back.** We want them to stay longer and to engage deeper.

Moreover, the right ecosystem will also provide non-customer facing benefits such as:

3   **Better cross-organisational collaboration.** While technology alone can't achieve this (I discuss this more in Chapter 8 on business change) it helps if the software, systems, and processes your organisation uses are aligned from one department to another.
4   **ROI tracking.** A quote often attributed to the 19th century Philadelphia retailer John Wanamaker is, 'Half the money I spend on advertising is wasted; the trouble is I don't know which half'. We want to know that we're spending our money in the right direction, and ROI tracking can help us with that.
5   **Time efficiencies.** Without wanting to open a discussion on artificial intelligence and machine learning at this point, the more automation we can deploy in our marketing processes, the more time we have to think strategy.

To achieve all of this you need more than just traditional CRM software for tracking the sales process. You also need to consider data management, analytics, digital marketing, and data visualisation.

Data warehouse versus single customer view

I don't mind admitting that when I first entered the world of data at the end of 2011, I didn't quite understand the difference between a data warehouse and an SCV, often using the references interchangeably.

I referred to an SCV in Chapter 2 as a centralised view of your structured and personally identifiable data: individual and unique customer records that provide the information your marketing, sales, and customer service teams need. Conversely, a data warehouse collects high volumes of both structured and unstructured data. It's usually an enterprise-wide tool, doesn't need to match to a unique customer, and therefore does not include any additional processing to make the data usable to marketers. This is different from a CDP, which we also discussed in Chapter 2 and which sits somewhere between an SCV and a warehouse; but as there are still many rights owners who have not yet managed to achieve an SCV, we'll focus on that for now.

The importance of your SCV really can't be understated. It's one of the most crucial elements of your technology stack. Without it, any other contributory components cannot function with full efficiency or efficacy. Imagine your marketing campaign platforms attempting to send the right message to the right person when the data in your SCV is incorrect or when your analytics count your fans twice or three times because of the presence of duplicates! Your SCV provides the hub of the data you need for your data-driven activities. When you combine your unique records with marketing technologies you can generate insights that support your marketing decisions. You can easily visualise and analyse your data at speed to identify the perfect audience for your targeted marketing, but only if it's been processed in the right format to make it usable.

Master data management: data in, data out

Master data management is the term given to the processes and technology that get you to your single point of customer reference – this sits within your data management strategy, discussed in Chapter 3. Within the process you need to identify the data that you need, collect it in a way that confirms to data-related legislation (more on this in Chapter 9), and finally, you'll probably need to transform and repair it to meet the format and standards of your database schema (the way your SCV is structured and designed).

The process of collecting data from your individual source databases (such as your ticketing systems, online store, website, landing pages, social channels, etc.) for input into your SCV, whether through an automated integration or a manual process, is commonly referred to as *ETL*.

Extract

Within the extraction phase the aim is to convert the outgoing data into the appropriate format for the transform stage. This is relevant whether the process is automated or manual. For example, your source database may provide you with the option to extract or export with a comma or pipe separator. Dates may be entered in a dd/mm/yyyy format, but the default on the extraction may be set with an mm/dd/yy rule.

Creating a data dictionary for each of your data sources (and the destination SCV) is a useful process that will help you identify the validation rules that need to be in place for efficient data extraction. When you write a data dictionary the purpose is to identify each data field within a database, describing the content and purpose, defining the format and field size, and identifying whether they're needed within the extract process.

They can be produced in a spreadsheet and are used to map out different stages of the ETL process, starting with the requirements of the business (e.g. what data does your marketing department need?), aligning with the design of your database, through to mapping into the appropriate field of your SCV.

Transform

In this stage of the process, the validation rules we identified in the extract phase are enhanced with further rules that enable the outgoing data to be integrated with, or imported into, the target database, in the case of this example, your SCV. Some of your data won't require any transformation and is referred to as 'pass through' data, but the remainder will be cleansed or 'normalised'.

Within the data transformation process, we often refer to data cleansing and normalisation; this can include various steps depending on the data in question, the processes used in the source systems, and its intended use. For example, for your email marketing campaigns you will want to ensure all email addresses are valid. If double opt-ins or captcha (a process used to tell whether or not the user is human or a machine) are not used in the data collection process, then I'd highly recommend running your imports against an email validation list. I talk about the importance of this in Chapter 6 on data-driven marketing.

An example of normalisation is that certain character sets that are available in the source database won't be available in the SCV. A common example is Cyrillic characters used in Eastern Europe and Asia, or perhaps the use of US dollars in a source system, and euros in the SCV.

Another common example is the first and last name fields – these should both start with a capital letter followed by all lower-case letters. If a customer uses all upper case when buying a ticket this is how the data will come to you when you export your ticketing data. It sounds like a trite issue, but when you want to use first name personalisation in your digital messaging, it will look strange if the format is 'Hey there MARK, have you thought about buying the replica shorts to match that shirt?'

Another common issue for rights owners, particularly IFs and NGBs, is the country field for those sports where teams from the UK compete as individual nations. This is the case for UEFA, who store data using England, Scotland, Wales, and Northern Ireland but whose third-party suppliers may use Great Britain, United Kingdom, or even the British Isles, all of which are different from each other.

An important point to note at this stage is that, if your data fails the validation rules, it means there are errors in the format. An easy temptation is to amend the offending records and continue with the process; but a better approach is to make corrections in the source database to avoid the need to constantly repeat the amendments. While this could be easily rectified in your own digital estate, when using third parties, such as ticketing systems and merchandise partners, to provide services it can be a little bit more time consuming to achieve the correct format – your partners may be happy to work with you, but if they use the same format across all their partners, they may all have different formats than you. This means you'll have to accept the data in the format it's sent to you and implement the transformation at your end. But time spent at this point will save a lot more in the future. We refer to the need for following processes in Chapter 2, and this is a classic example.

Load

The load, or import phase, requires further rules that deal with the way data is added into the SCV. These rules will differ widely, not only within each organisation, but also within each rights owner's source system. For example, when it comes to setting the frequency of the process, if you are a club that stages 20 or 40 events per year, your ticketing-system data may need to be loaded on an hourly basis, 365 days per year. But if you're an international or national governing body with just four to six events per year, the process may occur daily during the month of the event but increasing to hourly in the few days immediately prior. If you register your participating athletes on an annual basis but provide just a small window of opportunity for those registrations, for example one month, the ETL from your registration platform to your SCV may only need to be daily for that specific month.

When deciding what rules to put in place, you need to look to your business needs and the intended purpose of the incoming data. Using the earlier examples, ticketing data may be needed to ensure that your management can track sales performance, marketing may need it for promotional campaigns, and your merchandise team may want to cross-sell some merchandise.

Deduplicating your records

Having cleansed and normalised the data in the *Transform* phase, deduplication rules now need to be put in place. This is an SCV, the one place where we'll be able to see the 360-degree relationship your fans or customers have with you, so we need to be as sure as we can that each individual fan, participant, customer, or stakeholder is represented just once in the database.

Once the rules have been identified, algorithms can be designed to produce the required result by first identifying those records that could be considered duplicate. The identification of duplicates could be based on several different fields in the database, with the most common being email address. If there are multiple incidences of the same email address in a source database, it's reasonable to assume the same person has been represented multiple times. However, this might not necessarily be the case. The same email address may have been used by different members of a family, different friends in a group, or different participants in a grassroots club.

Another consideration is that not every customer in your source database has an email address. While nearly half of the population of the world uses email, there's another 4 billion who don't. In addition, the average user has 1.7 accounts, so we need to ensure we identify records that are duplicates even though email addresses may be the same (Campaign Monitor, 2019).

To ensure our deduplication works, we use additional data attributes to further narrow down the duplicated records, the most common being first name, last name, postal address, and date of birth. It's unlikely that further validation is needed after this point; after all, how likely is it that more than one customer will have the same name, live at the same address, be of the same age, *and* use the same email address? But there may be an instance when all the identified fields are not populated or are populated in a different manner, for instance, John Smith in one system may be Jonathan Smith, or J Smith in others. If your matching rules are too strict, these three instances will produce three different records even though they most likely belong to the same person. But if they're too loose, you may count them as the same person when they are actually two or three different people.

One final point to highlight is that when the data is imported and deduplicated based on your matching rules, you then must consider your merging rules. Using the earlier example, when you import a record with J Smith you don't really want the 'J' to overwrite the existing field that may say 'Jonathan' or 'John'.

I've again used the date of birth field as an example here, as this is a situation that occurs often. In your SCV you may want to store the date of birth field in the dd/mm/yyyy format if that's what's needed for your analytics program to identify age, and your email campaign platform to issue those all-important birthday cards. The *extract* process has ensured the right format has been exported, but if the data collection form at the source didn't use front-end validation to ensure correct dates are used, you could be attempting to import 12/09/0000 or 12/09/2030, neither of which are possible ages for your fans and customers.

I've highlighted here some data management issues to be concerned with when creating your SCV, but not the solution to addressing them. As with the rest of this book the intent is to bring to the forefront areas for further consideration, putting them into context with your CRM or digital transformation strategy. As your ETL processes are pivotal to this, I hope they receive the attention they deserve as you move forward. Your objective should be to constantly acquire more; *more* customers and *more* information about those customers. Your data management processes should ensure that the quality of your data is not compromised as you seek greater quantity.

Off-the-shelf versus bespoke build

While 'The Gartner CRM Vendor Guide, 2017' states that only 25% of new projects involve bespoke solutions, I'm comfortable admitting that for some of my rights owner clients I do advocate the use of a bespoke build, specifically when it comes to an SCV or data warehouse. If you read the MLS case study from the first edition that has been provided as bonus material in Chapter 2, you will know that MLS took this approach, building on a SQL database with additional off-the-shelf software and apps. Some of you might question this when there are long-established, market-proven, even industry-leading products that are out there and readily available, so I'd like to qualify my rationale:

1   While there are multiple products that are off-the-shelf, specifically when it comes to data warehousing, they're very rarely (in fact, I'd go so far as to say never) available as a plug-and-play. They need to be formatted to suit your current data sources and your business needs. They also need to be integrated with your incoming and outgoing data feeds. Some of you may be reading this thinking that I'm stating the obvious, but there are many unsuspecting individuals who will be sold on a dream, who believe there's a silver bullet and who will be genuinely shocked when they learn a software license is often only a percentage of the budget required to establish an SCV. Implementation and integration costs will, at minimum, double your budget.

2   If you scope your build to meet your specific business requirements, you can ensure that you're only paying for what you need; you won't be paying for a Ferrari if all you need is a Volkswagen. While I don't want to get too technical, if you use an open schema approach to your database it will be easier to build on it as your requirements, data flows, or data quantities grow.

3   The key is that while you're all in the sports industry, you're all rights owners, and with largely the same business models, the scale of your data requirements will vary significantly. Consequently, as with every element of your approach to CRM, you need to think about your business requirements first. List and detail out your use cases and then apply them to your resource and budget situation. Just because one of your peers licensed a particular software, it doesn't necessarily mean it's going to work for you – it's not a one-size-fits-all type of product.

A requirement that all rights owners have is the need for deeper engagement with fans, customers, and participants, so now we'll look at the layer of the tech stack that delivers targeted marketing.

Digital marketing platforms

When I think about the digital marketing channels that are informed by data and can provide a personalised experience (subject to the right data being available), I consider email, mobile app push messages, social ads, and web ads. I also include SMS marketing and personalised web content, as well as web push messages. We review each of these in the next chapter on data-driven marketing, but in the context of this chapter, I'd like to tell you where they sit and how they interact within your technology stack.

All these digital channels mentioned earlier can operate independently of each other to get the right message to the right person at the right time. They can all be personalised with the data you have in your SCV, so *ideally* these platforms will all be integrated with your centralised database so you can use your SCV to create, and then push, segments of the customers you want to message through that particular platform. Note that I use the word *ideally* as opposed to *definitely*. This is because, as with many tasks in the world of technology, there are manual workarounds that can be used temporarily to achieve the same aim. I say temporarily because the objective with your technology stack is to use automation that saves you time on certain tasks, freeing you up to spend your time in areas that can't be automated. Setting up automated integrations adds another layer of cost to your development, and while the time you save will more than pay that back, if you need to throttle the way you spend your budget, or need to demonstrate some quick wins before you ask for more, using manual processes as a temporary measure could assist with that.

An ideal solution is to use marketing automation software – these generally support multiple channels, usually always supporting email but with SMS, mobile app, and web push messages, and digital advertising functionality. This way you'll have all – or most – of your channels in one platform, reducing the number of integrations you need, coupled with powerful automation that allows you to build those customer journeys I keep referring to.

So if you now have all your digital marketing channels sitting on top of your SCV, you're in a perfect position to use them in a multichannel, crosschannel or omnichannel manner. Confused?

In the previous chapter I referred to the proliferation of different terms that can be sometimes confusing. Here's another case in point:

Since the term *digital marketing* was initially used in the early 1990s with the launch of Archie, the first search engine (Shedden, 2014), or when the first clickable banner made its debut in 1994 (Edwards, 2013), reference to multi/cross/omnichannel has grown at an incredible pace with The Huffington Post claiming *omnichannel* to be one of the 'Top Retail Buzzwords for 2013' along with *personalisation* and *mobile* (Cherwenka, 2013). But what do they actually mean? Are they the same thing or are they different?

Multichannel marketing means engaging with your customers using a combination of channels. For some rights owners this includes both online and offline (remember those days of stuffing catalogues into envelopes, processing paper order forms with cheques stapled to them?), but for many, the focus will be like this book: purely on the digital experience. Going back to the definition I use for CRM – right message, right person, right time, right platform – *multichannel* is knowing which channel to use at any given time, using multiple touch points to reach audiences and customers.

Cross-channel has a slightly different meaning. While it also refers to engaging across any channel or any device to suit the customer, *cross-channel* takes it one step further and takes the perspective of your customer. They see no distinction in the way they engage with you. For them, they just see the digital world as one big technology-enabled channel. Your fans might read a squad announcement on your optimised website, receive goal alerts through your mobile app, vote for their MVP (most valuable player) on your Facebook page, and then click on an email link to buy their next match ticket. They really don't know, or care, that they're in your cross-channel workflow, or that it's automated based on their last action.

Having highlighted the difference between *multichannel* and *cross-channel*, where does *omnichannel* fit? The key difference with *omnichannel* is that actions can be happening simultaneously because that's the way your fans behave. The second screen has been a talking point for the sports industry for some time, for example, using a laptop or a mobile to check for stats while watching a live broadcast. Another example could be your in-stadium point-of-sale tracking a fan's purchase, while their loyalty account in your mobile app is updated with the points earned, triggering a 'thank you' email to their inbox. With omnichannel, one platform serves another. They complement each other with the information they have about your fans and customers, providing the continuous and seamless experience they want and now expect.

A key process of all these digital touch points is that behavioural data funnels back into your SCV to enhance your individual customer records, produce insights into the efficiencies of your campaigns, and provide you with knowledge that enables improvements to the next one.

Analytics

I've already talked at length about the importance of acquiring and analysing data in previous chapters, reviewing the key areas of insight that are of use to sports rights owners, from marketing campaign metrics, to transactional behavioural analysis, including predictive analytics and RFV analysis, to name just a few. Here, I'll summarise where your analytics platforms sit within your ecosystem and the relative role in the data-in, data-out process.

Many of your digital channels will provide a level of data, demonstrating the effectiveness of your content and campaigns and the way your fans respond to them:

- Your email platform will show you how many, and which, of your fans opened your campaigns.
- Google Analytics provides a comprehensive level of analysis you can use to understand and improve the user experience, acquisition rates, and other actions taken across your website and mobile app (although the ability to

do this at a user level and match that back to your CRM system isn't 'out-of-the-box' functionality).

- Your ticketing system and online store provider will be able to provide you with the information you need to understand more about your fans' buying habits.

However, when it comes to creating a full picture of your fans, customers, participants, or other stakeholders across your multiple business units and digital touchpoints, the automated quantitative processes you can do with the bespoke SQL database I referred to earlier will not be sufficient: you'll need to use an analytics platform that sits across your SCV or is an integral function within it.

As I previously discussed, each of your source systems and databases will push data into your SCV, and the matching rules will ensure that all incoming data aligns to one unique record. Depending on the insight you're looking for, these comprehensive records can then feed into your analytics software, appending each record with the relevant tagging that can be used to create segments for your digital marketing campaigns.

Not all types of analyses that are relevant to a rights owner involve looking at individuals on a one-by-one basis. Understanding the movement of your fans around a stadium concourse (see Figure 5.1), how they might respond en masse to your next home match if it's raining, or how many fans might travel to your next away match are queries that are informed by different sets of data. Your SCV can pull all this together so your analytics application can do its work.

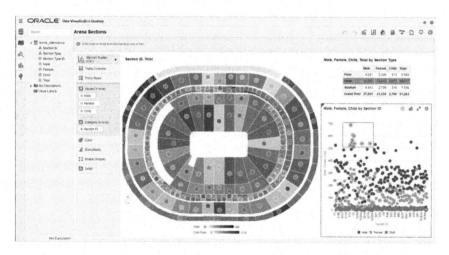

Figure 5.1 Tracking fan movement around a stadium (source: Oracle [online] www.oracle.com/technetwork/middleware/bi-foundation/ dvdarena-2997628.jpg)

The benefit of having this centralising analytics environment is that you can look for insights at a cross-organisational level – in the earlier examples, your stadium security team, ticket sales department, and away travel manager can all be informed through the same process.

With one central repository of the key data points needed for your analysis, the task of producing comprehensive dashboards that show these insights in a visual manner becomes instantly more achievable. This leads us to the data visualisation software in your tech stack.

Data visualisation

The role of data visualisation is exactly as it sounds. It's the visual presentation of your data, using graphs, charts, or other formats that enable the following:

- Communication of information clearly and efficiently.
- Easier and quicker analysis and assessment of situations.
- The identification of patterns or trends.
- More accessible, complex, and copious datasets.

Data visualisation is considered both an art and a science. It's an art because it involves the ability to draw focus and attention using carefully considered graphics, knowing which graphics to use for which datasets. It's a science because it draws on the data you have in your SCV or other source database, so you need to know which data will provide you with the visual you want to create or, more importantly, the insight you want to present.

Thanks to technology, not only do we have more data to inform these visualisations, but we have the ability to produce these graphs and charts for review in seconds and to view them dynamically, constantly in real-time, and with the ability to drill down, going deeper into different areas.

Many applications or software products will include a native level of reporting, or dashboarding, to support their core functionality. They know that users need to understand what's happening within their systems, but this is very different from having a dedicated and centralised reporting function that looks cross-organisationally and cross-platform.

For example, knowing your conversion rate once a fan is in the ticketing section of your website is great, but if you can link it to the responses to your email campaigns or social posts, then your insights will have so much more value. Imagine that these insights are also linked to behaviour within your sports registration platform – you can see how many active players buy tickets or how many online store customers are also registered coaches. When considering multichannel, cross-, and omnichannel marketing, the right data visualisation set-up can provide you with information about the customer journey across each of these, enabling you to make tweaks and changes to your journey as you learn more about your customers' behaviour.

Why is data visualisation so important?

According to the Visual Systems Division of 3M, the global conglomerate whose business areas range from health care and highway safety through to office products and adhesives, visual aids can improve learning by up to 400%. We can also process visuals up to 60,000 times faster than we can process text, so when it comes to ensuring we get value from our data work, and that our management and marketing teams can make the appropriate decisions, we need to ensure it's as easy as possible for them to see the insights we're producing for them (3M, 1997). I illustrated this in Chapter 4 using images to demonstrate the point, but in this chapter, I'll highlight some of the key considerations when using data visualisation.

Your data viz audience: who are they, and what are they looking for?

In the same way you have hierarchical levels in your organisation, and staffing levels with access to varying levels of company information, you can set up your dashboards to provide different information to specific users and user groups. You can imagine that your senior management have a need to stay abreast of key statistics like KPIs that provide a helicopter view of how each of the business units is performing, all available in one view. But at a department level you need to look at much more granular information. Knowing 'how much' won't be enough; you'll want to know how, why, what type, how often, and by whom.

Your visuals: what's the best format for the specific message?

Choosing the right chart for your particular message is important. Different views do a better job than others at presenting information. Graphs and charts should be used to show the information about data relationships, patterns, or how things are changing over time. Tables should be used when you must show precise value, and numeric data is best presented using dots, lines, or bars if you're looking to present a quantitative message. Maps are used when a physical location is key to the information you're presenting, and heat maps are used when different values within a map are shown using colours.

Correct and clear labelling is important when creating visual reports. Your objective is to ensure that the words you use are clear enough to explain what the visualisations represent but at the same time minimise the quantity of words to let the graphic speak for itself.

Choice of colours

Research shows that different colours generate different responses. The University of Melbourne demonstrated that the use of green boosts concentration

(Calligeros, 2015), while Feng Shui dictates that the colour orange is best for productivity (Ecker, 2013). However, in the sports world, it's more likely that team colours will dictate those choices. It's unlikely the German Football Federation would use orange in their reports or that the Rangers Football Club would make green their prevalent colour, but there are still some principles that could be easily followed:

- **Red versus green:** if you use these colours, make sure your red is for negative values and green for positive because of their natural association with traffic lights (stop and go).
- **Light versus dark:** it's easier to read text when light colours are used in backgrounds, and if you use dark colours to represent a specific finding, the reader might give unnecessary weight to it. I also recommend never using more than eight colours in your dashboard as they can become distracting at that point.
- **Colour differentiation:** while you want to use different colours to differentiate data points, it's important to use the same colour when referring to the same type of data. For example, the colour used for month-on-month comparisons should be consistent; year-on-year should use a different colour.
- **Use of axes:** you can use the same chart to present comparisons, correlation, or causality in your dashboards between two entities (periods, products, personas, etc.) instead of producing a different chart for each entity. However, it's important to remember to label your left and right axes clearly.
- **Order of data:** there should be a logical hierarchy in the way you present your data. If it's not appropriate to do it by value, you can do it alphabetically or chronologically. As with choice of colour, it's important that whichever order you choose, you remain consistent.

At the end of this chapter you'll read about the platform San Antonio Spurs use for data visualisation in their technology stack and how it quickly started generating insights, even within the first few months of their CRM implementation.

Where to go next

As a technology-neutral consultant, I'm not here to advocate one vendor over the other in any of these areas. For those readers who want to know more about the vendors that could meet your requirements, I recommend two sources of information:

1   The Gartner CRM Vendor Guide, which is published annually by Gartner, Inc., the world's leading information technology research and advisory company.

In the report, Gartner reviews and evaluates multiple vendors that provide the different components of a CRM ecosystem. In the 2017 edition, they also provide the worldwide market forecast through 2021, predicting that in the digital marketing category alone there will be an 18.5% growth, and in sales automation, 10.8% (Gartner, 2017).

You have to be a client (or a student) to access the Guide, but some of the vendors featured in the different categories will publish a licensable copy; you just have to provide some details to access it (a classic example of the value exchange I referred to in Chapter 3).

2   The CRM Watchlist is produced by Paul Greenberg – Managing Principal, The 56 Group, LLC, a customer strategy consulting firm, and the author of the best-selling book *CRM at the Speed of Light: Social CRM Strategies, Tools, and Techniques for Engaging Your Customers.*

Greenberg presents the CRM Watchlist as an 'impact award', identifying the strength, mindshare, and market share a company had in their market the previous year, along with the expected impact in the following three years.

The 2020 Watchlist was the award's 13th year, and it's now published for all to view on ZDNet.com, a business technology news website. The 2020 categories included Winners with Distinction, and Watchlist Winners with a nod to companies to 'keep an eye on'. Most usefully, access to the Watchlist is free, and the listing provides a link to each company, enabling you to read more about them (Greenberg, 2020).

Both sources will provide you with the direction to look in to understand which vendors support different functional requirements. Your journey into the world of CRM-related technologies has only just begun!

Case study: San Antonio Spurs

The San Antonio Spurs are a professional basketball team based in Texas, five-time winners of the NBA Championship. As with most sports, team performance is a critical factor in determining success in the NBA both on and off the court. Just as the players must perform well to keep winning their games, the CRM team behind the scenes must hold their edge as digital innovation is considered by some to be a priority within the industry.

When it came to creating their tech stack, the Spurs opted to work with KORE Software, a global software solutions provider specialising in the needs of the sports industry. KORE provided the centralised data warehouse, along with various ready-made integrations and applications that would work in tandem to provide the Spurs with the insights they needed to deepen fan engagement and increase revenue.

Jordan Kolosey joined the Spurs as Director of BA and Insights in 2016 with the immediate responsibility of building a data warehouse. In a KORE

Software webinar held on 12 December 2017, Kolosey shared his approach to such a major project:

> This data warehouse project was important to the early success of our department, particularly with me only recently joining [the Spurs]. So, it was really important to move quickly and to stay in budget. With that in mind we just got to work so that something could be presented to the executive staff in the first week.

The Spurs' philosophy on data analytics revolves around an easy-to-understand, three-step process. When presented to senior executives, it helped them understand more about the project and the process. The use of simple language to get stakeholder buy-in is reiterated by Mic Conetta, Head of CRM at Arsenal Football Club, in our case study from Chapter 8. Kolosey describes his process for us here:

> The first step is the data collection process, which is very time-consuming, not very much fun, but important to getting the end result. Then you get to analyse the information – the fun part – when you scour out what the insights are and what they are telling you. And then you have to implement whatever it is you learn to demonstrate why you are doing this in the first place. Just spelling out this three-step process really helped to demystify what analytics is and show that it's a science and not a magic trick.

In Chapter 2 we discussed the importance of ensuring that you have the right staffing capabilities. Kolosey had similar concerns and describes the infrastructure he has within his own team to help keep on top of their CRM needs:

> The data management analyst is really a data engineer-type role. We've all had data feeds fail on us; we've all had those connections and implementations take a lot longer than they needed to. So, it's very important for us to have somebody on the ground who can hold our partners accountable and be able to decipher our business needs to the data engineers.

> Our manager of business analytics is responsible for structuring our data – the tip of the spear, so to speak – and comes from a pricing scientist background, well-groomed in a lot of the very raw, more traditional areas of statistical and predictive analytics. Then we have a research coordinator to help provide more of the qualitative consumer-type research, to layer in with the heavy statistical skills of our Manager of BA.
>
> Finally, we have our marketing automation team, who jumps in after we've gained the insights and seen the different avenues that we could take to improve our business. They use AB testing in campaigns, generate the leads and get them to the appropriate sales reps, and so on and so forth. Once we get the results back from those campaigns, we make sure there's a lot more interaction between our team and our data management analyst, who's able to help us digest that information.

So, with the right people in place, the Spurs assessed various vendors to identify how they could scale quickly, and from that process, identified KORE Software, a company that also services several other NBA teams. This approach enabled the Spurs to benefit from the knowledge and integrations that KORE had already developed for Orlando Magic, Oklahoma City Thunder, and the Denver Nuggets, providing them with what Kolosey refers to as a 'solid foundation' and a strong level of confidence in the way they moved forward. This ensured that, from day one, they were more or less able to go live.

Kolosey highlighted another benefit of working with a provider so closely aligned with other NBA teams. He was able to support his second objective: staying in budget.

> We were able to share the cost burden with the other teams, and so it was much more cost-effective for us. So, not only were we getting started fast, with actionable data that we could actually utilise, but we were able to do it for a lower cost.

Moving on to their tech stack, with their centralised data warehouse in place, Kolosey was able to gain more information about the individual feeds (see Figure 5.2).

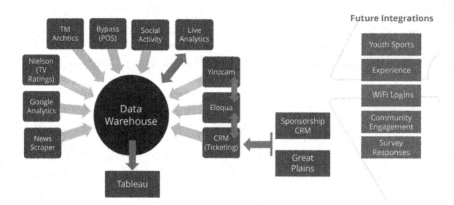

Figure 5.2 San Antonio Spurs – technology stack (source: San Antonio Spurs using KORE software)

This is a snapshot of the current data feeds we have active within our system. A number of these were native from day one, and you can't take for granted how important it is to have a reliable ticketing feed and having a reliable feed from your CRM. It just makes all the difference. Bypass (point of sale) was provided by KORE as an application with an existing integration, with Tableau for live analytics as well. Now we've been able to move to an on-demand scenario, and our data engineer has a checklist of different feeds we want to get into the warehouse. He's just been ticking them off one at a time from Nielsen data, Google Analytics, and a proprietary news scraper he's built out.

Other data integrations include Eloqua, which provides the campaign management platform. This allows the Spurs to create very dynamic campaigns and use the response data from those campaigns along with other data points relating to demographics or behaviour to trigger follow-up campaigns.

Kolosey highlights the benefits of this when it comes to targeted campaigning:

Previously when we would do a week of campaigns to all single-game buyers in order to warm them up for eventual pitches on group nights or anything else, we wouldn't really have any idea if we were producing quality leads for our sales reps or not. So, any business processes that we built out based on lead distribution for lead quality would break, and we had to come up with different scenarios, which doubled the work. So, being able to take for granted that every sales lead now has the same level

> of information allows us greater visibility and ubiquity with the processes that we put in place. This ultimately allows us to operate a little bit more efficiently when we don't have to create different scenarios for each [customer record] if they have data or not, if they're appended or not.

The Spurs have also integrated a YinzCam mobile app that provides valuable in-stadium behavioural data (something European teams continue to struggle to secure) and enables highly personalised push messages.

When asked about how he determined the order of their integrations (that is, which feeds to focus on first), Kolosey says it was a combination of the demands and vision of their various stakeholder departments.

> We wanted to get quick wins and then find our external evangelists in other departments, those that seemed much more engaged and forthcoming with needs and had kind of 'gotten' the process. We were able to spin up quick wins for those individuals, even if it was supplementing the work that they were doing manually so that we could point to clear victories for the executive staff – obviously, it was the revenue-generating departments, anything you can do to make more money and make the business better overall.

When considering how long it took the Spurs to create their data warehouse, Kolosey suggests that a project like this is never really complete, but he is proud that it took just three months after appointing KORE as their supplier to get their first data visualisations up and running.

Data visualisation

For Kolosey, the main focus of the tech stack was that Tableau was up and running for real-time reporting immediately after their project start. This is a sentiment shared by Momin Ghaffar, who fills the role of BA Manager.

The Spurs have created different rules for specific user privileges that match to the three different types of reports they produce and the different purposes behind them. Ghaffar describes them as such:

> First, you've got your standard bread-and-butter reporting for executives, the highest level of reporting, that shows how we look at the business

in three major revenue buckets: tickets, suites, and sponsorships. A lot of teams will look at tickets and their subtypes – plan, group, and gate sales – as well. And what becomes pretty informative, something that the end user can really pick up on, is what proportion of the overall budget is comprised by plan, group, and gate sales, and specifically, how we perform as an organisation according to those plan, group, and gate subtypes.

Then we have our game-by-game reports that show what [ticket] scans we saw for a particular game, what the Nielsen rating was, how these trend over the entirety of the season, and also from a food and beverage perspective. We can see on a game-by-game basis who are the marquis opponents or the non-marquis opponents, where we reach our budget goals or miss our budget goals, and specifically, what tends to be the huge revenue gainers from a food and beverage perspective, and what seasonality component figures into the equation here.

And so, we have a bird's eye view at a very high level. We're able to measure very specifically, game by game, and then we're also able to see things like the heterogeneity of ticket types in the arena bowl. How does this mix look from game to game? Is it something that's influenced by strategy, where you may want to be selling a certain type of ticket for a higher yield for certain opponents? Moreover, I think this report also starts to engage folks that may be on your service and retention team, where our season ticket members, our plan holders, are not scanning [as they go into games]; that should raise an alarm. What exactly may be driving that apathy, or how do we maybe try and deliver even more value so that they're showing up to games and scanning in?

And so, what I really like to look at here is that sort of tandem effect that this type of visualisation illustrates. Breaking it out by plan, group, and gate, ticket types and seeing what types, or how many folks scan into those types of games. And then where I think it gets really fun to look at this is comparing certain marquis opponents versus certain non-marquis opponents.

In Chapter 2 we referenced the need for cross-organisational collaboration. For the Spurs, the use of dashboards that combine data from multiple departments brings the focus of the different business units into one area, for example, using Google Analytics to identify where and how a sale was generated, whether it be through Spurs.com, Ticketmaster, through a search engine, or via social channels. Individual business units can use daily sales reports to see day-to-day changes and isolate where the organisation can see quick wins and track against budget on a year-to-date and month-to-date basis.

When it comes to the value of sales management, Ghaffar was able to offer further insights:

> We're able to specifically point out different products that reps are selling and where they're tracking against their goals. And something like this really elucidates exactly what it is that we're doing from a sales force effectiveness standpoint. I think where this becomes incredibly powerful is being able to slice and dice different reps' names and come up with some sort of general conclusion about the effectiveness of the sales force and how they may be achieving sales force excellence – how they may be really leveraging their different skill sets to be able to sell different types of products, and do it in a relatively effective manner.

Tech stack developments

Ghaffar is quite clear about what he thinks is next: the ability to look at different business efficiencies, specifically the area of what he refers to as the 'industrial engineering' that goes into staging an event and parking efficiencies around it.

> There's undoubtedly a tremendous amount of ingress and egress, and I know vendors have popped up here and there with artificial intelligence products to help teams and organisations better manoeuvre, or better navigate how to configure an arena so that it's conducive to revenue maximisation. And so, where we really want to go is, by using something as simple as looking at concessionaires and kiosks and realising where there may be certain transaction depressions and densities in the arena, and really be able to understand perhaps an underlying consumer behaviour or consumer psychology that could unearth an entirely new revenue stream. How might we configure our arena so that more and more folks are able to get their burger on time, get to their seat on time, and ultimately improve their fan experience? I think that's something that we'll always be marching towards, and that's quite honestly where we're trying to go next.

He also believes sentiment data will be the next set of information that rights owners will try to integrate into their tech stack, proposing that game–by–game analysis could open up a new avenue of opportunities.

Perhaps a cold hot dog led to some kind of engagement attrition in subsequent games. Or perhaps a parking concern was raised. Those are the types of sentiments that we would hope to be able to capture. It's something that we have an eye for, something that we would like to build towards, and something that we've put on our data roadmap.

Kolosey sees the value in the integration of concession data as the start of a drive to provide one universal truth for the organisation.

With this kind of integration, everyone's on the same page; there's no level of scepticism by our executives based on rosy reports they're receiving. The reports show the way it is, and then the conversations can begin based on that one universal truth that everyone understands. And from there, it allows us to have a little bit more of an organisation of strategists and implementers really focussing on how we are working, as opposed to having so many man hours in so many different areas of the business spent collecting reports and then publishing them. That turnaround time makes things that much more sticky, and so it allows us to be a lot more flexible and dynamic in both of those realms.

(Source: KORE Software, 2017, 12 Dec.; Kolosey, 2017; Ghaffar, 2017)

Key chapter ideas

1　There is no single piece of software or a stand-alone CRM system that will provide you with all your needs. Instead you need to think about a CRM ecosystem made up of different products and platforms which are integrated to work together.

2　The holy grail of CRM is the SCV. This is a powerful view held in a centralised database that enables you to have a 360-degree view of all your fans, customers, participants, and other stakeholders.

3　When you are a data-driven business there is a constant movement of data around your environment, so you need a data management strategy to inform the way you approach this. The strategy document will inform the processes you need for a uniform approach to the way you acquire, transfer, store, and use your data.

4　The way your data is visualised needs to be planned so that it is grouped meaningfully and presented in a way which has the greatest impact on the end users.

5   Your ecosystem should be future-proofed to deal with the vast pace of digital technologies. As you move forward with your development, you'll want to integrate your technology stack with other applications.

6   Planning, designing, and implementing your technology stack is not an IT project and should be led by your business needs. Technology is an enabler not a driver.

References

3M. (1997). *Polishing your presentation*. Austin, TX: 3M.

Calligeros, M. (2015). Seeing green boosts your concentration, research shows. *The Sydney Morning Herald* [online]. Available at: www.smh.com.au/technology/sci-tech/seeing-green-boosts-your-concentration-research-shows-20150525-gh8udh.html.

Campaign Monitor. (2019). *How many email users are there in 2019?* [online]. Available at: www.campaignmonitor.com/resources/knowledge-base/how-many-email-users-are-there-in-2019/.

Cherwenka, A. (2013). Top retail buzzwords for 2013: Omnichannel, personalization, mobile. *HuffPost* [online]. Available at: www.huffingtonpost.com/andrew-cherwenka/top-retail-buzzwords-for-_b_2506997.html.

Ecker, S. (2013). Best color for concentration and productivity is orange. *HuffPost* [online]. Available at: www.huffingtonpost.co.uk/entry/best-color-concentration_n_3949427.

Edwards, J. (2013). Behold: The first banner ad ever – from 1994. *Business Insider* [online]. Available at: www.businessinsider.com/behold-the-first-banner-ad-ever – from-1994-2013-2.

Gartner. (2017). The Gartner CRM vendor guide, 2017. *Gartner* [online]. Available at: www.gartner.com/en/documents/3738036/the-gartner-crm-vendor-guide-2017.

Ghaffar, M. (2017). R & D and Analytics, interview by email, 12 Dec.

Greenberg, P. (2020). CRM watchlist 2020: And the winners are. . . *ZDNet* [online]. Available at: www.zdnet.com/article/crm-watchlist-2020-and-the-winners-are/.

Kolosey, J. (2017). Sr. Director of Insights and Analytics, interview by email, 12 Dec.

KORE Software. (2017). Data warehousing in action: Spurring efficiency & collaboration with the San Antonio Spurs [Webinar]. *KORE Software Customer Insights*, 12 Dec. [online]. Available at: https://info.koresoftware.com/data-warehousing-in-action.

Shedden, D. (2014). Today in media history: The first Internet search engine is released in 1990. *Poynter* [online]. Available at: www.poynter.org/news/today-media-history-first-internet-search-engine-released-1990.

Chapter 6

Data-driven marketing

In Chapter 1 I introduced the definition of CRM as getting the right message to the right person at the right time. We also included Don Peppers' definition of treating different customers differently, as well as Gartner's longer, more detailed definition ('a business strategy [that] optimises revenue and profitability while promoting customer satisfaction and loyalty'). In Chapter 8 you'll also read the following definition from Mic Conetta, Arsenal's Head of Digital Experience: 'the automation and technology to better deliver fan experiences, customer interactions and the provision of services'.

Each of these definitions represents the essence of data-driven marketing: ensuring your marketing is customer-centric. This means securing, maintaining, analysing, and using your customer data, then actively segmenting it to enable better targeting and engagement with your customers. As we discussed in Chapter 4, your analysis could be used to predict future behaviours, but the intention at all times is to enhance and personalise the experience for your customers.

But why has this suddenly become such a big deal? I don't think there are many people out there who would disagree that marketing has experienced a fundamental shift, that many of the techniques and approaches that worked for the past 50, 40, or even 30 years are no longer relevant in today's digital world. The shift has been driven by the customers' demands that we now listen to them and, more importantly, give them what they want, not what we think they want. It's been enabled by technology and the data that it generates. In turn, marketers are expected to quantify and measure their actions like never before, demonstrating data-driven decision-making along with customer-centric campaigns. In the same way a chief financial officer (CFO) looks at the decimal points in their analysis of P&L, so too are chief marketing officers (CMO) expected to assess the ROI of their actions. They now have the tools to track this information, and they're expected to do so.

There is also an expectation that, despite the most savvy marketers advising that now is not time to be cutting marketing budgets, the coronavirus may result in just that, compounding the need to be accountable and to be able to track the marketing ROI (Ritson, 2020).

What customers really want

When delivering my 'Introduction to CRM' workshops, I'm often asked by clients whether I believe their fans and customers really want us to know who they are. They ask, 'Do they like us to have this level of awareness, or do they find it creepy?' If you recall in Chapter 1, I referred to the Orwellian 'Big Brother is watching you' notion that is no longer the theme of a book but an everyday reality; so my response to this question is always the same and is two-fold:

1   If your fans, customers, participants, or any of your stakeholders don't want to be part of your engagement strategy, they don't have to be (at least that's the case if you're following the appropriate legislation and implementing a best-practice approach). They can opt out of your email campaigns, web and social remarketing; they can disable advertising cookies and ensure they are sitting outside any of the data-driven activities you use.

2   Research seems to suggest they want it. The results of a survey taken by SmarterHQ in 2019 showed 72% of the 1,000 respondents will only engage with personalised marketing messages, even though 86% of them are concerned about data privacy (SmarterHQ, 2019).

However, there's a big difference between watching your customers because you can versus watching them to enable you to provide them with great customer service, and it seems our fans and customers might agree with that. So, let's look at a few examples that could resonate with rights owners:

- **Timing is key.** If a fan has just purchased a season ticket, they might not appreciate being asked if they'd like to buy an individual match ticket. But you could expect an email with a 10% discount for your online store the morning of their birthday to be greeted with delight.
- **Help your customers progress.** Sending a congratulatory message to a coach who has completed your Level 1 might also be followed up by a message to let them know they can progress to Level 2 at the click of a button.
- **Give them information they need.** If you have a goal to increase participation, one of your registered players might stay in the game after they've moved to a new house if you advise them that their nearest club is located just two miles away from their new location and is looking for members.
- **Use TripAdvisor-style recommendations.** While a fan would never pay attention to someone else's recommendations when it comes to which team they should support, they might appreciate being advised that the matching shorts are a perfect complement to their recent purchase of the replica shirt or that upgrading their ticket purchase to a one-off corporate

hospitality pass would provide them with the opportunity to meet their favourite player.

- **Make their lives just that little bit easier.** Advising to your event attendees the location of the concession stands in relation to their seats, and which one has the shortest queue at half-time, might be appreciated by your fans keen to get back to their seats as quickly as possible. If local highways management is aware of the distance your fans are likely to have travelled, they can ensure the traffic flows minimise the risk of jams or other disruptions to their journey.

- **Exercise joint benefit and value.** This is the exchange value: when a customer feels they'll receive something of value as a result of you having their data, they'll be more receptive to the notion of sharing it. This of course includes providing them with access to content and is more relevant in the sports industry than some others. Behind-the-scenes footage, interviews with star athletes, exclusive competition entries, and previously unseen footage and photos are just a few ideas that can entice a fan to tell you what you need to know. Privileged access to tickets for that all-important event, or a meet-and-greet with the team, is sure to entice people to hit the 'submit' button if they've previously resisted.

This chapter is going to look at how we take the data we're now collecting and analysing, applying it to the way we market to, or more importantly engage with, our fans and customers. We're going to take a look at the different formats of marketing that are enhanced with this data-driven approach and the different channels that can be driven by data. I'll focus on those that enable the use of segmentation and personalisation, specifically those that are considered online as opposed to offline.

Email marketing

I had been selling and leveraging the benefits of sponsorship, merchandise, and TV rights in the sports industry for over 25 years before I moved into my current field. When I did so, I recall surprise at the constant chatter about the death of email marketing. I also met several social media marketers who were so obsessed with their own field they couldn't see the frailty in placing all of their marketing focus in this area.

The reality is that email isn't dead, nor is it dying. Email continues to be a requirement for registration of social networks, app stores, competition entries, and online purchases. But, as with all communication methods, the challenge is to do it well, to use email to get the right message to the right person at the right time. This is a view shared by leading CRM practitioner Russell Scibetti, Senior Vice President of Strategy and BI at New York Football Giants and founding editor of The Business of Sports, a blog dedicated to discussing new ideas and current events in the sports industry. Scibetti shared the following with me in a discussion in January 2018:

> People like to make the comment that 'email marketing is dead', which I vehemently disagree with. One of the main premises of that belief is that email has been overtaken by social media as a primary communication channel to fans and customers, and while we shouldn't underestimate the impact of social media, different channels are better at different things.
>
> One area where email marketing still has a clear advantage is in direct consumer monetisation, so whenever this topic comes up in a group setting, there's a simple exercise I love to run. First, I ask everyone in the room to raise their hands if in the last 12 months, they've purchased an item directly from clicking a link on Twitter or Facebook, and very few hands are raised. Then I ask the group to raise their hands if in the last 12 months, they've purchased an item directly from clicking a link in an email, and nearly every hand pops up. This creates a clear demonstration of email marketing and direct marketing in general maintains its effectiveness in generating sales.

When I start working with a rights owner client who hasn't yet used any form of data-driven marketing and has no CRM capability within their organisation (there are still many out there), I introduce them to email marketing as a starting point. My reasons are:

1 **Email marketing is cheap.** I know that term is relative but when you compare it with the other digital channels like SMS, mobile app push messages, web and social retargeting or remarketing, the cost of entry to develop and to deploy are all lower with email (assuming you've selected the appropriate platform for your needs).

2 **You don't need special skills to get started with email marketing.** Most commercial platforms provide a drag-and-drop option, meaning that anyone in marketing who knows how to use PowerPoint can quickly adapt their skills.

3 **The database format (usually) allows you to replicate some CRM functionality.** As an example, building list segments based on data attributes and merging lists on a unique ID to create an SCV will introduce you to some key CRM principles.

4 **The email campaign introduces workflow automation.** Functionality will (usually) include triggered campaigns and other formats that will introduce you to the efficiencies of marketing automation.

5 **The reporting functions introduce you to the benefit of using actionable insights**. In turn this will help you to inform your decisions, for example, what to do differently, or the same, in your next campaign.

6   **The landing page has various functions.** These introduce the importance of data standardisation and correct data mapping. Free landing pages
are usually available on commercial email marketing platforms.

The point I'd like to make here is that if you're at the beginning of your journey into the use of data-driven marketing, starting with email campaigns is a
great place to be, and everything you learn will be applicable as you continue
to progress. However, it's important you select a system that is future-proofed,
providing you with enough bandwidth to grow in capability for at least 12 to
18 months. If your website developer offers you an email tool within their
website build, unless they're referring to integration with an external commercial provider, I'd recommend you think twice. You'll never get the appropriate
level of email function from a company whose core role for you is to build
your website. And this isn't just your website provider – it's the same for any
software you contract for a specific use. If you license an athlete registration
platform, contract with a ticketing vendor, or licence an online store partner,
their system emails will not replace the functionality you'll get from an email
marketing platform – and of course their approach will never take into account
your cross-organisational business objectives. They're more likely to focus just
on the purpose of the platform they provide.

Key considerations for email campaign planning

I'm going to talk you through some key steps when using email marketing
because, as I mention earlier, this process, once adopted, can be readily applied
to the evolution of your use of data.

Aligning with business objectives

In Chapter 2 we talked about the importance of a strategy to ensure your individual business units are all heading in the same direction and your operational
delivery is aligned to your business objectives.

We practice the same approach when planning email campaigns. Each
broadcast represents one minor cog within a significant wheel and should be
treated as such. The individual purpose of the campaign, the action, or the
'why' should align directly or indirectly with your business objectives.

List segmentation

After determining the purpose of your campaign, the next step is to consider
the target audience. Who do you want to send it to? This is where the use
of list segmentation comes into the planning. While you can send emails to
your full database, and there may be occasions when this is both necessary and

desired, sending your emails in a more targeted manner is a key way to increase engagement and therefore ROI. Even if you're not yet at the stage where you have customer personas, you'll probably know who buys your tickets and who doesn't, who attends your events or volunteers at them, who has previously opened a campaign and who hasn't.

Building on this, the different types of segmentation considered could include gender, age, geography, or purchase history. For example, if you're promoting last-minute ticket sales to an event in London, your fans in the US are less likely to respond to a request to 'buy now' than those that live in the UK. If your objective is to seek out female coaches or referees, your message should exclude the males in your database (unless, of course, you include a message to that segment that starts with 'Do you know a woman who'd be interested in this?').

Content and design

In Chapter 1 we highlighted how our ability to concentrate on one thing at a time is being challenged; so when it comes to the content and layout of your email, you need to be thinking about how you can grab your customer's attention before they move onto the next. Most importantly, you need to make the content interesting. If your objective is to sell tickets, use content to support this instead of a blatant sales message. For example, if the match you're focussing on is against a team you've played before, remind your fans of the result the last time you met, or your full history if you've met them more than once.

'Less is more' is often the case when it comes to email content. The recommended approach is to include a small section of the story and provide a web link to the remainder on your website, or an alternative destination page, as this is the objective of your email campaign: to get the recipient to click on content in the email and go to your website, your ticketing platform, your sponsors' websites, etc. This should be through a clear call to action (CTA) button that inspires the reader to 'buy now', 'read more' or 'watch here'. Never expect your recipients to be curious enough to click anyway – you must pique their interest.

In the image-rich world of sports, the use of high-quality images consistently throughout your email campaigns will draw your recipients' attention and help keep them engaged. If you include ones that haven't yet been published on your website or social channels, you can expect higher open rates as your customers start to expect this unique content.

Finally, the type of content you include should be varied, not just to support your different business objectives, but also to reflect the multiple opportunities the digital world presents. People love to interact, even more so when it comes to their sport, event, or club, so you can expect links to videos, polls, quizzes, and competitions to be a big hit with your fans.

Personalisation

If you're using the right email platform, you'll have the ability to easily personalise your messages. Here are three easy tactics to start you off:

- **Personalisation in a subject line:** Dale Carnegie, the author of *How to Win Friends and Influence People*, believed that a person's name is the sweetest sound in any language for that person, and that it was important to use it whenever possible. He stated that as a name is the core part of our identity, when we hear it being used, it validates our existence, which makes us feel more positively about the person using it (Carnegie, 2006). With this in mind, try using the recipient's name in a subject line and see if Carnegie was on to something. Experian Marketing Services suggest that personalised subject lines generate 27% higher CTRs and 11% higher CTORs (Experian, 2016). The personalisation doesn't have to be limited to the recipient's name. You can refer to their favourite athlete or team (if you know it), their response to your last campaign (if your system provides it), and even their transactional status (whether they have or haven't bought a ticket to your next game).
- **Content:** expanding on the themes presented, you can personalise the text and images within the email content to reflect what you know about the recipient: for example, whether they've already purchased a ticket you know they plan to attend your event, or if they live on the other side of the world and will need to watch online or on TV. While beginners can use a simple manual process to do this, advanced marketers can use dynamic content to reduce the amount of time needed to achieve this.
- **Date and time of send:** if the campaign you're sending is not time-critical, unlike a squad announcement, then you can segment your list so that different recipients receive the email at a different time. Imagine providing a window of opportunity for your most loyal fans to be able to purchase tickets to the must-attend match or the launch of a new piece of merchandise in your online store. And, if you have an international fanbase, personalising your campaigns using local language, references, or even time zones could make your fans feel you really care about them.

When it comes to personalisation, you're only limited by what you know about your customers, the data you have in your database, and the functionality of your email broadcast platform. Your objective is to ensure that every person in your database feels like they are an individual, that you are marketing to a segment of one.

Email marketing as a specialism

While I mentioned earlier that if you're using the right platform, you don't need any specific skills to start using email marketing, it goes without saying that the more you learn about this channel, the better you'll be at it. Email marketing is a specialism, and while products like Mailchimp, Campaign Monitor, Constant Contact, and many others have made it easy for users to get started, there are still issues to consider that take a deeper level of skill. These include tactics to avoid your emails being treated as spam, keeping your email addresses clean to avoid a high bounce rate that could lead to your domain being blacklisted, and the use of HTML templates for more creativity and flexibility.

As I highlighted at the beginning of this book, *Winning with Data* is intended to give you an introduction to multiple areas in CRM, data-driven decision-making, and marketing. If you believe a career in email marketing is for you then I recommend you continue your studies with other publications and training courses.

Other data-driven marketing channels

While we consider email marketing the cornerstone of CRM, there are many other communication channels we can use.

SMS marketing

SMS marketing costs quite a lot more than email marketing but is nevertheless a valuable channel that supports the use of segmentation and personalised messages. While there is a natural limitation on how much content can be used, SMS is great for last-minute notifications as response rates tend to be quicker – an average of 90 seconds for a text message compared to 90 minutes for an email (Campaign Monitor, 2019). It's also a great channel to use when your fans or customers are on-site if you have no Wi-Fi and their own 3G or 4G is unavailable. And, as CRM is all about the right message on the right channel, if someone is not responding to your emails then you try another channel – if you have their mobile number you can use SMS. As with email marketing, response tracking in SMS marketing is possible at an individual level, but unlike email, text messages don't run any risk of getting caught in spam filters.

Mobile app push messages

A mobile app message is content that is 'pushed' through a mobile app to alert a recipient to news, events, special offers, or any other content you wish to share with your fans or customers. There are two types of mobile app messaging – push and in-app –both are used in most territories around the world, and the user has to have 'opted-in' to receive such notifications. You can read more about opt-ins across different platforms in Chapter 9, on data and the law.

With push messages, the content will be sent even when the app is closed, whereas in-app messages can only be seen when your customer is actually using the app. For this reason, push messages are a great tactic to remind customers that they've downloaded your app.

Unlike email campaigns, but similar to SMS marketing, you can guarantee 100% deliverability to your list of opted-in customers as your app messages don't get caught in spam filters.

Behavioural responses to push messages can be tracked, including interaction times and device used, as well as the content that produced the most engagement. However, while the actual cost of mobile app push messages is negligible, unlike with the use of email or SMS, you have to start with a mobile app, so the costs to get going are more significant.

Web push messages

Web push messages operate in a similar way to mobile app messages – you can either receive them when you're on a specific website or you can receive them when you're not on the website, nor indeed on any website, but your device is connected to the internet. And as with all forms of targeted message, a user has to opt-in to receive them. You will have seen these yourself as browsing websites – you see a pop-up box, usually in the top left-hand corner that states something like 'This website wants to send you messages' and you then select BLOCK or ALLOW.

These push messages can be used in a silo or (as with email, SMS, and mobile app) can be used as part of a cross-channel customer journey. However, unlike email and SMS, but as with mobile app messaging, you can send targeted and personalised messages even if you don't have the individual record in your database – they can work with 'unknown' data or anonymous web visitors.

Digital retargeting

Digital retargeting is key to implementing cross-channel marketing automation and enabling the full customer journey, but in this book we're just going to look at how we use our databases to support digital advertising programmes. This is important to improve your advertising ROI – enhancing the 'custom audience' function that advertising platforms providing by including customers and fans that have visited your website and/or are known to you and are you in your database(s).

Unlike normal website banner ads, retargeted ads are presented specifically to people who have already visited your website or are in your contact database, perhaps your email marketing database, athlete registration database, ticketing system, etc., or your centralised database/SCV if you have one.

There are two main forms of retargeting: pixel-based and list-based. Both work on the principle that a customer visits your website, leaves it without completing the action you wanted them to (for example, buying a ticket, visiting your sponsor or registering to play), and continues visiting other websites, including social channels. Your digital ad is then displayed on one (or many) of the websites they visit, which aims to then draw them back to your site so they can complete the target action. When you apply this process to your digital advertising plans, we call it 'retargeting', and it can sit within a data-driven marketing plan – when you just place advertising without the retargeting, it operates more as a siloed function without the benefit of the data you have about your existing customers to support your decision-making.

Pixel-based retargeting allows you to show your advert or message to any of your website visitors, whether they're anonymous or known. When someone visits your website, assuming you have your cookie policy in place and your user accepts it, a pixel will be dropped into their browser. This will follow them as they browse your site, and other sites including social platforms, allowing ad platforms to serve your adverts to them. These ads can be personalised based on the pages they visited on your website. For example, if they visited your ticket sales page but didn't purchase, the ad you can serve them will promote your next match. If they visited the section of your website that discusses how someone gets into your sport, but they didn't register or complete any forms, the ad you serve can invite them back to your site to sign up for a course, to join a club, or to enter a competition.

Pixel-based retargeting can generate fast results as web visitors can be retargeted almost as soon as they leave your site. However, subject to the way you manage your site, it may take some time to implement the coding on the different pages that you want to include in your retargeting campaign. Bear in mind that if your website doesn't generate a lot of traffic, then you won't be retargeting many users through this method. Another consideration when planning your retargeting strategy is that you want to avoid 'spamming' – serving too many adverts to the same people. This is the same consideration when sending email campaigns – we have to respond to what the data's telling us about frequency of messaging.

With **list-based retargeting**, your list of customer email addresses is used to identify those users who are to be served your ad. While this form of retargeting is less common than pixel-based, because it involves the use of a database; your campaigns can be more targeted because you choose, at an individual level, who sees your advert. This allows you to use more than just behavioural data as targeting criteria. For example, you can create a list of email addresses for fans who read your email campaigns but haven't yet purchased a ticket for the next match, pre-ordered the new home shirt, or registered to play for your club next season. You could also use this tactic to re-engage your customers who aren't responding to your emails. For example, if you use a list from your email platform of anyone who hasn't opened a campaign in 90 days, you could use a digital ad to remind them of the great news and exclusive content they can get from you.

Your list is imported to an ad platform where the data is anonymised (usually through a process called hashing). The ad platform then uses that list to find these fans on other websites so your advert can be served. This is important as it means your targeted segment will naturally be smaller than the original list because not only is it expected that not all users accept cookies or may delete them, but the retargeting platform has to match your email addresses with users of other digital platforms, and the email address they gave you may be different to ones they've used elsewhere.

Also note that with this process you can either include or exclude the list(s) you're importing, i.e. target these users in my customer audience or exclude these users from my custom audience. This enables you to then use digital advertising to serve a message for a second time to the same customer but through a different channel.

Unlike pixel-based retargeting, it takes time for the ad platform you use to match email addresses, so advance planning and preparation is very important here. Another difference with list retargeting is that you are in charge of uploading and maintaining the lists you use, so this form of retargeting, for all its benefits, is less automated and takes up more of your time. The caveat to this is if you're using marketing automation software that integrates with a DMP, that can support the digital channels you want to use for paid advertising. If you recall, we introduced you to a DMP in the MLS case study in Chapter 2 and again referenced its role in your ecosystem in Chapter 5.

Retargeting can also be used in social channels such as Facebook, Twitter, Instagram, and LinkedIn, as well as in mobile apps and based on keywords used when using a search engine. As with email marketing, dynamic content can be used to ensure the message can be personalised to a very granular level.

You can use a dedicated retargeting platform for either of these techniques, or you can go directly to the ad networks or exchanges themselves (i.e. advertise directly with Google, Facebook, etc.). Using a dedicated platform streamlines the process but as my mantra is to minimise the need for more technology unless there's a clear need and benefit, I would recommend using the native functions in each channel first, to familiarise yourself with the opportunity before investing in any technology.

A big advocate of Facebook's list retargeting services is the NFL's Miami Dolphins, having transferred 80% of its marketing budget from 2015 to 2017 to using Facebook's Custom Audiences, Lookalike Audiences, and Lead Ads. According to Jeremy Walls, the team's Senior Vice President and CMO, 'Overnight, Facebook has become our largest lead-generation source for season tickets' (Ourand, 2017).

The Dolphins' strategy is based on creating unique content and using Facebook as the distribution platform. During the 2016 season, the Dolphins created eleven online shows that ranged from two-minute videos to a three-day-per-week podcast, supplemented by montages of the season's most popular videos accompanied by music from artists such as Ella Fitzgerald and Johnny Cash.

Instead of buying a TV commercial or radio ad last season, we bought music rights for social media for a week or two weeks at a time. . . . Millions of people would watch that, then we would retarget them with an ad to generate a lead for us. . . . That was a big shift for us on the marketing side. We were reaching a lot more people doing that versus making a 30-second TV commercial that was outdated a week after we started airing it.

(Ibid., 2017)

Not only does Walls credit the Facebook campaign with generating 30% of all-season ticket sales, the Dolphins generated about $10 million in sponsorship revenues around the content. And, because the programming has been so well received, the strategy provided sponsor opportunities as well. Walls always intended to seek sponsorship for the shows, but he was keen to ensure they approached this in the right order: 'We wanted to build really good content franchises first – build them up, build up the audience and then assign a brand to it, not the other way around' (Ibid., 2017).

Moving from silos to multichannel

Each of these channels on its own can provide incredibly powerful results when used in conjunction with data to deliver a personalised experience. But when they work together to provide a multichannel experience, the user has a better experience and your results are improved.

Multichannel marketing means engaging with your customers using a combination of channels. For some rights owners this includes both online and offline. (Remember those days of stuffing catalogues into envelopes and processing paper order forms with cheques stapled to them?) For many, the focus will be like this book: purely on the digital experience. Going back to the definition I use of CRM – right message, right person, right time, right platform – 'multichannel' is knowing which channel to use at any given time, using multiple touch points to reach audiences and customers.

Moving from a silo approach in digital marketing to multichannel can be challenging, but it's not just factors such as an absence of collaboration, commitment, or integration that prevent progress – it's a reality that getting the right team with the right skills can also be difficult. I referenced the fact that data and analytics are at the top of the list of critical skills shortages in Chapter 1. By its nature, the use of data in marketing is still a niche role so securing the experienced staff, particularly with the types of budgets and head counts that most rights owners have to play with, can be difficult. However, there is a process in your approach to digital marketing, the use of data, and multichannel marketing that can help increase your chances of success: the use of testing.

Test and learn

Elon Musk, the billionaire founder of PayPal, SpaceX, and Tesla, said:

> I think it's very important to have a feedback loop, where you're constantly thinking about what you've done and how you could be doing it better. I think that's the single best piece of advice: constantly think about how you could be doing things better.
>
> (Ulanoff, 2012)

Musk wasn't talking about data-driven marketing when he made this statement, but it's still highly relevant. One of the many benefits of marketing in the digital world is our ability to test our theories or ideas before we commit to them.

Consider the process of printing a poster to promote ticket sales for your event. You produce the design based on all the information you have at the time. You show it around to colleagues in your office and maybe a few other people whose opinion you respect. Then you order a hundred, a thousand, or ten thousand of them and have them printed. At this point, you're committed. The poster includes an offer code, so when your fans book their tickets you can track your ROI. But what you don't know is your conversion rate: how many people saw the poster and then went on to use the code. Furthermore, you don't know how much your conversion rate would have increased had the wording or imagery been different, if you'd placed the posters in different positions, or if you had placed them on a different day.

Compare that to the process of producing an email campaign, a banner ad, a landing page, or indeed any piece of digital content. In any of these instances, while you will again produce the digital asset based on the information you have at the time, by using a testing process you'll be able to amend it based on the information you gather as your customers engage with it. In many instances you can automate that process for added efficiency.

When you use testing, you make an informed decision based on an objective, not subjective, data-driven process. You'll increase your chances of making an incredible breakthrough and reduce your chances of implementing a bad idea.

A/B test versus MV test

In an A/B test we set up two different experiences, with A representing the current state or the champion, and B having been amended to reflect the elements you want to test – therefore considered the challenger. The A and B versions of the digital asset are served up randomly, and the key metrics are compared to see which performed the best. The winning version is then used.

In email marketing you first select the quantity of recipients you want to use in the test samples, for example 10%, then consider the amount of time you want to run the test for. A key consideration here is that if an email campaign is time sensitive, for example a squad announcement or an exclusive window of availability for ticket sales, the period of time you select for the test will mean a delay in the time your recipients receive their campaign. I know that sounds obvious, but I've seen clients get so excited at the thought of using testing protocol they forget that certain tests only work in certain conditions.

The KPI tests that can be impacted in email marketing are:

1   **Open rates**. Using different from names, subject lines, preview text, date of send, and time of send can all have an impact on a recipient's propensity to open. Interestingly, among our sports clients at Winners we have been surprised to find that when it comes to a subject line, 'Official news from' often outperforms text that actually describes the content within the email. We wonder if this is representative of the importance placed on the value of official status when *fake news*, the Collins Dictionary Word of the Year for 2017, is now so commonplace.
2   **CTR**. Placing content in different positions within the email, using different text or colours on your CTA, using different images or text, and even using a recipient's first name in the content can produce different results.

One final point to note when using testing in email marketing is that most platforms provide this as an automated process. That is, the test segments are picked randomly by the system and at the end of the test period, the winner is automatically sent to the remainder of the database who were not included in the test segments. This is referred to as the 'roll out'.

Multivariate (MV) tests operate with the same principle but compare a higher number of variables and look at how these variables interact with one another. It's a bit like running multiple A/B tests, on top of each other, like a waterfall – one A/B test, that then leads to another A/B test, followed by another A/B test.

Testing data collection forms

My clients regularly ask me how much information they should ask for in their sign-up forms. My answer is pretty much always the same: test different versions and see what your fans think.

As with the email testing process described earlier, you can apply the same logic to your data collection forms. Produce any number of versions using different tactics, see which one performs the best over a period of time, and then 'switch off' the other versions. Different tactics include the number of questions you ask, the use of mandatory fields, personalisation if you're using dynamic content, different CTAs, and opt-in consent wording, among others. If you add Google Analytics to your landing page, not only can you look at which format of the form produces the most opt-ins, you can also track conversion from visitors to the page itself.

When you apply MV testing to a landing page, you can first A/B test one element, for example the header text used to draw customers in, but then layer the test with another element such as a sign-up form, and then finally the landing page footer. In this example you might create three different header texts, two different sign-up forms requesting varying amounts of data, and two different footers. You would then funnel visitors to all possible combinations of these elements to see which converts at the highest rate.

While I've specified two particular use cases – email marketing and a landing page – the principle can be applied to pretty much anything within your digital estate like text content, images, and videos, but a key consideration is that you need to be confident the application you're testing can support the testing method. For example, you can't test both a subject line and a CTA in the same email campaign as you won't know which of the different elements impacted the result. Also bear in mind that while setting up tests increases the amount of time needed to implement and deliver a campaign, the results more than outweigh the additional resources required.

Most importantly, you can see the results of digital marketing tests really quickly, so not only are you able to fail and then improve, to use the different mantras of Silicon Valley you can 'fail fast, fail often', 'fail better', or 'fail forward', all of which put you in a stronger position to deliver your target KPIs.

A/A testing

Advanced digital marketers may also consider the use of A/A testing. This is a process used before A/B or MV testing to check the validity of the test you're about to implement. In this instance, you use two versions of exactly the same asset to ensure that the tools or processes you're using are running correctly. When using an A/A test you should see no difference between the two variations and can be confident there will be no external factors impacting your A/B or MV tests.

From last action to next best action

In Chapter 4 I talked about the role of predictive analytics to help you understand what's likely to happen in the future. When you apply this process to digital marketing, you're able to move from just tracking a customer's last action to predicting their next one. Most importantly you can prepare for it, anticipating their needs and presenting them with the right message at the right time and on the right channel. We call this 'next best action'.

This process works by assessing all the potential next best actions for your fan or customer (for example, buy a ticket, upgrade to VIP hospitality, extend to a season ticket, buy the matching shorts, train to be a coach) and selecting the one that they're most likely to take, given the results of your analysis. Irrespective of your customer's response (i.e. did it work or didn't it), you'll learn more about that customer. This in turn will improve the efficiency of this process as you continue to use it. The key to successful use of this process is ensuring you strike a balance between what your customers expect from you and what you're trying to achieve.

Applying a next-best-action approach involves quite an advanced use of analytics, so by nature it would be part of a cross-channel marketing automation programme – i.e. if you're still just using email marketing then you're unlikely to have access to advanced analytics in your environment – so I won't go into too much more detail at this stage. But this is the link to the 'crystal ball' I referred to in Chapter 1.

Data-driven marketing: the utopian state

The extent to which you use data-driven marketing will depend on a number of factors relevant to your specific organisation, the most important of which is your business need. As with any form of marketing, the costs have to be taken into account and considered against the potential gains. For example, if your objective is to sell 5,000 tickets and you have 100,000 previous ticket buyers in your database, you can be relatively confident of a 5% conversion rate using some basic processes. However, if the numbers are reversed and you have 100,000 tickets to sell, and a starting point of just 5,000 customers, your plan will change. In addition to converting existing customers you'll be looking for new ones.

Thinking more strategically, if your mid-term organisational objectives include increasing your engagement within a specific segment of fans, extending your global reach into new territories or doubling your participation base, then it's reasonable to assume you'll need the appropriate resources to deliver this. This could include a combination of more people with more skills, more software, and more processes to support that software. And it's also reasonable to assume that you'll need more content to support more progressive marketing and messaging.

Some rights owners have gone beyond data-driven marketing and are talking about complete digital transformation. This is the change associated with the application of digital technologies across the whole of a business. This digital usage inherently enables new types of innovation or creativity, as opposed to simply enhancing and supporting an existing method. I've already discussed how the sports industry is moving at a slower pace than other industries, not just the pure plays; but let's assume that this is your objective: to achieve digital transformation that delivers significant increases in KPIs over a three-year term. In this case your utopian state would be fast and accurate cross-channel and cross-device engagement, with attribute tracking at every touch point. This would enable you to know the exact contributing factor at every step of the customer journey, so you could continue to improve on the efficiency of your processes.

In reality no one is actually achieving this yet, not even Amazon, Netflix, or Spotify, and the reason is the pace of technological change, which is providing our customers with more choice, more frequently. According to Scott Brinker's annual review of the marketing technology landscape, 2020 saw an increase in 25% of solutions resulting in a total of 8,000, with data-related technologies representing 1,258 of them, a 25% increase within its own category (Brinker, 2020).

The key for every rights owner is finding the appropriate ways to optimise the channels they use to achieve their KPIs and, along the way, improving the level of engagement they have with their fans, customers, or participants. Equally as important is that the fans feel valued along the journey and that rights owners know and care about the fans and are talking to them individually.

Case study: Lincoln City Football Club

In the first edition of this book Derbyshire County Cricket Club provided a case study. You can download that from www.winnnersfdd.com/winningwithdata-first/ch6casestudy.

For this edition, I had a phone interview in June 2020 with Liam Scully, CEO of Lincoln City Football Club, a team in the English Football League's League One. Lincoln City is quite well known by football fans around the world having made it to the FA Cup Quarter-Finals as a non-League club in 2017, a feat not seen in English football since 1914, only to be beaten by Arsenal at the Emirates Stadium. This led *The Sun*, one of the UK's leading tabloids for sports coverage, to proclaim 'Lincoln City won the hearts of millions' (Allen, 2017) and also resulted in three times the usual number of Google searches for the club. It is still the Google Trends peak for search frequency.

Armed with the knowledge that Lincoln City has more than demonstrated its ability to 'punch above its weight' when it comes to on-the-field performance, I started by asking Liam what he thought of their approach to the use of data-driven marketing: how does it compare to other clubs in their League of their size/status?

I think Lincoln City has always had the potential to be bigger and do more. We started using email marketing in 2015 when we were in the National League; that's a full two years before I arrived, but it's fair to say we started to really focus on it from April 2019. I look at the way we use fan data now to personalise our interactions with our fans, how we think about automation and the fan experience, and I can't imagine many clubs of our size and at this level – both in football and in other sports – doing what we're doing. Having said that, we've still got a long way to go, so we look at the new Juventus website with a single sign-on and Man U's database of 36 million, and we realise we're just at the beginning of our own digital transformation.

As we've discussed earlier in this book, the use of CRM and data has to be linked to business objectives – it can't just be 'data for data's sake' – and on that point Liam was quite clear about the impact he's seen as a result of their increased focus on data-driven marketing.

I'm too young to remember what it was like before football clubs had websites, but I can imagine how difficult it must have been to get your story across when all you had was a press release and interviews with journalists to rely on. Back in 2011 the EFL came up with the original FLi [Football League Interactive] proposition, where 86 clubs worked with a website framework provided by the League, and it was quite a game-changer, not just for Lincoln City but for all of us. We already had our Facebook page, set up in 2009, so the natural progression was to then add email marketing to our digital channels, and I have to say, it's been pretty transformational.

Putting aside the importance of revenue generation, the level of engagement we can get through email is incredible – our fans see that we know them, we understand what they're interested in, we know that they've already bought a ticket or a lottery, and we can thank them for it. Yes, you can get this level of one-to-one through Facebook, but the costs are a lot higher. We do use Facebook advertising, but only when we can't reach fans through email. And, while the EFL is continuing to develop the functionality of our websites, it's still a very much static environment – we don't yet have a dynamic website that responds to each of our fans individually, and until that happens, email provides us with a personalised experience that makes a real difference.

League One football in England drew to a premature close in March 2020 as a result of the global pandemic, with Lincoln City playing their last game on 7 March. At the time of writing, it's expected the new season will start in September 2020, but there has been no confirmed start date. The club usually operates with a digital marketing team of two staff but, as a result of coronavirus, they've had to rely on just one team member to keep the club's communications going when it can be argued that engagement is now more important than ever. Here I ask how email marketing has helped Lincoln City maintain that close connection with their fans when they're not playing week in and week out:

> The task has been quite significant – we've recognised the need to maintain, even increase, that level of engagement to remind our fans we're still here and we still value them, but we haven't had any of our natural content. It's been a case of more engagement needed, less content to do it with. The manager and players have been great, plus we've been using a lot of our archive videos to remind fans what it's like to watch us play – we've also used competitions and promotions to maintain that close relationship with them. When you look at the number of email campaigns we've sent since the start of [coronavirus] lockdown, it's actually double the number we sent out across the same months in 2019, so that's both representative of how much better we are at using email, along with our awareness of the need to stay in touch until our fans can watch us play again.
>
> We also have a few automations going – the traditional onboarding approach to new fans signing up to hear from us, as well as a birthday email – so there's been a consistent stream of campaigns going out.

I discussed the principle of 'test and learn' earlier in the chapter and asked Liam about their approach to testing, and what they have learned from it:

> We're primarily testing subject lines, as our focus has been on our ORs – our click-through rate is already more than double the industry average, and while our ORs are also higher than average, we want to focus on that metric as a priority.
>
> We're learning a lot about our fans and what drives them, and you won't be surprised to know that the use of *win* and any subject lines that include a sense of urgency such as 'Don't miss' generally outperform the others. Use of a fan's first name consistently wins, although we don't use it every campaign; but sometimes a mention of the manager or a player's name will beat it. But, interestingly when we tested the announcement of a new signing against the unveiling of our new home kit, the home kit won. And generally, the content areas promoting our online store really do generate a high percentage of clicks in our campaigns.

When it comes to personalisation, Liam was able to provide a very relevant and valuable example – the need to address season ticket holders who had paid to watch their team play for the whole season but ended up losing one-third of the action they paid for.

When we first knew for certain that we wouldn't be playing any more matches in the 2019/2020 season, we decided that while it would hurt to lose a third of our season ticket revenue, our fans were also hurting. Many will have been furloughed or lost their jobs altogether, some will have suffered emotional and physical issues, and some may even have lost a friend or family member through COVID-19. We didn't want to add any further burden to them by suggesting they let us keep their money – we wanted them to put themselves and their needs first, and we really meant it, so we had to work hard to get that message across.

In addition to posts on our website and in our social channels, we created a very focussed series of email campaigns. It started with a plain message from our chairman to our season ticket holders that introduced the options we were considering but more importantly that we wanted them to think about their needs over ours – and we meant it. We then gave them 24 hours to digest that and really think about what we said, and then we followed up with further information about the three options we'd be providing – a refund directly into their bank account, the opportunity to convert the value of their refund into shares in the club, and finally a donation to the Red Imps Community Trust [The Supporters Trust] to enable them to increase their shareholding in the club. The last email provided the platform for them to choose that option – a link to a personalised landing page that enabled them to quickly select the option for each of the tickets they had purchased. Some of our season ticket holders have just one ticket in their name, many have several, and we have one fan with 18, so the landing page had to be both personalised and user-friendly for each instance. To ensure we reached as many of our season ticket holders as possible, we did re-sends to anyone who hadn't opened their emails or completed their forms and, as of today, we have just 4% who haven't responded.

I don't know whether it's a response to the way we communicated the options, the relationship our chairman has with our fans, or the close affinity our fans have with us, but only 22% of our season ticket holders requested a refund. While we were genuinely prepared for all of them to want their money back, their option to convert to shares or donate to the Trust was indeed gratefully received.

That exercise alone demonstrated the value of personalised and direct engagement with our fans. And because we used email as the main channel to talk to our fans, providing an easy-to-follow digital process supported with automation, we were able to do this at scale and at a relatively low cost. When you combine those facts – reduced manpower and minimised errors, but fans feeling that you really care about them – you get an unrivalled ROI when looking at cost-to-deliver versus income retention.

With the club experiencing the value of data-driven marketing at such a challenging time in its history, we asked Liam to share his next steps in this area and his vision for the club's own digital transformation:

It's going to be very much 'one step at a time' here. Yes, we're pleased with the progress we've made, and yes we realise the importance of the use of data, but we have to put that into perspective with our immediate challenges – and right now that means understanding what the 'new normal' will look like, not just for us or just for football but also for our fans and indeed the rest of the population. Having said that, we're definitely not going backwards, so in the immediate area of email marketing it'll be more of the same, but then extending that out to our different communication channels. We don't have a mobile app, but we've got mobile numbers for SMS marketing, and we have been working with the League to introduce web and social retargeting. So, investing more in paid advertising will be a part of our strategy – subject to us generating the right level of returns. We're also using our data to support the commercial team – through sponsorship, corporate hospitality, and events – and have started using Tableau to ensure we can see our results and progress at a glance.

I'd like to think that in the same way we showed our peers that playing on the same field as the big boys is achievable for Lincoln City, we'll do that with the way we engage with our fans – we'll look at what Man U and Juventus are doing, and we'll keep heading in that direction.

(Source: Scully, 2020)

Key chapter ideas

1   While your software vendors – for example your ticketing system, online store, or athlete registration platform – will no doubt provide you with a system for email function, this is not the same as using a dedicated campaign management platform for your targeted marketing. Always use a separate email or multichannel marketing system for this.

2   Using segmentation and personalisation in your direct marketing channels will increase engagement and should therefore increase your ROI. It
should enable you to make your fans feel valued.

3   When it comes to retargeting with digital advertising, you can use a dedicated platform that allows you to use pixel and list-based retargeting or you
can work directly with the ad networks or exchanges themselves. Using
native applications first will allow you to get used to the functions and
understand how they work before making an investment in technology.

4   When you use testing processes in digital marketing you make an informed
decision based on an objective, rather than a subjective, data-driven process. This will increase the chances of your tactic, concept, or project having a successful outcome.

5   Ensure you use the right testing process for your objective – for example,
testing a subject line to increase email ORs or trailing a CTA to test landing page conversion rates.

References

Allen, J. (2017). COW-CH! Lincoln city won the hearts of millions with their FA cup run last season – but it cost their manager £740 and a fancy car. *The Sun*. Available at: www. thesun.co.uk/sport/football/4838232/lincoln-city-fa-cup-arsenal-danny-cowley/.

Brinker, S. (2020). Marketing technology landscape supergraphic (2020). *Chief Marketing Technologist* [online]. Available at: https://chiefmartec.com/2020/04/marketing-techno logy-landscape-2020-martech-5000/.

CampaignMonitor. (2019). *ROI showdown: SMS marketing vs. email marketing* [online]. Available at: www.campaignmonitor.com/blog/email-marketing/2019/01/roi-showdown-sms-marketing-vs-email-marketing/.

Carnegie, D. (2006). *How to win friends and influence people*. London: Vermilion.

Experian. (2016). *New insight from experian marketing services helps brands prepare for the holiday season* [online]. Available at: www.experianplc.com/media/news/2016/q2-2016-email-bench mark-report/.

Ourand, J. (2017). Dolphins plow marketing budget into content and get results. *Street & Smith's Sports Business Journal* [online]. Available at: www.sportsbusinessdaily.com/Jour-nal/Issues/2017/03/27/Media/Sports-Media.aspx.

Ritson, M. (2020). The best marketers will be upping, not cutting, their budgets. *Marketing week.com* [online]. Available at: www.marketingweek.com/mark-ritson-marketing-spend-recession-coronavirus/.

Scully, L. (2020). Chief Executive, in a personal interview, 7 Aug.

Scibetti, R. (2018). Personal interview, 22 Jan.

SmarterHQ. (2019). *Privacy & personalization: Consumers share how to win them over without crossing the line* [online]. Available at: https://smarterhq.com/privacy-report.

Ulanoff, L. (2012). Elon musk: Secrets of a highly effective entrepreneur. *Mashable* [online]. Available at: https://mashable.com/2012/04/13/elon-musk-secrets-of-effectiveness/#D DVq740.3aqt.

Chapter 7

The role of CRM and data in sponsorship

I started selling sponsorships in sports 30 years ago. From shirt, match, and ball packages for Notts County FC (formerly the oldest Football League club in the world, but since the 2018/2019 season, now in England's National League) through to European Championships and World Cups on behalf of UEFA and FIFA. Two of my last major deals in this area were the 2003 signing of Thomas Cook as the shirt sponsor for Manchester City, the catalyst for the launch of its sports travel business, and the 2008 naming rights to Sophia Gardens, home of Glamorgan Cricket Club, to the utility brand SWALEC. But these were many years ago, and a lot has changed in the sponsorship industry since then. One of these changes is the role of data.

Looking back to the negotiations between City and Thomas Cook, I recall that the club's fan base played a role. The driver of Thomas Cook's sponsorship wasn't ad boards, match tickets, or meet-the-players opportunities; it was the ability to sell holidays to City fans. And boy did it work. When they went on to renew the deal two seasons later, Thomas Cook reported that 'the club's supporters are four times more likely to choose Thomas Cook over their rivals' (Gibson, 2005). But here's the thing: while we talked about City's fan base, we didn't talk about its database. We referred to more traditional above-the-line advertising methods to engage en masse. When we looked for one-to-one opportunities, it took the form of a leaflet in the club shop's carrier bags or placed on the seats in the stadium.

Skip forward five years, and I remember the late Paul Russell, the former Chairman of Glamorgan, going through his sponsorship wish-list. He wanted a Welsh company (he was very patriotic through to his passing in January 2018), a brand that would work as a naming rights sponsor (short and not a word that could be considered 'descriptive' in any manner), and finally, a company that could help extend the reach of his favourite sport, which was naturally overshadowed by rugby in Wales. It couldn't have gone better. SWALEC, a regional brand of Scottish and Southern Energy met all the criteria and, on the last point, had a customer base of one million residents in Wales. Most importantly, as part of the sponsorship deal, SWALEC agreed to help promote the Glamorgan Cricket brand to its customers via their monthly bills and statements.

Looking back, I didn't realise then that what I had successfully negotiated, with Thomas Cook for Manchester City and SWALEC on behalf of Glamorgan Cricket, would resonate so closely with where I am now – knee-deep in the use of customer data to support a rights owner's business objectives. In this chapter I'll be looking specifically at sponsorship, one of my favourite areas of the sports industry and one to which every rights owner in sports will be able to relate.

To reiterate my words in Chapter 1, when I deliver client workshops, I start the section on sponsorship by joking that in my previous years, had I known the impact the use of data could have on sponsorship sales I'd have made a lot more commission. I believe I'd have sold sponsorship far more quickly and with a lot more ease. In reality, 10 to 15 years ago the industry didn't have quite as much access to data as we do now, but I use the statement to make a point and to grab the attention of the salespeople in the room.

Here's when I usually have to revisit the meaning of *CRM*. If you recall from previous chapters, the term has evolved from the use of software to manage the sales funnel to the definition that we use at Winners: getting the right message to the right person at the right time and incorporating five key elements, of which software is just one. So, while the right software can ensure the process is more efficient (it helps you track your actions, highlights next-step tasks, and manages your inventory), the bit that makes the real difference is when you can match your fanbase to a prospective sponsor's target market, demonstrate how you can engage with them on a one-to-one basis, and show how your sponsorship proposal enables the direct delivery of their message to your fans, individually and with relevance.

Sponsorship use cases

Consider beer – The ubiquitous Heineken has a target customer audience of males aged 18 to 24 (InfoScout, 2017), so imagine how much more powerful your sales pitch is when you can tell the company how many of that audience you have in your database and that you can ensure they see your co-branded message. You are then able to give Heineken a reason to look closer at your proposal and, as many sponsorship salespeople know, sometimes just getting a foot in the door – or a proposal on a desk – can be a challenge.

Retail outlets – The checkpoints in Figure 7.1 represent the location of a rights owner's fan database, at a postcode level, in Wales. The checkpoints in Figure 7.2 show the location in Wales of SPAR stores, the international food retailer. Now, this rights owner can go to SPAR and show the relationship between its shops and its own fan database. Figure 7.3 shows that nearly 45% of the database live within one mile, and over 95% live within 5 miles of at least one SPAR branch. That's quite a powerful message to incorporate into a sales pitch. It shows that the rights holder understands the potential sponsor's objective to get more consumers visiting its stores. Later I'll look at the next stage: leveraging this type of fan data to generate customers for the sponsor.

Figure 7.1 Location of fans (source: Winners FDD Ltd)

Figure 7.2 Location of SPAR outlets (source: Winners FDD Ltd)

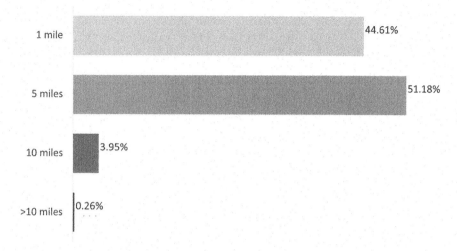

Figure 7.3 Percentage of fans and their distance to a SPAR location (source: Winners FDD Ltd)

Airlines – In 2012, just before signing a £150 million extension to Emirates Airlines' sponsorship of Arsenal, Divisional Senior Vice President for Corporate Communications Boutros Boutros made the following public declaration:

> Data on customers is important to us like it should be for any business. The price of media is increasing every year and having detailed data on customers allows us to work out where we spend our ad budgets and who we target as well as what markets we focus on through the club's channels.
>
> (Joseph, 2012)

It's probably an exaggeration to say that Emirates invested this amount just because Arsenal was starting to understand who its fans were, but it went a long way in helping secure the deal. Emirates is interested in people with a relatively high disposable income such as long-haul travellers who like business class, or business travellers whose employers are footing the bill. With its approach to CRM, Arsenal would be in a position to give Emirates' marketers what they wanted: sight of their target customers and the ability to communicate with them directly.

Entertainment – Manchester United, Arsenal's competitors on the field but its peers off it, when it comes to commercial prowess and aspirations, is just as effusive about the role of data in making decisions regarding its sponsorship strategy. As Tom Hill, former Head of Partnerships and Operations at Manchester United, espoused at the 2016 SportsPro The Brand Conference:

> When 20th Century Fox (a global partner since February 2016) wanted to create awareness for their films on a global scale we adopted a non-traditional route, working with them to create content that would appeal to our fans. With ten seasons' worth of TV viewing data we had valuable insights into our global fan base of over 659 million followers.
>
> (Hill, 2016)

This informed the decision to make a video where United player Wayne Rooney met the superhero Deadpool, which was viewed over 12 million times on social media. Showing the video during a match resulted in a 39% increase on searches for the film than on non-match days, with a further 15% increase in the 60 seconds after the promotion of the film on Old Trafford's digital advertising boards. Hill went on to say:

> The key thing for Fox was the ability to analyse how good the relationship with Man United was film-by-film, and how successful the promotional activity was compared to traditional advertising. This enabled them to convince their CEO in LA that this was a good use of money.
>
> (Hill, 2016)

Case study: the Warriors and NBA jersey sponsorship

Another example of the use of data to secure a sponsorship is the $60 million sponsorship between the Golden State Warriors and Rakuten (Brown, 2017a).

In 2017, the NBA created a ruling that would allow the placement of a 2.5-square-inch advertising logo on jerseys above the left breast (NBA, 2017). While kit advertising may be commonplace in other parts of the world, most notably in European Football, it was still almost unprecedented in major American sports, with just teams in MLS presenting a full complement of shirt sponsors.

The Women's National Basketball Association (WNBA) adopted jersey ads back in 2011, and these did indeed generate an increase in revenue, but the NBA still hesitated to give the advertising proposition a green light. The WNBA has fewer than half the fans of the men's game so, for the NBA, it was much harder to anticipate how fans would react, with the key worry being a backlash to this commercial move. With the NBA already making significant use of branding opportunities for sponsors, from stadium names and mid-game entertainment to arena panelling and branding in special seating sections, there was concern that jerseys were the last bastion of non-commercialisation.

At the time of writing, only 16 out of the 30 NBA teams have brokered a deal for a jersey patch. The Warriors' agreement is with Japanese ISP and e-commerce giant Rakuten, a deal projected at being worth $20 million annually over a period of three years. This deal is the biggest patch agreement to date, doubling that of the Cleveland Cavaliers and Goodyear, which is the next biggest deal in terms of value.

The players

So, who are the players in one of the NBA's most lucrative new sponsorship deals?

The Golden State Warriors team was founded in 1946 as the Philadelphia Warriors, and it is a charter member of the NBA, moving to its current base in Oakland, California, in 1971. Its history includes five NBA Championships, an NBA-record 73 wins during the 2015/2016 season, the best post-season run in NBA history (16–1 in 2017), six of the NBA's 50 Greatest Players, and 27 members of Naismith Memorial Basketball Hall of Fame.

Founded in 1997, Rakuten is the biggest e-commerce site in Japan with 90% of Japan's internet users registered as customers. That's more than 100 million users. It currently hosts 40,000 different businesses and services, all of which know they need to be on Rakuten to reach Japanese residents.

In addition to its globally renowned Viber messaging app, Rakuten has acquired leading Canadian e-reader Kobo. But despite establishing its American headquarters in the Bay Area in 2015, Rakuten remains a largely unknown entity to American sports fans. It recently became the shirt sponsor of Barcelona FC, as well as a broadcast partner of the NBA, providing live coverage of the sport in Japan, so these deals will help increase its European and American brand awareness.

But the Warriors deal will provide further exposure for Rakuten, and not just through the placement of its logo on the team's jerseys. The Warriors' practice facility will be renamed the Rakuten Performance Centre, and the company will be the Warriors' official e-commerce partner, video-on-demand partner, and also the team's affiliate marketing partner.

Chip Bowers, the Warriors' chief marketing officer, revealed that Rakuten's offer was not the most lucrative that the team received, but it had to align with a global brand in order to grow its global vision.

How data helped broker a deal

Despite the Warriors' successes and star power, the team had to make sure it had real data to support key elements of any sales pitches to potential sponsors. While its celebrated players are one element of its value, according to Bowers the right processes had to be in place to show the added value of both the team and its fans.

> The Warriors organisation wanted to look at this through a very responsible lens. This is not a typical sponsorship asset. You're placing a brand on the chest of your players – the most valuable asset of your organisation.

To support this approach, the Warriors teamed up with Wasserman Media, using their proprietary Scorecard-Analysis and Regression-Analysis metrics to build an estimation of the team's value to potential sponsors. They looked at market dynamics, fan purchase behaviour, team performance, and franchise reach, as well as visibility to fans and within the sport. They compared the values of other sports properties, both in the US and worldwide, in order to compare trends of similar deals and make comparisons based on these markets, and similar brands, within the NBA. The jersey patch itself was analysed for exposure. The brands would be most prominent during televised games, via digital streaming channels, and (most notably) when a player was at the foul line.

> It was really important to understand the Warriors brand both nationally and globally. We could see that through our own channels and our own media on the return we and our partners were getting, but the jersey sponsorship deal was all new. We kind of expected the league would want us to be one of the first to reach our deal, but we took a cautious approach to it.

Using Wasserman's analysis, the Warriors could refine the sponsorship proposal to suit the needs of potential partners. With a more in-depth knowledge of where the team's appeal was centred, it became clear that what was needed was a global partnership, furthering this by performing international fan insight research to gauge the team's appeal to international brands.

> For Rakuten, it was about people alignment and philosophical alignment as much as brand alignment. They are very focussed on the future, innovation, and positivity. And when you look at our team, our players, our brand, they felt there were some natural alignments between their company and the Warriors.

Conversely, Rakuten's CEO Hiroshi Mikitani understood that his company lacked brand awareness in the US, despite its North American headquarters being based in San Francisco. A partnership between the two would provide good exposure for the sponsor. With the Warriors' location near Silicon Valley and its use of analytics demonstrating a like-minded approach to understanding their customers, it was clear to Bowers that the partnership had potential.

> When you think about it, one of the biggest reasons for brands to wish to align with an organisation like the Warriors is the power of sports. We represent a region, and in many ways California. We need to make sure that our fans are going to be fine with a brand we align ourselves with, and Rakuten met that criteria.

Over the course of their partnership, the Warriors' deal will help Rakuten increase its brand awareness through television, digital and social media channels. With the Warriors' expansion of e-commerce platforms for ticketing, merchandise, and digital content delivery, Rakuten delivers benefits back to the team and, more importantly, their fans. In addition to this, as the sports industry is pursuing more and more technological innovations, not only to improve the experience of their fans but also to collect valuable fan data through digital channels, the Warriors can expect to benefit from Rakuten's extensive knowledge, experience, and technical infrastructure.

The future of NBA jersey sponsorships

The $60 million Warriors-Rakuten partnership is set to provide the blueprint for all future NBA deals of this type, with data informing the approach while also enhancing the rights owner's ability to generate and use data as an output of the relationship. But rather than commit to jersey sponsorship in perpetuity, the NBA has instead decided to run the patch partnerships on a three-year trial basis. If fan backlash is detected, the NBA can change its mind with very little damage to its reputation. So, with the possibility of an extension after the trial period, it will be interesting to see how this data-driven partnership can help two global brands achieve their respective business goals.

With huge potential revenue and lucrative sponsorships on the horizon, it not only seems that patches will be here to stay, but that the NBA's decision may open the doors for other American major sports leagues, perhaps even the NFL, to take the plunge (Brown, 2017a).

Using data to leverage sponsorship

Moving on from data to inform sponsorship decision-making to data to maximise the value of sponsorships for both parties, let's look to ESP Properties' 32nd annual year-end industry review to understand where this is heading:

> As a growing number of properties pursue data-driven audience engagement plans – and the potential they bring for personalised marketing – sponsors rated access to audience data as one of the most important benefits their rights owner partners can bring . . . about one-third of sponsors rated the benefit a none or 10 on a 10-point scale of value, ranking it the seventh most valuable benefit.
>
> (ESP Properties, 2017)

So, how do we ensure we provide our sponsors with the opportunities they want without compromising the rights owner's relationship with the fan? The industry of brokering data has been around for a very long time, whether it be collecting and selling information about your newspaper subscriptions; the type of car you drive; your choice of pet, holiday, or breakfast cereal; whether you use credit cards and have a mortgage; or even your contact details. But that's not where the value of data as part of a sponsorship programme lies.

Referring back to the ESP report, the right to use property marks and logos is identified as the third most-valuable opportunity, confirming that building brand positioning through associative imagery continues to be a major driver (Ibid.). We know that selling or giving a fan database to our sponsors and partners won't achieve this. Therefore, the message to the fan has to be carried by the rights owner incorporating the sponsor's content in order for that association to remain intact.

Let's return to our SPAR example seen in Figures 7.1, 7.2, and 7.3. This particular rights owner has the contact details of fans; in this case, an email address with an opt-in to receive direct communication. It can provide highly targeted messages on behalf of SPAR, incorporating content that matters to the fan with a CTA that increases the chances of a sale. For example, consider the power of the fan receiving an email that tells them where their closest SPAR branch is, particularly if it's with a message that fans get a discount on purchases.

But there are other forms of targeted marketing that a rights owner can provide a sponsor. In April 2017 it was announced that Coca-Cola had replaced Pepsi as the sponsor of MLB, a move that, while not sending shockwaves through the industry, certainly did raise a few eyebrows. It wasn't just that two leading brands in their categories swapped position; it was the change in emphasis for Coca-Cola from its traditional '3 Ss' (seats, suites and signage) approach to sponsorship. Instead, it chose to enter into a deal based almost entirely on digital and empowered by data.

Bob Bowman, MLB President, Business and Media, said about it: 'This partnership is focussed on . . . connecting Coca-Cola with our fans through digital, mobile and social' (Brown, 2017b). Coca-Cola activating its sponsorships through digital channels is nothing new. London 2012 saw the emergence of this trend, where online and offline combined to provide the ultimate leverage program. Indeed, Coca-Cola 'outdid themselves' according to *Forbes* (Peterson, 2012). The 2017 contract would still enable creative offline executions, however, such as the Houston Astros 2017 World Series win commemorative edition can (Coca-Cola, 2017). But the focus of this deal would be the activation of tie-ins through MLB Advanced Media and its owned and operated digital platforms: mlb.com, its 30 club websites, its At Bat and Ballpark mobile apps, MLB's multiple social accounts, and MLB.TV.

Similarly, in 2016 when Telefonica UK renewed its longstanding partnership with England's Rugby Football Union (RFU) for a further five years under the O2 brand, it was emphasised that the deal was a departure from the more traditional sponsorship objective of increased brand awareness to the opportunity to engage more closely with rugby fans. As reported in *The Drum*, Nina Bibby, the CMO at O2 said: 'When we first partnered up years ago it was about raising awareness of the brand but we've moved beyond that so we're now looking to shape new experiences for our customers and engage with them through those experience' (Connelly, 2016).

The telecommunications industry places a lot of focus on reducing churn, that is, minimising the number of service subscribers who discontinue their subscription to that service within a given time period. Bibby credits O2's

Priority programme as a driver behind halving contract churn from 1.8% to 0.9% over the last ten years. Not surprisingly, this Priority offering will play a key role in O2's partnership with the RFU, with a focus on creating integrated, connected, and personalised experiences across mobile devices along with special offers such as tickets to England matches (Ibid.).

The RFU's approach to CRM

To enable O2 to achieve this, it needed the RFU to have a handle on its own fan data. Mark Killingley, then the RFU's Head of Digital and CRM, told 2015's Festival of Marketing that this was an area the RFU had been working on for some time (Davis, 2015).

The RFU's CRM technology stack includes an SCV from data integrations with its player registration platform, marketing data from its social channels and the RFU website, and commercial data from England team matches and other related activity. With this in place, the RFU is able to know nearly all its stakeholders across several digital and non-digital touch points, identifying which customer falls into which profile, for example a coach, a fan, a pitch-side father, or a club player.

This optimised approach to customer data enables the RFU to send the right message to the right person at the right time, and it's this foundation and approach to engagement that will power the partnership with O2, providing the information O2 needs to ensure its Priority offering for rugby fans is in line with expectations, that it's what the fans want and what they need. Personalised opportunities will include pre-match content that's available 48 hours before anywhere else, and behind-the-scenes and match-day digital content, along with access to priority tickets for all England matches at Twickenham.

In addition to engaging with the RFU's fans, Bibby says that O2 witnessed an increase in the interest in rugby among its customers, particularly after the 2015 Rugby World Cup, which was hosted in England:

> We saw a big jump after the World Cup last year which tells us more of our customer base are becoming active fans. We know customers love live experiences we offer them with rugby and concerts so now we're focussing on how digital can enhance those experiences before, during and after [events]. That's really what we want to try and do more of, that whole end-to-end experience from live to digital and back.
>
> (Connelly, 2016)

For O2, this also means pushing its use of technology even further and exploring live streaming and virtual reality (VR); and it's in the implementation of the latter that the RFU's extensive archive of performance data will demonstrate its commercial potential.

Performance data for commercial use

I mentioned in my introduction to this book that, while data is an area I'll be looking at, it's not performance data that I work with. It's the statistics that enable a rights owner to make business decisions and send targeted communications. My caveat to this has always been that, when the natural silos between sports performance teams and their marketing teams are broken, when we can use that rich player data to entertain and engage our fans, then we at Winners can start to enter that market.

A great example of this is in O2's VR offering, made possible by the RFU's TryTracker, a web-based predictive analytics platform for rugby fans produced in collaboration with IBM through a partnership that started in in 2013 (IBM, 2013). During live matches, TryTracker produces data to inform three dashboards that are displayed on the RFU's website: momentum, keys to the game and player influence. Each dashboard presents different datasets that provide real-time insight to fans. In describing this approach, Nick Shaw, Head of Digital at the RFU, said:

> We saw a major opportunity to bring the rich data we had on past rugby matches to life on RFU.com and tell the story of a match in real time. By creating a platform for insight using the latest business analytics technologies, we realised that we could transform RFU.com into the destination site for anyone interested in rugby and reach new fans around the world. The 'keys to the game' dashboard highlights specific areas where teams are over- and under-performing, and identifies three targets that a certain team needs to achieve to increase their probability of winning a match. On a match day, these three keys to the game are surfaced on the TryTracker hub page; if a team hits all three, then their probability of winning increases dramatically. This feature of TryTracker shows new fans exactly what to look out for as a match progresses – helping them to get more from the experience of watching live rugby.
>
> (Ibid.)

The 'momentum' dashboard provides a live, interactive timeline of a match and shows statistics, such as possession, to show a fan which team is most likely to score next, with 'player influence' demonstrating the impact a player entering or leaving a match has on a team's chance of winning, using historical data and the status of the current match.

So, having built this application over the past four or five years, the RFU is now able to enhance its partnership with O2 even further to power its VR offering with this deep archive of player and match performance data. Unveiled in March 2017, O2's VR rugby experience provides gamers with the opportunity to compete against England's best rugby talent in the form of interactive

CGI characters, created using accurate player movement along with England players' weight, mass, and average speeds (Ellison, 2017).

> We believe in live and using the latest VR technology we can showcase our live experiences to O2 customers in our stores across the country. Through a combination of world first CGI characters and unique interactive gameplay, each experience has been designed to give the user unprecedented access our relationship with the England Rugby team. We're excited to roll our new VR into O2 stores nationwide and at Twickenham Stadium on match days.
>
> (Ibid.)

While this example stood out as being particularly innovative and forward-thinking, it's also one of the few out there as the performance staff at clubs and teams continue to remain protective of this type of data. However, I do wonder if the impact the coronavirus has had on our heightened need to engage in creative ways will force this issue when teams are training again, but doing it behind closed doors. We may even see that occur before this book hits the shelves!

Changing the sponsorship dialogue

While coronavirus has caused (or enabled) rights owners to come up with creative and innovative engagement programmes, the impact it had on our sponsorship revenues cannot be overstated, with the European Sponsorship Association suggesting the industry is predicted to be down by $61 billion (Bradford, 2020). This suggests we need to take the same approach to sponsorship as we have to content and to reframe our offering – at Winners we've created a model that we title 'Changing the Sponsorship Dialogue'. The principle behind the framework is that it allows you to add a valuable asset to your sponsorship discussion: the guarantee that you'll drive your fans to your sponsors' websites.

Think about it – rights owners are accustomed to selling boards, shirts, stands, tickets, unique experiences, and more recently, exposure through digital channels; but the dialogue continues to be about the number of tickets, the number of impressions, and the number of broadcast minutes – our model allows you to talk about the number of *your* fans that you can help convert to *their* customers.

Our starting point is that whatever reason a brand will give for sponsorship – brand exposure, brand association, community relations, staff relations, etc. – their business is generally after one thing: to sell more; more products to existing customers or more new customers.

Our second point is that if a brand has a website (which they normally do), then when someone visits the website the brand has a process for converting that person to a customer. Pure plays will have a detailed customer journey and an exact conversion rate for each website visitor, and while 'brick and click' businesses may be a bit further behind, they'll still know how they convert a web visitor to a paying customer, even if they go offline in the process.

The third point, one of the most important points for me – the one that's the game-changer for selling sponsorships and getting more budget from your brands – is that marketing budgets and, more importantly, digital marketing budgets, are generally WAY BIGGER than sponsorship budgets. This suggests that *if* you can speak to brands in the same language as the digital marketers and digital ad agencies, if you can talk about generating guaranteed traffic to their websites, and if you use the right content that combines your sponsors' offerings with your sport/team/league event, they can expect a MUCH HIGHER CTR on their banners resulting in a better landing-page conversion rate.

And the fourth and final point to consider – if a rights owner has a leverage budget of X, and spends 40% of that leverage budget on digital marketing linked to their sponsorship, somewhere out there an ad agency is making a commission on that 40% of X. With the right internal skills, the rights owner themselves can be making that commission. Whether you charge it as part of a leverage fee, absorb it as a cost-of-sale, or increase your sponsorship rights fee to incorporate it, the net result is a positive impact on your sponsorship strategy.

With the Winners' framework you identify the exact number of visitors you can generate for your sponsors' websites. This number can then be added into your sales pitch, negotiations and contract as a key deliverable and, while it won't replace nor negate the value of boards, shirts, stands, tickets, unique experiences, and digital channel exposure, it provides a tangible number that the brands can convert into actual customers. You can read about this approach in the next case study.

What can your sponsors do for you?

The last point I want to make in this chapter is that while securing the right value for your sponsorship has always been a priority, most of the time we want to steer away from value-in-kind (VIK) deals, instead focussing on those deals that provide us with cash, as highlighted in the Warriors-Rakuten deal, sometimes the right partner can support you in your own CRM and data-driven quests.

Sponsors who operate in the financial services, telecommunications, ISPs, travel, and indeed any other B2C category, where they focus on personalised offers and messaging, could provide you with different areas of support (of course always operating in compliance with the GDPR or any other relevant regulatory authority):

- **Data acquisition:** why not consider asking them to use a 'third-party opt-in' when implementing co-branded promotions using your logos or trademarks through their channel? Or, perhaps you can be a common data controller, giving both of you the right to use the data they collect.
- **Data enhancements:** there's a very good chance your sponsors' technology stacks will be more advanced than yours, and the insight they carry on each of their customers will probably be deeper. In the same way you might use a third party such as Experian or Acxiom, perhaps your sponsors could help you in this area, enriching the customer profiles you have in common with the information they have in their database.
- **Knowledge sharing and training:** from assistance with ad-hoc, data-related tactics, to sessions on advanced use of digital retargeting, supporting with technology consulting, to advising on an IT procurement process, your sponsors could provide a stop-gap resource until you've managed to increase your own headcount.

Case study: UEFA sponsorship

The following case study demonstrates how all the considerations discussed in this chapter combined to help UEFA secure a major sponsorship deal with global pure play Booking.com and how the tactics discussed can be used by a sponsor to target the fans of the property with which the sponsor associated, replicating the framework I refer to as 'Changing the Sponsorship Dialogue'.

In October 2017, Booking.com agreed to a four-year global partnership to become the Official Accommodation and Attractions Booking Partner for all UEFA national team football competitions from 2018 to 2022 (UEFA, 2017).

Booking.com is one of the largest travel e-commerce companies in the world with over 15,000 employees in 198 offices in 70 countries worldwide. A pure play online retailer, its mission is to: 'Connect travellers with the world's largest selection of incredible places to stay, including everything from apartments, vacation homes, and family-run B&Bs to 5-star luxury resorts, tree houses and even igloos' (Booking.com, n.d.). Its websites and mobile apps are available in over 43 languages, offer 1.4 million properties, and cover 120,000 destinations in 228 countries.

One of the aims of the sponsorship for both parties is to help UEFA improve fan experiences with tailored travel deals and recommendations. With ten competitions and more than 500 matches over the next four years, there are plenty of opportunities for advertising, promotion, and digital engagement, but the focus will be on using data to ensure the experience is relevant for each football fan. Both parties will also collaborate to organise various campaigns and events to make the most out of their partnership over the next four years, with UEFA's database playing a central role in the planning.

In an interview that I conducted on 5 December 2017 with Peter Willems, then Head of Marketing Activities and Sponsorship at UEFA, he shared some interesting insights into the way that the discussion over this sponsorship differed to others. 'It was the first negotiation we've had where there was more talk about data and digital than anything else', he said.

Traditionally, negotiations for sponsorships have evolved around the more common rights that UEFA could provide, such as advertising, tickets, corporate hospitality packages, and exclusive access. When partnering with Booking. com, it was the way that fans were digitally engaging with UEFA that played a significant role in brokering the deal.

> We're in a very fortunate position. We could see the direction the sports industry was heading in the way it dealt with sponsorships, so three years ago we started to build our own data capabilities. As we progress through the group stages of our club competitions, as European qualifying matches take place for our national teams, we continue to generate more traffic to our various platforms, adding more fans to our database in the process. And it's not just about the number of fans, but also the quantity and quality of information we have that allows us to improve their experience with us.

The collection of fan data is an ongoing job, but at that point UEFA could pinpoint the gender of 70% of its fanbase, the age of 73%, the country of residence of 82%, and the preferred language of 50%. Willems said that with such a strong foundation UEFA would move on to focussing its work on other areas such as pinpointing favourite clubs, national teams, and the nationalities of fans. Of course, there are hurdles to overcome in any task of this scope, but he planned to use those to his advantage.

> It's quite possible that a person of a particular nationality could support a different country while living in still another country. This provides us with three different references that can all be used to ensure we provide them with the content they want when they are most likely to want it.

UEFA almost certainly has the most extensive database of known fans in sports that has provided direct contact details. Consequently, it truly knows who its fans are and can pinpoint their interests at a 'per record' level.

This is invaluable information for a sponsorship deal and will be fully utilised by Booking.com to provide an experience individually tailored to UEFA's fans.

Two-way collaboration with sponsors

UEFA has a global fan network, and tailoring its service to make sure that all fans feel involved and engaged is no easy task. As an example, stadiums can only accommodate a small percentage of the overall fan base, so UEFA has to use digital channels tactically to ensure that even if a fan can't be present, they still feel like they're part of the events that interest them. However, this service spans so much more than just match days and specific events. Whenever and wherever there are fans, all day, every day, the team at UEFA has to ensure that fans can get their football fix and actively engage in their favourite sport.

To support this approach, UEFA has been exploring ways in which collaborating with sponsors and partners can help in its data acquisition and enhancement strategy. An early example of this came in June 2016 when Coca-Cola ran a co-branded promotion of its EURO 2016 Panini sticker collection. Using their own digital and offline channels, Coca-Cola and Panini targeted fans of the European Championship, and in doing so were able to secure a significant number of opt-ins from football fans for UEFA's database.

Conversely, Booking.com has a very deep, very rich database, but a lot of its customers simply don't have the same relevance to UEFA as the fans collecting Panini stickers or the fans it organically acquires through its own channels. While there will be a crossover between the two companies, not every traveller is a football fan and not every football fan is a traveller. However, when a customer goes through a transaction on Booking.com, the action of the purchase will produce rich, up-to-date, and relevant data that would be of use to UEFA, particularly when matched to its own database. Consequently, over the term of the sponsorship, both parties will benefit.

The more information that UEFA has on its followers, the better service and fan experience it can offer, tailoring news the fans want about the teams they support, their favourite players, and their history in UEFA tournaments. And when it comes to the fans that have bought tickets to attend UEFA matches, this collaboration with Booking.com will provide relevant travel information, further supporting the personalised approach.

Steps taken by UEFA

In the lead-up to the Booking.com discussions, UEFA focussed on learning more about its fans and implementing a centralised database, ensuring the continuing health and consistency of its data. Having started the build of an SCV, where each fan exists as an individual, UEFA layered this with an interactive dashboard to provide a 360-degree view and present the data in a way that enabled immediate access to information. Most important, the data visualisation is presented in a way that's relevant for UEFA's team of marketers, providing the key insights that answer their internal questions and provide information to sponsors as demonstrated during the Booking.com negotiations.

> We could tell you how many viewers in Brazil watched the EURO 2016 Final on their televisions, how many social followers we have in Indonesia, and the age groups of our website visitors. But for Booking.com, and all our negotiations moving forward, we need to know more than that. We need to know our fans by their names, where each and every one of them lives; we have to understand their interests at an individual level, and we have to know how they like to engage with us. We're in an environment now where we're marketing to a segment of one. It's how Booking.com runs its business, so to be a valuable partner, we had to do the same.

The partnership in action

Booking.com's ad management platform and algorithms ensure accuracy in its approach to remarketing and retargeting, which, when combined with UEFA's active database, will be a powerful partnership. One of the challenges of being a great digital marketer is ensuring that the parameters or conditions that you set on your ad delivery platform work hard for you. When brands don't use experienced marketers, the results are often the opposite of those desired. Instead of effective, targeted advertising, it's easy to fall into the trap of irrelevant messages or spamming the user with too many ads. Willems is already well aware of this problem.

> As any good digital marketer knows, we have to ensure a balance of providing the adverts that will genuinely benefit the fans and won't become intrusive or annoying. That's one of the many benefits of our digital world; we can track the number of times our fans see these adverts to ensure they're kept to a minimum, we can ensure they only see the ones that are relevant to them, and once they're no longer relevant we can turn them off.

By partnering with Booking.com, UEFA can use its vast experience to ensure that its fans see only relevant messages.

For the first time in history, the 2020 UEFA European Championships [now to be played in 2021 as a result of the coronavirus] will be played across 13 different countries. Let's assume that Romania qualifies. What if one of their games is played at the Millennium Stadium in Cardiff? There will no doubt be thousands of Romania fans, including their diaspora, needing accommodation in Wales. We will ensure Booking.com's information about its accommodation deals in Cardiff at the time of the Romania match gets to those fans seamlessly – making it easy for them to complete their travel plans.

UEFA will share Booking.com's message in a way that's the most relevant to the fans, through their chosen digital channels. For example, when fans have applied for tickets through UEFA.com, the email notification to confirm success could include Booking.com's recommendations for accommodation. These messages can be tailored right down to the distance from the stadium that is hosting the match they're attending. This same approach can be taken through social channels, UEFA's website, and even its web remarketing programme. UEFA will be able to identify the customer segments that suit the message that Booking.com wants to share and use its personal information on fans such as location, supporting team, and match preferences to make sure the fans get the right messages.

Fans first

But what is the cost of this tailored experience to the fan? With the growth of targeted digital marketing, consumers are now savvier about the security of their data and the way in which it's used. This negativity has the potential to cancel out any gains from a sponsorship deal like this.

To ensure the integrity of the relationship UEFA has with its fans, Willems stated categorically that Booking.com will not have direct access to UEFA's database or its fans' information.

Our fans trust us with their data, and we're not going to do anything with it that could compromise our relationship with them. We won't sell their data, and we won't give their personal information to our sponsors. Everything we do is with our fans' express permission – not only do we comply with all the relevant regulations on the way we collect, store, and use our fans' data, but we use it to ensure the best possible experience for our fans. We put our fans first.

Instead, UEFA will maintain full control of its data. Booking.com will provide the message, and UEFA will ensure that the message gets to the right people at the right time.

So, what does Booking.com gain from this? The answer is simple. UEFA will provide the message, but Booking.com will provide a point of sale. Once fans move from UEFA's digital channels, they will become Booking.com customers. This allows Booking.com to manage all transactions as it would with any other customer – but having committed to ensure that UEFA's fans get the best service possible. Clearly defined terms in the sponsorship agreement outline the way Booking.com will engage and manage its relationship with any customers coming via any of UEFA's digital channels, such as website, email, mobile app, and social accounts. UEFA doesn't just want to sell products and services to the fans; it wants them to be provided with a valuable service. That makes these contractual terms a crucial part of the Booking.com agreement and any other sponsorship deals UEFA might secure in future.

Looking forward

Data-driven sponsorship for sole customer targeting is a long-term goal. Pure play online retailers such as Booking.com have a long history of collecting customer data and basing its business structure on these principles, but this is an area that's still quite new to the sports industry. Through this partnership, UEFA can expect to learn quite a bit about Booking.com's approach and methods, but conversely, sponsorship is a very new area for Booking.com, and it can also expect to learn from the experience.

> We'll be looking to replicate the same type of opportunities for all our sponsors, based on their particular needs and, more importantly, what they can do for our fans. We'll be able to target their messages so they're relevant to the receiver and, in turn, provide greater return for the sponsorship dollars, ensuring their continued investment in football. However, we believe our approach to data is a two-way street. The more we have, the greater value our sponsors receive, so a logical next step will be to work together to ensure we're getting more data, more insight, and more knowledge with all our partners.
>
> (Source: Willems, 2017)

Key chapter ideas

1   Using data in your sponsorship strategy can help you cut through the clutter of the many proposals your prospects receive by demonstrating you can deliver their target audience.

2   Once engaged, you can then use your approach to targeted communications to increase your sponsor's ROI.
3   Sponsors can support your data and CRM strategy – for this, include some data-related obligations in your contract negotiations.
4   As it is vital to maintain the trust of your fans, data-driven deals must be designed sensitively to not jeopardise this trust.
5   Performance data is valuable content for your fans and can be commercialised with your sponsors through innovative applications.

References

Booking.com. (n.d.). *Booking.com: The largest selection of hotels, homes, and holiday rentals* [online]. Available at: www.booking.com/content/about.en-gb.html [Accessed 27 Nov. 2017].

Bradford, J. (2020). *Covid-19's impact on sport*. European Sponsorship Association [online]. Available at: https://sponsorship.org/covid-19s-impact-on-sport/.

Brown, M. (2017a). Inside the golden state warriors' $60 million Jersey patch deal with Rakuten. *Forbes* [online]. Available at: www.forbes.com/sites/maurybrown/2017/11/27/inside-the-golden-state-warriors-record-60-million-jersey-patch-deal-with-rakuten/#72a34d307b59.

Brown, M. (2017b). Multi-year deal reached with Coca-Cola to be 'official soft drink of MLB'. *Forbes* [online]. Available at: www.forbes.com/sites/maurybrown/2017/04/03/multi-year-deal-reached-with-coca-cola-to-be-official-soft-drink-of-mlb/#4017fa075ae2.

Coca-Cola. (2017). *Coca-Cola® releases commemorative championship can to celebrate the houston astros world series victory* [online]. Available at: http://stylemagazine.com/news/2017/nov/03/coca-cola-releases-commemorative-championship-can-.

Connelly, T. (2016). O2's chief marketing officer on its digital plans for English Rugby sponsorship extension. *The Drum* [online]. Available at: www.thedrum.com/news/2016/10/29/o2s-chief-marketing-officer-its-digital-plans-english-rugby-sponsorship-extension.

Davis, B. (2015). How the RFU manages CRM & personalised messaging. *Econsultancy* [online]. Available at: www.econsultancy.com/blog/67180-how-the-rfu-manages-crm-personalised-messaging.

Ellison, H. (2017). O2 unveils new virtual reality experiences. *Campaignlive.co.uk* [online]. Available at: www.campaignlive.co.uk/o2-unveils-new-virtual-reality-experiences/%7Bsubjects%7D/article/1427514.

ESP Properties. (2017). *What sponsors want and where dollars will go in 2017* [ebook]. Available at: www.sponsorship.com/IEG/files/7f/7fd3bb31-2c81-4fe9-8f5d-1c9d7cab1232.pdf.

Gibson, O. (2005). How the Thomas Cook /Manchester city shirt deal came about. *The Guardian* [online]. Available at: www.theguardian.com/football/2005/sep/22/newsstory.sport.

Hill, T. (2016). *SportsPro the brand conference*. Available at: https://www.sportspromedia.com/analysis/the_brand_conference_2016_five_reasons_to_attend.

IBM. (2013). *Rugby football union uses predictive analytics to drive fan engagement*. Portsmouth: IBM [ebook]. Available at: https://www-935.ibm.com/services/uk/bcs/pdf/RFU_YTC03611GBEN.PDF.

InfoScout. (2017). *Heineken consumer insights and demographics* [online]. Available at: https://infoscout.co/brand/heineken.

Joseph, S. (2012). Emirates: CRM data key to £150m Arsenal deal. *Marketing Week* [online]. Available at: www.marketingweek.com/2012/11/23/emirates-crm-data-key-to-150m-arsenal-deal.

NBA. (2017). *Warriors and Rakuten form Jersey partnership* [online]. Available at: www.nba.com/warriors/news/rakuten-partnership-announcement-20170912.

Peterson, B. (2012). Beyond the logo: How to win at olympic sponsorship. *Forbes* [online]. Available at: www.forbes.com/sites/onmarketing/2012/08/21/beyond-the-logo-how-to-win-.

UEFA. (2017). *UEFA announces global deal with Booking.com* [online]. Available at: www.uefa.com/uefaeuro-2020/news/newsid=2511295.html.

Willems, P. (2017). Chief Executive, personal interview, 5 Dec.

Chapter 8

Business change, change management, and culture

Pre-coronavirus, when we worked from a central office, we would have a basket of fruit delivered every week from which the team could help themselves. I remember some hours after one delivery a former colleague bemoaned the absence of bananas. When the basket was first delivered there had been plenty, but by the time he got to it, they were all gone. I remember the resulting exchange his comments generated between the team members, so I made a mental note that this colleague didn't like the other fruit. He only liked bananas. My intention was to ask HR to change the fruit choices to make sure everyone was catered for.

So why am I starting a chapter on business change with this seemingly unrelated incident? Because in an article in the *Harvard Business Review* (HBR) titled 'To Get People to Change, Make Change Easy', the authors start with a story about fruit choices. And guess what? Everyone wants the bananas! According to HBR, they're easy to peel and therefore easier to choose (Luna and Cohen, 2017).

This mirrors a research article published on eLife in February 2017 that suggests, in essence, that we're lazy, or at least that the path of least resistance really is the one most trodden. More accurately, it says, 'the effort required to act on a decision can influence the decision itself' (Hagura, Haggard, and Diedrichsen, 2017).

In the second chapter of this book, we highlighted process and culture as two key elements to implementing CRM as a business approach, and this is where business change and change management come in. Business change is the process by which our employees (and other relevant stakeholders) adopt new ways of doing things, perhaps also adjusting their attitudes and behaviours and developing new skills as the business changes.

Change management is about the way we support individuals affected by business change. The reason it's such an important part of implementing a CRM framework is because moving from an experience-driven business to one that is data-driven – one that uses evidence-based decision-making – involves a significant shift: a shift of attitudes, behaviour, and skills. In line with the HBR article, and as many change practitioners will attest, we have to make it easy for our stakeholders to change with our businesses.

And finally, while culture is a huge subject in its own right and could justify a dedicated book, or indeed several books, in the context of this discussion we mean 'the way we do things'. Aligning that with business change and change management, culture is the environment we've created to adapt to that change.

I had my own lesson in that at Winners in early 2020 when I introduced the use of Microsoft Teams, the collaboration platform that incorporates chat, file sharing, project planning, and video conferencing facilities, to name just a few. We'd been using multiple different platforms ever since the business started and across the years had continued to add to them. I made the decision to switch us to Teams over Christmas 2019 and spent some of the holidays teaching myself how to use it and setting it up based on the way we operate. When the office re-opened in early January I was raring to go. I demoed the platform to my colleagues, waxing lyrical about all the different functions, showing them how easy it was to have everything in one place, and then going through the way we would use each of the different sections based on our internal and external projects and tasks. We talked through each of the functions, their benefits to us, and the relevant use cases, and before long we were all using the platform with ease. I had introduced a change to the way we would work in our business, demonstrated the process to support that change, and most importantly, created the environment in which to make that change; we had cultural acceptance.

The importance of change

I remember working with a client in early 2016 who said something that resonates with me to this day. My role was to assist with the production of a request for information (RFI) for a rights owner looking to develop its digital real estate in order to support a drive to become a more data-driven organisation. The new environment would be powered by a centralised database, enabling the creation and delivery of personalised experiences across multiple channels, from websites and social channels to mobile apps, SMS, and email campaigns (the marketing automation environment we discussed in Chapter 7). The client was starting on a journey which many of you have already commenced, and many more are yet to embark on.

A few weeks into the project, a senior member of the client's team sat back and said, 'What if we don't actually have to do all this — what if all this talk about the need to provide a personalised experience and working with data is made up?' At first we laughed at that, but we also acknowledged that there could be something to it. In reality, we don't know what would happen to our individual businesses if we didn't 'get the right message to the right person at the right time'. We can all see the downward trajectories of our attendance figures and participation rates, but would the trend line really hit the x-axis if nothing changed?

That's the challenge our senior management have when we go to them asking for investment in CRM. Whether we're asking for budget, people, or time, ultimately it adds up to an expense that has to be accounted for and an investment that has to generate a return. But, as we've already discussed in Chapter 2, CRM is a journey not a destination, and when it comes to business change, you're in it for the long term. It's a marathon, not a sprint. So, if you can't show your management an immediate return, it's reasonable to expect a tougher sell-in than if you're justifying the purchase of a new format ad display, more replica kits for your online store, or the addition of a friendly event to your fixture schedule.

So, how do we know that it is necessary? How do we convince our management of a need for change? I guess the answer to that is that if we didn't have to change, we probably wouldn't. But our fans and stakeholders are changing, and they're demanding that we change with them. Their expectations are being shaped by the digital leaders in other industries such as Amazon, Netflix, and Spotify. These are the brands we aspire to emulate (but within our own frame of reference), the ones that are repeatedly held up as champions who understand the customer journey in this omnichannel/cross channel/channel-neutral environment. Customers of these brands are used to the immediacy, entertainment, and engagement that Facebook, Twitter, and Instagram provide. These customers like being in control of what they watch, listen to, and read. They also like being in control of when they do it, and when it comes to spending their time, their attention or their money, they have an abundance of choice.

In order to address this, to give our fans what they want when they want it, not what we want them to have in our timeframe, we have to change the way we work. We have to be agile. Being agile means being flexible and having the ability to rapidly adapt and respond. And this needs to be organisation-wide.

How many rights owners do you know who sound just like that? I'd guess not many. The transformation from a traditional hierarchy, formal meetings, and committees; along with the politics of voting in and voting out; and the pressure of needing to win each match, each week, or each season are just a few reasons why change in the sports industry can be so challenging.

Change in the sports industry

In the same way the use of data has been prevalent in sports performance for some time (see our reference to *Moneyball* in Chapter 3), so too has the consideration of business change and change management. In 2012, The University of Central Lancashire published *Change Management: The case of the elite sports performance team*, which concluded that, with the intense pressure faced by incoming managers and coaches to create a high-performing culture at lightning speed, the role of change management is 'both an applicable and highly pertinent construct for the optimisation of elite sport team performance' (Cruickshank and Collins, 2012).

Earlier still, in 2005, Nova Southeastern University published *The Examination of Change Management Using Qualitative Methods: A Case Industry Approach*, where 29 sports managers from Australian national and state sporting organisations and clubs were interviewed to provide the industry case. The key findings in this paper suggested the following:

> Subject to the strategic whims of their leaders as well as the pressures forced upon them by their institutional environment . . . Australian sport managers were inclined to be flexible in both their view of the origins of change, and its effective management.
>
> (Evans, Smith, and Westerbeek, 2005)

The paper went on to further define the different types of change prevalent within Australian sports organisations. Do you recognise any of them in your own environment?

1 **Fast change** – The report cited that this typically occurs when sports organisations are under-performing to a significant extent. The changes made are in direct response to the perceived crises. This sounds to me like the classic change of team management when you're six games and no points into the English football season. To demonstrate that point, across the 2019/2020 English football season, 51 of the 92 professional club managers were sacked.

2 **Slow change** – The report defined this as the type of change that continues indefinitely on an almost daily basis in the form of minor amendments to policies and practices. An example that we've referred to several times could be the changes you implement every time you look at your engagement metrics after you've sent an email campaign.

3 **Accidental change** – The report classified this form of change as something that didn't fit into either the fast or slow category where the change occurred without design or strategic intent, without specific thought to the outcome of the improvement or any other implications. A specific example provided involved a change in the way club merchandise was distributed (Ibid.). Although the policy was to sell club merchandise from the club only, as a result of an accidental change where a mail order was accepted and discharged promptly by an unknowing work placement student, sales of merchandise almost doubled as additional mail orders arrived.

In my years in sport, I've been witness to some significant change when it comes to revenue generation and event formation. Let's look at some examples.

1992: formation of the English Premier League

When Sebastian Coe, gold Olympic medal winner and a newly elected Conservative MP, said, 'I think it is wrong that only 2 million [satellite] dish owners get access to such major sporting events' (Nicholson, 2015), he set the tone for concerns about the changes to the traditional TV rights deals. With subscription TV operator BskyB securing a five-year contract for the best live matches, BBC being awarded highlights, and ITV leaving the table empty-handed, there was genuine concern for the future of English football.

One of Britain's leading newspapers, *The Guardian*, carried a piece that suggested fans would be the biggest losers. 'A lot of people who want to watch matches regularly in future are going to have to buy a bond or a dish' (Lacey, 1992).

Alex Ferguson, then Manchester United manager, also made his feelings known:

> A deal was stampeded without consultation with the most important people in the game, the managers and the players whose livelihoods are at stake. . . . It's the most ludicrous and backward decision football has taken. We managers must seriously question its wisdom.
>
> (Potter, 1992)

But now, the Premier League is the most-watched sports league in the world. The UK-only TV rights to cover three seasons from 2019 to 2022 were sold in February 2018 for £4.46 billion, international rights generated £4.2 billion, and Amazon also secured a package of 20 matches per season for a reported £90 million (BBC, 2018).

2000: creation of Major League Baseball Advanced Media

It's impossible to write about changes in the sports industry, particularly when we focus on digital technology and data, without referring to the behemoth that is MLB Advanced Media, or BAM for short.

Back in 2000, Bud Selig, the commissioner of MLB at the time, created BAM as a vehicle for building the MLB clubs' websites and managing their digital rights. The approach was intended to ensure parity among the teams, regardless of their size or status within the sport, and BAM was set up as a stand-alone company with an initial budget of $120 million: $1 million per year from each of the 30 clubs for the first four years of operation.

From humble beginnings that included the broadcast of a game to 30,000 fans, BAM led the way in over-the-top (OTT) broadcasting in sports (i.e. using the internet to bypass traditional broadcasters). The next big step came with the evolution of MLB.TV, which launched in 2003, with a digital viewing package for $79.95. Over 100,000 customers signed up in the first year, and now BAM streams to over 25 million digital viewers.

In my opinion, the real shift came when BAM stopped being just about baseball and started servicing other organisations including the NHL, Home Box Office (HBO), World Wrestling Entertainment (WWE) Network, the Professional Golfers Association (PGA), and the New York Yankees' YES Network. It was this combination of services to third parties, coupled with BAM's development of digital products for baseball, that led *Forbes* in July 2014 to name it 'The Biggest Media Company You've Never Heard Of' (Brown, 2014).

As a demonstration of how much MLB's business really did support change, 2015 saw BAM create a spin-off, BAMTech, which focusses on providing streaming video technology, particularly for OTT content services. Then, in September 2017, Disney topped up its original $1 billion investment with a further $1.58 billion to take its share from 33% to 75%.

BAM now focuses purely on baseball, having retained a 15% share of BAMTech, but according to Commissioner Robert D. Manfred, Jr:

> Major League Baseball will continue to work with Disney and ESPN to further grow BAMTech as it breaks new ground in technologies for con-sumers to access entertainment and sports programming.
>
> (Business Wire, 2017)

2003: launch of Twenty20 cricket

With the global success that is Twenty20 cricket, it's hard to believe that the launch of cricket's short form almost didn't go ahead. In a 2003 interview for cricket website www.espncricinfo.com, the chairman of the ECB, Lord MacLaurin, recalled the following:

> From the feeling there, we weren't going to win the votes. I had a list of chairmen and called them the night before. I said, 'All I ask is that you give it a chance. After three years we'll have a review. If it's not successful we'll pull the plug'.
>
> (Williamson, 2012)

The vote eventually went in favour of this change by just eleven clubs to seven.

The cricinfo article also covered the views of other press members, most of whom echoed the sentiment of *The Times* journalist, Simon Barnes, who commented:

> It's the trappings I can't stand. The garnish. The gimmicks. The wrapping, the ribbons, the packaging. The noise. Music should be banned from all

sporting occasions, live and televised. Never mind keeping politics out of sport; if we can keep music out, I'll be happy.

(Williamson, 2012)

While some believe the divide between Twenty20 and Test cricket (the longest form of the sport) is getting too wide, there's no denying its success. In July 2017, *The Guardian* claimed, 'T20 is evolving so fast it is radically redefining cricket' (Wigmore, 2017).

2007: NFL games in the UK

Over ten years ago, the National Football League (NFL) played its first regular-season game in London. The city now hosts four games per year with attendances of over 80,000, and it boasts a fan base of 40,000 individuals who regularly buy tickets. That's more than many EFL teams. But, this level of success has not been a fast change. It's the result of a slow and steady presence of NFL teams, staff, and management and a dedicated NFL UK office in London.

According to a 2014 article in *Sports Illustrated*, the NFL in London is already an unmitigated success:

The NFL has jumped from the 16th to the 8th most watched sport during England's football season on Sky Sports, Britain's subscription sports channel. Last season 13.8 million UK viewers watched NFL programming, an increase of 60 percent over the previous year, and the NFL also says more than 12 million people in the UK identify themselves as NFL fans. Amateur football participation has grown an average of 15 percent each year since '07, and there are now 77 university teams playing American football.

(Vrentas, 2014)

However, not everyone is singing the NFL's praises, with *The Guardian* proposing that the selection of teams sent to play represents the NFL 'dumping mediocrity on UK fans', citing that the thirst of their international fan base allows the NFL to treat people in this manner (Caldwell, 2016).

Where you go from here: change literature

We're in the middle of a global pandemic right now and, at the time of writing, many of us have no clue what the 'new normal' will look like. You can read more about the impact the coronavirus has had on the sports industry in Chapter 11, but regardless of what the ultimate outcome is – whether the way we play, watch, or follow sports has changed forever or has to pivot 180-degrees – business change will be a factor. So, what are your next steps?

In the aforementioned NSU paper, the following statement was of particular interest to me:

Respondents frequently lamented that while change had to be dealt with, they were uncertain about the best way of dealing with it. In the first instance, it was commonly admitted that a 'tried and tested' approach to change is noticeably absent from the operations manuals of most sporting organizations. This lack of information concerning the best methodology for initiating and sustaining long-term changes is indicative of a general confusion about the two fundamental elements in any change program: what to change and how to change. Thus, not only are sport managers unclear about where to direct their energies in order to initiate change, they are also hesitant when it comes to nominating their preferred tools and techniques for managing, directing, and controlling.

(Evans, Smith and Westerbeek, 2005)

The change industry has been around for many decades. The first documented reference to the study of change appears to be in Kurt Lewin's 1947 publication *Frontiers in Group Dynamics – Concept, Method and Reality in Social Science; Social Equilibria and Social Change*, where he refers to the following three-step process:

A successful change includes therefore three aspects: unfreezing (if necessary) the present level, moving to the new level, and freezing group life on the new level. The 'unfreezing' of the present level may involve quite different problems in different cases. The same holds for the problem of freezing the new level.

(Lewin, 1947)

Fast forward 56 years, and psychiatrist Elisabeth Kübler-Ross wrote the book *On Death And Dying*, which outlined the five stages that terminally ill patients experience: denial, anger, bargaining, depression, and acceptance (Kübler-Ross, 2003). This model, later named the Kübler-Ross Change Curve, became widely accepted as valid in many situations that relate to change, including those in a work environment.

When you think this one through, you can actually understand this relationship. Consider the thoughts a stadium gate steward might go through when he hears that his employer is purchasing an access control system:

1   **Denial** – *It'll never work; they won't get it up and running while I'm still here.*
2   **Anger** – *I've worked here for 17 years; every match day, rain or shine, I've stood on post and now they want to replace me with a piece of kit.*
3   **Bargaining** – *If I get here half an hour earlier and don't take a break, would you keep me on instead?*
4   **Depression** – *Why have I wasted 17 years of my life here when they clearly don't appreciate me?*
5   **Acceptance** – *OK, so it is a pretty impressive system. Maybe they can train me to use it?*

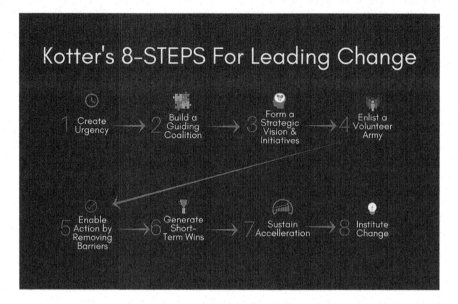

Figure 8.1 Adapted from *The 8-Step Process for Accelerating Change* eBook (source: reproduced by Winners FDD Ltd with permission)

This might seem trite, but when you consider the role of all your stakeholders in making your businesses a success, including the gate steward who's the first to greet your fans as they turn up on a match day, you can understand how and why change management is so important.

I personally subscribe to the view shared in John Kotter's 1996 publication, *Leading Change*, which features his seminal 8-Step Process – since updated and expanded in 2014 (Kotter, 2014). I've had permission from Kotter to reproduce his literature here, but I have expanded on his words and added some sports industry context. My hope is that you can align his eight steps to your current state, whether you're just tiptoeing around the edge of CRM and data, are at an intermediate level, or have progressed to a more mature stage. Please see Figure 8.1 for reference.

John Kotter's 8-Step Process for leading change

Step 1: create a sense of urgency

Kotter suggests that if you can identify and describe an opportunity that will appeal to individuals' heads and hearts, you will have 'a breadth of focussed readiness across the workplace that is unprecedented in your organisation'. Let's consider the occurrences that might prompt a sense of urgency:

- For clubs, a new stadium or stadium refurbishment (particularly if the outcomes include increased capacity, more/new corporate hospitality facilities, additional functional areas, etc.) would produce that critical focus against a specific timeline.
- For NGBs, qualification for a world championship event would provide the perfect focus, as it would have a finite start point.

But there doesn't have to be a specific event or occurrence on the horizon. Senior management can create a sense of urgency tied to financial goals, a multi-year strategic plan, or a set of KPIs.

Step 2: build a guiding coalition

According to Kotter, a guiding coalition would ensure that 'the linchpin of your entire transformation is in place: an accountable, diverse group bound by opportunity, strategy and action'. What's key in the creation of a coalition, or a committee, is that the members are skilled and respected by others in the organisation and have a level of influence. Of equal importance is the need for senior management to support the coalition, providing them with the tools they need to succeed, from resources to power, processes, and guidance.

The departments that are represented in your coalition should be cross-organisational and, most importantly, be relevant to Step 1. For example, a focus on increased revenue would dictate the need for commercial staff to be represented. Increased participation would involve your sports development team and, on the basis that data will be integral to your transformation, you would need support from your legal team and technology staff.

Step 3: form a strategic vision and initiatives

The benefits of a strategic vision and initiatives, according to Kotter, is that 'you have a single vision of the future with a credibility and authority that comes from being crafted by a diverse set of employees and validated by senior leaders'. This is something I talk about on many occasions with my colleagues and clients. Working without a vision is like driving a car without a destination. Without destination we just go through the motions; we implement a series of tactics without an end goal.

While senior management might be needed to create a high-level description of the strategic vision, the coalition can complete it using relevant data to inform the past and project the future. The key challenge here is to ensure that the vision is simple and that it can be described easily to other colleagues, possibly even sponsors, and maybe even fans.

Step 4: enlist a volunteer army

Enlisting a volunteer army will provide you with 'a sizable body of employees excited and able to take action on critically important initiatives linked to your business strategy' (Kotter, 2014). If you can find the colleagues in your team who are excited by what you're trying to achieve; if they buy into the vision and respect the coalition, you'll have a group of people who will change because they want to, not because they have to. They will build on the achievements of the coalition and champion the strategic vision, supporting and perhaps even driving the change initiatives.

Imagine how powerful that could be in your organisation! We already know how passionate people in the sports industry can be. If you can take that passion and combine it with their enthusiasm for your change process, you'll already be en route to great success.

Step 5: enable action by removing barriers

Enabling action and removing barriers can be a challenge because it involves empowering your team members. But as Kotter reminds us, when you do this, 'you have tangible evidence of employee innovations stemming from collapsed silos and new ways of working together'.

When I think of some of the natural barriers we have in the sports industry, my mind turns to the following:

- **Gender barriers:** so many of our activities are focussed on male participation as opposed to female. This is changing and at quite a pace, but perhaps there is something more that can be achieved in this area.
- **Economic barriers:** money makes the world go 'round, but can we do something differently, even as a pilot, to support one of the identified initiatives?
- **Knowledge barriers:** within any organisation there are knowledge gaps, so we need a training plan to counter this. We need to equip our volunteer army in the same way we equip the coalition.

Step 6: generate short-term wins

While every one of Kotter's steps is vital to successful change management, generating short-term wins is what resonates most. What we need is 'a body of wins data that tells the story of your transformation, that is validated in quantifiable and qualifiable terms'.

When we have those WOW! moments – tangible milestones that have been reached – we must communicate them before we can celebrate. Quick wins keep us motivated and excited; they help ensure momentum is maintained and support a positive attitude across the organisation.

Consider some of the quick wins applicable in the sports industry, like surpassing your target attendance for an unattractive fixture, increasing the value of your next sponsorship sales contract, or retaining your volunteers from one event to the next. How powerful would these achievements be for ensuring your transformation stays on track?

Step 7: sustain acceleration

At this stage of Kotter's process, 'you have confirmation of organisational threats and stamina that enable the reinvigoration of your mission and help you and your employees stay the course of change over time'. This means you've successfully worked through Steps 1 to 6 and are celebrating your quick wins. The task now is to maintain this momentum, to keep moving forward, implementing change after change until the strategic vision of Step 3 looks set to become a reality.

This is where I believe we may encounter a real problem. One of my observations from 30 years working in the sports industry is our natural inclination to focus on the short term. I've even tried to coin a word to represent this: *sport-termism*. It hasn't caught on yet, and I hope it never will, because it refers to our quest for the next win we're aiming for (the end-of-season trophy we hope to lift, even the next election we lobby for) when really, we need to be thinking about and planning for the next three to five years.

When we get to this point in Kotter's plan, when we've started to see the quick wins (increased attendance, more or higher-value sponsors, a squad of volunteers), we risk forgetting about Step 7 and derailing all our achievements so far. We need our senior management, the guiding coalition, and the army of volunteers that have driven the change up to this point to ensure we stay on track so we can implement the last step.

Step 8: institute change

You've made it! At this point in Kotter's process, 'you have collective recognition that your organisation has a new way of working with speed, agility and innovation that directly contributes to strategically important business results'.

To institute change and to ensure that it's sustainable and ongoing, you must have the right people, processes, and systems in place to support the change vision. This could involve a continual process of training and development, technology upgrades and, in line with Chapter 3 of this book, continuous data collection and analysis. We also need to communicate the changes we've implemented, the successes and behaviours, and the relevance to our business and vision in order to ensure we have continued, long-term buy-in.

With a clear strategic plan, change management becomes a much less daunting task. Failure is often a consequence of a lack of focus, but Kotter's 8- Step Process provides a fantastic roadmap to successfully instituting change, resulting in a positive outcome for your entire organisation (Kotter, 2014).

But, 70% of change projects fail – or do they?

If we Google it, we can easily discover plenty of repetitions of the common misconception that '60 percent of all CRM implementations fail' (Gould, 2015). If we do the same for business change or change management, we'll get an even less favourable result at 70%. So, let's start by dispelling that myth.

In 2011, Dr Mark Hughes, a reader in organisational change at Brighton Business School, published an article that unequivocally announced the following:

> Whilst the existence of a popular narrative of 70 per cent organizational-change failure is acknowledged, there is no valid and reliable empirical evidence to support such a narrative.
>
> (Hughes, 2011)

Hughes' work critically reviewed five separate published instances that proclaimed a 70% organisational-change failure rate and demonstrated that in each instance there was no 'valid and reliable empirical evidence in support of the espoused 70 per cent failure rate' (Ibid.).

With that myth dispelled, we can focus on one of Hughes' key points: the absence of empirical evidence. The challenge we have is that the data we generate, when setting out our approach to business change, tends to be qualitative as opposed to quantitative, generated from a cultural analysis workshop or subsequent root cause analysis. These human behaviour factors can't be quantified in an empirical manner. This is in itself another reason why it can be difficult to justify investment in change management and why the sell-in I referred to previously can be more challenging.

With the use of predictive analytics and access to the systems and processes we now have, we can start to transform our approach to change management. We've all heard variations of marketing pioneer John Wanamaker's quote, 'Half the money I spend on advertising is wasted; the trouble is I don't know which half'. Thankfully, being able to track our ROI means we have less money wasted. By applying data-driven approaches to it, we can see what works and what doesn't. This same thinking can, and should, be applied to our change management practices.

Until then, we must rely on our management's absolute faith in us or the consistent delivery of Step 6 of John Kotter's process: those invaluable quick wins.

Case study: Mic Conetta

Mic Conetta, Arsenal FC's Head of Digital Experience, is a former Accenture consultant with a great deal of experience with customer databases and their associated technologies: data warehousing, data management, campaign management, reporting, and analytics. Throughout his career, Conetta has encountered change projects on various scales, so he's acutely aware of the challenges but also the opportunities and benefits that come with getting it right.

Mic provided me with this case study in the book's first edition, and then updated it with me through a telephone interview on 24 July 2020. As a starting point, I asked Conetta to share his very interesting take on where we are when it comes to the use of data in the sports industry:

> CRM is nothing new in sports; there's always been an interaction with a customer or a fan. It's just the automation and the technology to better deliver experiences, customer interactions, and services that's new. Ultimately, everyone's always been doing CRM in sports; it's just we're now doing it in a way that helps us leverage a better benefit from that relationship.

In another highly relevant observation, Conetta summarises the uniqueness of our industry:

> Sports properties, unlike many other businesses, are both content generators and product and service providers, which is very different to just being a high street retailer, for example, who is purely focussed on selling products. We're doing all three. We're trying to combine those experiences, and CRM helps blend that together.

In this case study, Conetta combines his extensive experience from outside the industry with his unique insights from within it to build on the some of the principles discussed in this chapter. But since we last talked to him, his business unit has undergone a restructure – he was previously Head of CRM, so is his new title representative of some of the key changes?

> When you look at the role of a website for a traditional retailer or something similar, it's for commerce but for a sports property; it's the way we put out content that sits outside our broadcast deals. So, traditionally in

sports, the objectives of the media operation could be out of sync with the traditional CRM organisation. What we've done is look at how we bring those two areas closer together, and that resulted in the need to create a digital experience function. With this approach we can now bring together the direct fan touch points, whether that's the core Arsenal.com platform, the Arsenal mobile app, or the marketing automation platform. This enables the team to deliver against a common set of objectives, regardless of how the solutions are being used. So, the media team can still use Arsenal.com to put out its content, but the actual delivery of the site is aligned to the expectations of the business. At the heart of it this is how we engage our fan base, give them unique individual journeys, and really personalise their content in the way that they want. And so that is a slightly nuanced approach to why we created the new function.

This approach is reflected in the Deloitte 2020 Football Money League report that states, 'It seems clear that any club that understands both its fans and their related data has a greater chance of moving up the Money League in the future'. The report further highlights that while global fans engage with content, match-going fans want to 'engage with their club in a way that provides them with easy, seamless access to everything the club can deliver' (Deloitte Sports Business Group, 2020). And with such different needs and expectations, clubs face a challenge that goes way beyond the traditional focus of team performance and in-stadium experience. We asked Conetta how the new responsibilities and global focus on digital experience have changed his role:

It's about ensuring that we take the principles of what we've done in delivering an excellent CRM programme within the club and extending that out to reflect the new technology advances that allow us to take the same approach, but across a broader digital footprint. Now that I have responsibility for Arsenal.com and our mobile app, I can look at them through the lens that emphasises improving fan engagement and customer journeys. So, not only do I have responsibility for guiding the journey, but I have responsibility for managing our membership schemes and influencing the way that we use technology on Arsenal.com and the app to orchestrate customer engagement.

We're also getting more into insight-driven content and informing strategy both on our own platforms and other platforms, looking at how we engage our fan base across their platform of choice. The focus is not necessarily on moving people to our own platforms, although that is still important; it's also around creating engaging content that sits in the platform they've chosen to use. My team is responsible for all of the insights that we deliver as a digital operation within the club, understanding what content is working and where it should be played out – then, in turn, informing what content we should be producing.

Earlier in the chapter we talked about the importance of ensuring our stakeholders change with our business, and when it comes to implementing CRM or driving towards digital transformation, it will often involve significant retraining and a wholesale change of mindset. In a typical sports club environment, the key stakeholders are anyone who has a customer or fan touch point. Ticketing, hospitality, meetings and events, merchandise, stadium tours, and membership schemes are just a few examples of the business areas that can become stakeholders of a CRM project. While some may drive a higher proportion of revenue than others, breaking down those silos and combining data will provide a single customer view that benefits everyone. Add to this other elements, such as web presence and media channels that combine known individual data with unknown data within CRM, and you have a cross-organisational database that supports multiple business units. But, Conetta tells us that knowing this and engineering its delivery can be two very different things:

Stakeholder management is absolutely critical to the implementation of a CRM platform. Depending on where the transformation is being driven, you effectively need to get stakeholder buy-in. If you're driving an implementation, you're doing that on behalf of a number of business areas, and if those business areas don't fully buy in to what you're doing, that is going to leave you open to failure and make it very, very difficult to do successfully.

Everyone knows managing silos in businesses can be challenging, but there are lots of stakeholders who are purely driving for their specific area when you're trying to run a cross-functional service line that meets natural challenges. Your CRM function is providing a service to all of your commercial silos that exist within an organisation. You've got to be prepared to work across that and engage with all of those stakeholders.

Changing the way in which you deal with people based on their abilities and level of understanding is paramount to ensuring the best level of collaboration from stakeholders.

> Like any part of the business, dealing with stakeholders is a relationship – a two-way street. The user community needs to be confident in what you're proposing and be willing to be open with you and your team. The only way you can consistently deliver success is if you truly understand the wants and needs of your stakeholders and they in turn understand the same from you.

To assist with stakeholder buy-in, Conetta ensures he has one-on-one time with department heads. This not only means that he and his team are providing the services that meet the needs of the stakeholders, but he also makes sure that his project team is conforming to some of the requirements set by those stakeholders. This ensures that successful implementation is continuous and open-ended.

Regular meetings allow the project team to see how they're performing with campaigns and whether targets are being met. It allows him to take something concrete to his stakeholders to show where they are making gains and where they might not be making as much progress as they'd like. Ultimately, they can draft creative ways in which they can drive value back into the business.

I asked Conetta how frequently he has these meetings and how much time was actually needed to break down these silos and get the buy-in he needs.

> My approach is to engage with the main stakeholders once a month in a one-on-one meeting, with my team then running operational meetings on a bi-weekly basis. Generally, they have tended to be popular, or not, dependent on the time of year. As you would expect, people are excited about attending when they've got something in mind that they want to discuss.
>
> The format we adopted ensured that once a month there would be a set agenda, then the other will be more like a drop-in session – 'how can I do this, what's best practice' – that way we would know that people will come and bring their challenges.
>
> This approach also ensures my team doesn't do all the talking in these meetings – the objective is to try and instil some confidence in our user community to be open with us. The only way we can continue to deliver success is if we truly understand where they're coming from, but also for them to understand where we're coming from. Like anything, it's a two-way street. It's a relationship.
>
> Admittedly since taking on additional responsibility I've found it really challenging to recreate these meetings – and not because of the subject

matter, but because of the coronavirus. During lockdown we were all working from home, so trying to deliver a new project that involves workshops is much more difficult across Zoom or Teams, particularly when we need cross-organisational engagement in a subject matter that can be quite difficult to some, and quite new to many.

You can read more about Conetta's take on the impact of the coronavirus in Chapter 10.

We've already heard Conetta mention success a few times so it's clearly an important part of managing a change programme. I asked where he tends to see the biggest success, in the smallest amount of time.

Building personas that represent our fan base, bringing them to life, is one of the greatest areas for growth. You can easily lose people if you get too into the details of data, clustered models, big data, and data science. It's actually the ability to bring data to life and have a consistent way of talking about it, be that for Christmas retail campaigns, season ticket renewals, or ticket sales on a per game basis. If you can start bringing that to life a bit, and help departments understand a bit more about the makeup of our transacting fan base or our international fan base, it helps to deliver a stronger creative play into the message that we're trying to get across. It helps them think about the products and services we bring to market to meet those fans' wants and needs when they have different personas to work with.

I introduced personas in Chapter 2 with a great case study from Charlie Shin of MLS, but if you're not familiar with them, and to help put Conetta's prior statement into context, a simple definition is 'the cosmetic manufacturing of your ideal customers based on the information you have about them'.

An example of how Conetta might put this in action is with something as simple as changing an image in an email for a different persona. For example, a young family is likely to respond to an image of a child's replica kit in the online store more than a persona that doesn't have children. Using a simple example like that makes it much easier for stakeholders to understand how data and personalisation combine to 'get the right message to the right person'.

Knowing where to place your focus when initiating CRM can be a significant challenge, and there are many different approaches to this. Some businesses select MVPs – that's *minimum viable product*, not *most valuable player*, as some of our trans-Atlantic readers might think (although both could be used when you think about it). An MVP approach is a development technique that dictates that a new product is developed with just enough features to provide the feedback, learning, and data needed to support future development. But, this isn't an approach to which Conetta subscribes:

> There isn't a single MVP. What we tend to do is sit down and work out what the objectives are, and then try to put some measurable targets against that– whether it's looking at year-on-year improvement in the success of a campaign, driving more traffic to a site to support a campaign, reducing churn on a seasonal renewal, increased revenue, the number of people entering a competition, or brand awareness, to name just a few.

But, on these success measurements Conetta again has an interesting take – almost calling into question the efficacy of using data to enable the tracking of ROI unless you have the right technology.

> It's really hard to say in sports, 'You know what? This year we renewed 95% of our season ticket holder base because we invested in CRM'. We know that's unrealistic. You could have the best season, you could have the cup-winning season, you can finish second in the league and win no trophies, or you can finish fourth or fifth. It's really hard to understand, day to day, what the impact is of signing global superstars or how the team is playing versus what you're doing. All you know is that you're working in a way that was different from the way that you were working a few years ago; and with that, it naturally feels that the more sophistication you're putting into your campaigns, and your data-related activities, the more you're able to drive a greater benefit.
>
> But, this is where we see an opportunity for improving our business intelligence – if the business wants answers to these ROI questions, we need the right technology to be able to deliver those answers. At the moment we're in a situation where we're churning out reports on a weekly or monthly basis, but we ideally want to get to a place where people can self-service their everyday questions.

However, Conetta does subscribe to the principle of test and learn – an approach credited to financial services company Capital One, which in 1998 carried out 28,000 individual experiments across advertising and products (Fishman, 1999), and is now the standard approach for data-driven marketers.

With that approach naturally comes failure – some new things may not work – so, in that instance, Conetta will try other new things that may work. And, those that do are expanded and rolled out.

I asked Conetta his top tip for setting out corporate governance when undertaking a change such as the one he implemented, and will now be progressing, at a greater scale in his new role. Unsurprisingly, his number-one recommendation is not unique to the sports industry.

> Focus on high-level objectives. You've got to create a governance structure that understands, and buys into, those benefits and is also able to see and monitor how you're progressing against those over time. You want to a) to prove that it's working; but b) give your team perspective on how they are performing.

As CRM and the use of data in any business operates as a cross-functional service provision, it often doesn't bring in any direct revenue; so Conetta has a model for giving his team a sense of worth, providing the performance measurement he refers to earlier.

> We measure the benefits that we deliver to each of our departments, and then we also measure the soft benefits. An example of this is our ability to reduce churn. So, the business target might be to hit a certain churn target, but then we beat the target and reduce churn further. But, because we always knew we could cope with x amount of churn, and churn has never gone above that amount, there's no physical benefit. So, while beating that churn target was never in the business case, it's still a huge benefit – it's our soft benefit.

Building on this sentiment, Conetta comes back to the value of having regular meetings with the stakeholders and regularly asking the following questions:

1   We can see where we're behind. What can we do?
2   Is there something more creative we can do with the offers we're making?
3   Do we need more campaigns?
4   Are our current campaigns working?
5   Is our channel mix right?

This approach introduces the governance that Conetta subscribes to, focussing on objectives, measuring success, and meeting and sharing with his stakeholders.

We talked about making change easy (and why we choose bananas) at the start of this chapter, and when I asked Conetta to provide his recommendations on how to approach our natural resistance to – and fear of – change, he again focussed on communication.

> Education in the right language is essential to business change. Not everyone is going to be at the same level of understanding. It's easy to forget that CRM and the use of data can be quite a difficult subject for some people, especially if they've not come across it before, or haven't worked in marketing, or don't understand some of these principles. Explain it in layman's terms, short and sweet.

This reiterates Conetta's earlier point about personas. Creating a fictional ticket buyer or international fan, summarising their key characteristics, and then calling them Jeff or Jack already helps with the challenge of industry-specific language that's unfamiliar to our stakeholders, the very people we need to understand us and buy into the change.

I moved on to asking Conetta about training – a key aspect of implementing change to understand his approach:

> It's train-the-trainer for me – it's what we've always done, even with the implementation of Microsoft Dynamics [contact and sales automation software] and our organisational training. I always ask two questions: will the training develop the individual or is it improving the team performance? If it does both, brilliant; but as long as it does one of them I'll put the budget into it. I encourage a healthy balance, so it's about creating an environment in which our teams feel like they are developing, being mindful of their career paths and supporting them, but also balancing that out with the needs of the business.

Building on his very first point, that CRM is not new in sports, Conetta goes on to explain that talking about what people are doing in other organisations that your stakeholders may already be familiar with is another way of achieving that necessary level of understanding. This is a tactic we use at Winners. With Amazon, Netflix, and Spotify now so ubiquitous, we use them as the standard-bearer for services that make you want to engage or buy more. They make it easy for you.

In reality we're not expecting rights owners to perform at that level. These are pure play organisations (they only operate in the online world), so operating at the leading edge in digital experience is their only option.

> Hardly anyone out there hasn't had an online buying experience, buying with their mobile phone or being advertised to by Google and any sites that they visit. They're all being exposed to CRM on a daily basis they just might not realise it – it's about finding a context that they'll understand.

Conetta's other recommendations include knowledge sharing: ensuring that whatever your stakeholder's level of understanding, whether beginner or sophisticated, you support them to learn more. Of course, the best way of keeping everyone on point, focussed in the right direction, prioritising and taking action at the right time is sharing successes, both within your team, the wider group, and the business as a whole.

In Chapter 1 I told of the occasion when a senior Microsoft executive explained the business no longer used the term *CRM* and instead used *intelligent customer engagement*. I broached the same subject with Conetta – was his new title representative of him also making this three-letter acronym redundant?

> Yes, we got rid of it, and it was the hardest thing to do. So now I'm no longer Head of CRM, I'm Head of Digital Experience. People got blindsided with CRM, and then CRM became email marketing, and of course it's not, it's so much more. And, it doesn't help when people like Microsoft rebrand their whole platform to Dynamics and don't talk about CRM anymore, so now we are about digital engagement. It's about building relationships with the fans and also internal stakeholders. But, what we do is we enable better dialogue through our digital touchpoints. We manage the experience that our fans have digitally.

On this point I ask Conetta if he feels that using just *digital experience* is sufficient, for example, when it comes to those digital practitioners who are just in love with social, but don't think about known data. Should it be data-driven or data-informed digital experience? And I love his answer:

> I think in my mind now, people understand that behind every digital touchpoint there is data. Without the data, the digital – the front end – is meaningless.

And, as Conetta highlighted earlier in our talk with him, the reason he calls it 'digital experience' is because unlike CRM, which was just about his own platforms, it's now also about Facebook, Google, Twitch, and TikTok, to name but a few.

In one final fix from Conetta, we share what could be the shortest-ever definition of business change in the context of digital and data:

Essentially, it's the automation and technology to better deliver fan experiences, customer interactions, and the provision of services. The most important thing is to make sure that everyone understands it, to make sure it can be implemented in a way that helps leverage a better return from your relationships.

(Source: Conetta, 2020)

Key chapter ideas

1   Change has to be easy to ensure that it's successful; but change management has been around for many years, and there's a lot of documentation for further reading to guide you through it.
2   Moving from a traditional business to one driven by data and digital technology is a fundamental shift and requires an informed approached. This comes from understanding business change and is brought about by implementation of a change management programme.
3   There are established models that you can follow, but the main elements of a change management programme centre on the creation of groups, continuous communication, the documenting of success stories, and the sharing of these successes.
4   CRM is not new in sports. It's been around for years, and even if you didn't know it, you've been on the receiving end if you've ever bought anything online or on a mobile app. To facilitate implementation, work to find the context that your stakeholders will understand and use clear language.

References

BBC. (2018). Premier League TV rights: Five of seven live packages sold for £4.464bn. *BBC* [online]. Available at: https://www.bbc.co.uk/sport/football/43002985.

Brown, M. (2014). The biggest media company you've never heard of. *Forbes* [online]. Available at: www.forbes.com/sites/maurybrown/2014/07/07/the-biggest-media-company-youve-never-heard-of.

Business Wire. (2017). *The Walt Disney company to acquire majority ownership of BAMTech* [online]. Available at: www.businesswire.com/news/home/20170808006428/en/Walt-Disney-Company-Acquire-Majority-Ownership-BAMTech.

Caldwell, D. (2016). Why the NFL can get away with dumping mediocrity on UK fans. *The Guardian* [online]. Available at: www.theguardian.com/sport/2016/dec/15/nfl-london-games-international-series-wembley-twickenham.

Conetta, M. (2020). Head of Digital, interview by telephone, 24 July.

Cruickshank, A. and Collins, D. (2012). Change management: The case of the elite sport performance team. *Journal of Change Management*, 12(2), pp. 209–229.

Deloitte Sports Business Group. (2020). *Eye on the prize – football money league* [online]. Available at: https://www2.deloitte.com/uk/en/pages/sports-business-group/articles/deloitte-football-money-league.html.

Evans, D. M., Smith, A. C. and Westerbeek, H. M. (2005). The examination of change management using qualitative methods: A case industry approach. *The Qualitative Report*, 10(1), pp. 96–121 [online]. Available at: http://nsuworks.nova.edu/tqr/vol10/iss1/6.

Fishman, C. (1999). This is a marketing revolution. *Fast Company* [online]. Available at: www.fastcompany.com/36975/marketing-revolution.

Gould, L. (2015). Characteristics of a failing CRM project. *C5insight.com* [online]. Available at: www.c5insight.com/Resources/Blog/tabid/88/entryid/605/characteristics-of-a-failing-crm-project.aspx.

Hagura, N., Haggard, P. and Diedrichsen, J. (2017). Perceptual decisions are biased by the cost to act. *eLife* [online]. Available at: https://elifesciences.org/articles/18422.

Hughes, M. (2011). Do 70 per cent of all organizational change initiatives really fail? *Journal of Change Management*, 11(4), pp. 451–464.

Kotter, J. (1996). *Leading change*. Boston, MA: Harvard Business Review Press.

Kotter, J. (2014). *Accelerating change* [online]. Available at: http://go.kotterinc.com/get-the-8steps-ebook.html.

Kübler-Ross, E. (2003). *On death and dying*. New York: Scribner.

Lacey, D. (1992). Future sold for pie in the sky. *The Guardian*, 20 May, p. 16.

Lewin, K. (1947). Frontiers in group dynamics. *Human Relations*, 1(1), pp. 5–41.

Luna, T. and Cohen, J. (2017). To get people to change, make change easy. *Harvard Business Review* [online]. Available at: https://hbr.org/2017/12/to-get-people-to-change-make-change-easy.

Nicholson, M. (2015). *Sport and the media*. London: Routledge, p. 29.

Potter, D. (1992). Premier TV deal under attack. *The Independent*, 22 May, p. 32.

Vrentas, J. (2014). Why London? And can it work? *Sports Illustrated* [online]. Available at: www.si.com/2014/10/02/nfl-team-in-london-international-series.

Wigmore, T. (2017). T20 is constantly evolving and is no longer held back by traditionalists. *The Guardian* [online]. Available at: www.theguardian.com/sport/2017/jul/11/t20-twenty-20-tradition-the-spin-cricket.

Williamson, M. (2012). Crash, bang and Pandora's box is opened. *ESPN Cricinfo* [online]. Available at: www.espncricinfo.com/magazine/content/story/579245.

Chapter 9

Data and the law

This chapter is intended to give readers insight into how the various data protection regulations around the world impact the way sports rights owners can use data to drive decision-making and digital marketing. I focus primarily on personally identifiable information (PII) or PII data which has traditionally been defined as data that can identify an individual (name, address, contact data, etc.) but more recently has included IP addresses and any other online identifiers.

At the time of writing over three-quarters of the world either has specific regulations in place, regulations due to come into force, or regulations in discussion (see Figure 9.1). The United Nations Conference on Trade and Development states that while 132 out of the world's 194 countries have data legislation, there are 5% that not only don't have data legislation, but they don't even have data. These countries are primarily in Africa and South America, but – unsurprisingly – North Korea, or DPRK, is also identified as having no data (UNCTAD, 2020). I think they not only have data – and lots of it – but neither their residents nor the rest of the world are allowed to know about it!

So while data legislation is as prevalent across Europe as it is across North America and Oceania/Australasia, the focus of this chapter will be on the GDPR, which is the legislation governing the European Union (EU) plus Switzerland, Iceland, Lichtenstein, and Norway. The UK will also be maintaining GDPR as the data legislation once the Brexit transition rules are effective from January 2021. The reason I focus on the GDPR is two-fold:

1   It's the most comprehensive and cohesive set of data laws that are consistent across multiple countries.
2   It's considered the most stringent of legislation (although Australia, Brazil, Japan, South Korea, Thailand, and the USA have comparable data privacy laws).

On this point, the USA's approach is of particular interest to me. As with many of their laws, there is no data privacy law applicable to all industries at a country or federal level; every state in the union has its own data privacy laws.

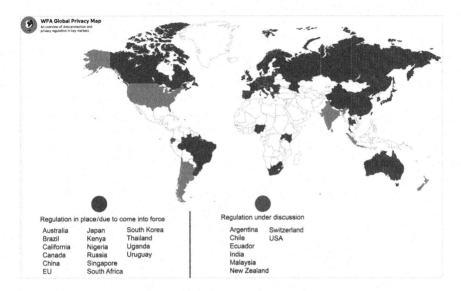

WFA Global Privacy Map
An overview of data protection and
privacy regulation in key markets

Regulation in place/due to come into force

Australia	Japan	South Korea
Brazil	Kenya	Thailand
California	Nigeria	Uganda
Canada	Russia	Uruguay
China	Singapore	
EU	South Africa	

Regulation under discussion

Argentina	Switzerland
Chile	USA
Ecuador	
India	
Malaysia	
New Zealand	

Figure 9.1 Map of the world showing where data legislation is in place or in discussion, or where there is no legislation (Winners FDD Ltd.)

The most stringent of these is California's Consumer Privacy Act (CCPA), which has many provisions that overlap with the GDPR, and many states are expected to eventually replicate their approach.

Focus on the GDPR

When I first submitted the manuscript for this book, it was February 2018 and the introduction of the EU GDPR was three months away. I mused how enforcement was expected to be a gradual process so regulators would be looking to see that organisations were making progress, showing intent, while also taking care of those issues that can be addressed relatively easily.

In addition to the acknowledgement that data compliance would be a slow evolution, I stated there are many areas of GDPR that can be considered 'grey', and solutions will only be discovered through case law. That led me to state that this pace of change would help ensure this book remained relevant in the same way that seminal works such as Mark McCormack's *What They Don't Teach You at Harvard Business School* (1989) or Paul Greenberg's *CRM At The Speed Of Light* (2001), now in its fourth edition, are perfect examples of books that, despite the passage of time, remain as relevant now as the day they were published.

So fast forward two years, and where are we now when it comes to our compliance with these seemingly draconian laws that we had to adopt in

May 2018? According to a 2019 report produced by the Interactive Advertisers Bureau, over 50% of digital marketing and media practitioners who use audience data believed that government regulation or the threat of regulation was the top obstacle threatening their data projects. Within the sports industry, Law in Sport's 2018 survey suggested that 43% of sports organisations did not feel their business was supportive in complying with GDPR (Cottrell, 2018). So, there's a good chance that some of you reading this will still have a little bit of work to do, but the purpose of this chapter is not to explain the GDPR but to highlight some questions that it continues to raise, even though we've been working with it for over two years. I start by looking at some of the key differences between the former EU Data Directive and the GDPR.

The threat of fines of up to €20 million

The change that ensured the subject got the attention of the most data-weary management teams was the scope for potential fines. Under the EU Data Directive, the maximum possible fine was £500,000; but under GDPR it's €20,000,000 or 4% of turnover, whichever is greater. At the time I asked whether fines of that magnitude would ever really be issued or whether it was simply an amount set to incentivise compliance. It definitely wasn't a ruse because in July 2019 British Airways was fined £183 million, Marriott International £99 million, and Google €50 million. This compares to the previously largest fine of €500,000 issued to Facebook for the Cambridge Analytica scandal, which, had the breach been caused under GDPR, could have been 4% of Facebook's turnover – a potential €4 billion (Privacy International, 2019)!

I moderated a panel in 2017 at a Sports and Entertainment Alliance in Technology (SEAT) conference that focussed on the GDPR. When talking about the fines, one rights owner asked if we could only be fined once a year. It was an interesting question, as there aren't many rights owners who could handle a €20 million fine the first time, let alone a second. Even if their insurance covered it, their premiums would become prohibitively expensive when it came to renewal. The question led to a discussion that, regardless of the value of the fine, the reputational damage for rights owners could often be more damaging than any financial loss. When something goes wrong in other industries, the story might be limited to the trade press. In the world of sports, however, we provide fodder for everyone from the world's elite publications to the gutter press. We're not restricted to the sports pages.

Later, on a panel with me discussing GDPR's implications at the March 2018 Fan Engagement Conference in Dublin, I remember a young marketer (who was perhaps in his first role in sports) dismissing me with a derisive 'I didn't graduate from my sports marketing degree at university to sit on a stage and discuss this boring stuff'. I'd say it's a shame that university courses are not introducing our future sports industry executives to this area, as already La Liga has been handed a €280,000 fine (McCaskill, 2019) and one of €525,000 to the Royal Dutch Tennis Association (Bodewits, 2020).

When a player transfers, how much data has to go with them?

Rights owners' use of data can go beyond their fans, ticket buyers, shop customers, and staff. If you're a club, national governing body, or even a league, you'll also have participation data to be concerned with that includes players and athletes, referees, coaches, medical personnel, and other paid or voluntary support staff.

The key question here is the impact of the right to data portability, one of the few articles in the GDPR that is not updating or refreshing an existing clause of the EU Data Directive. It means that the data subject (any individual whose personal data you hold) has a right to request a copy of all their personal data that is processed electronically to be passed from one data controller to another, in effect allowing them to take their data with them when they move from one environment to another.

Imagine this scenario in the context of a player transfer. Clubs must ensure that *all* personal data they have on a player can smoothly transition from one club's system to another. What's the limitation on the extent of that data? For elite athletes on a professional team, does that mean all their biometric data and the results of the coach or manager's training regime (which is usually proprietary), and for what period of time?

Consider this: Club A wants to buy a player from Club B and, knowing about the right to portability, asks the player to bring ALL their data with them. Club B refuses because they consider it their data, and Club A says, 'If you don't get me your data, I'm not going to buy you'. Club B would then be restricting the player's ability to get a job. This goes to the heart of the Bosman ruling, involving the former Belgian football player, Jean-Marc Bosman, who challenged UEFA, the Belgian Football Federation, and RFC de Liège in the European Court of Justice. He won his case with a decision that would see a ban on restrictions placed on foreign EU players, allowing them to move to another club at the end of a contract without a transfer fee being paid (Brand, 2015). Add another level to this: if the player wins the argument and gets their data over to Club A, they then have the opportunity to reverse-engineer the data points and get an insight into Club B's training methods!

A further question is the right to erasure, the right that all data subjects have for their information to be completely erased from your systems if they request it. What about a player or athlete's performance data that you post on your website as part of your content offering to fans – do you have to erase it entirely from your archived stories?

Would *Moneyball* be allowed if Billy Beane tried it now?

We talked about the role of data analytics in selecting a winning team in Chapter 3, but under the GDPR, data subjects have the right to object to any type of processing of their information. While that's clear-cut when it comes to the use of unsubscribes from communication and opt-outs from retargeting, another objection right is the use of profiling that results in an automated decision that has a legal or otherwise material impact. As an example of this, the financial services industry might use automated decision-making to determine that a customer doesn't qualify for a mortgage but, in the sports world, does that mean a player or athlete could object to their performance data being used to assess whether they're on the squad? If Billy Beane were to apply the same approach, could a player demand the team no longer process his information the first time a player is rejected? In reality, it might not be a major issue. If a player objects to this, then the chances are they won't be selected anyway; but it throws up an interesting point. Could the right to object to profiling, along with the right to data portability, and indeed the right to data erasure, have a far-reaching impact on professional athletes and their contracts?

What about rights owners outside the EU?

The focus of the GDPR is not just the organisations that operate in the 31 countries that collectively make up the EU and EEA (European Economic Area). The GDPR was written with the *residents* of the EU in mind, not the businesses. This means it's not just rights owners who operate in this territory who need to be concerned with these legislation changes; it's any rights owner who provides and offers services to residents of the EU and EEA, regardless of where their business is located.

In Chapter 2 you heard Charlie Shin, VP of Strategy and Analytics of MSL, state that MLS doesn't provide an offering for EU residents (it doesn't schedule matches in EU territories or provide a streaming service targeting Europeans). Even so, he will be keeping an eye on the GDPR, as he believes it will be the direction the rest of the world will take. Several years ago, I had a conversation with a US lawyer who suggested that if the US ever decided to take Europe's approach to data protection, it would put a lot of businesses out of operation. Essentially, this still leaves this question unanswered. In addition to the definition based on the provision of services (which is irrespective of payment), the GDPR article suggests that any non-EU business with a website using cookies that could be visited by an EU resident not only has to be GDPR-compliant but has to appoint a representative in the EU. Surely that's unsustainable?

What do we do about legacy data?

When you started collecting your opt-ins however many years ago, you were probably asking your fans and customers to opt in for one thing: to hear from you, either by email, SMS, phone and maybe even direct mail if you've been doing it for a while. This is the principle of consent – securing consent from your fans and customers to send them marketing messages. Then we started using cookies on websites, so your digital terms and conditions had to be amended to accommodate this, including a cookie opt-in policy. There aren't many of us who would have had the foresight to ask for an opt-in to retarget our fans with digital advertising. But as we discussed in Chapter 3, now we can use email addresses for remarketing using not just our own websites but networks of websites like Google Ad Networks, Facebook, Instagram, and LinkedIn.

So, what do we do about our 'legacy data': all the email addresses we've collected over the previous years? Can we use them to remarket through a different channel to the ones we've been using thus far? Can the condition of 'legitimate interest', a framework in the GDPR that can be applied instead of consent, be applied here?

For our purposes, what does 'legitimate interest' mean? The GDPR allows for the processing of data for legitimate reasons not specifically discussed within the legislation itself, so long as it doesn't infringe on the rights and freedoms of your fans or customers as far as their data is concerned. In the case of the sports industry, I would argue that if a rights owner has been using an email list to share news and stories of interest with a fan base, having secured the right to do so through an opt-in, then it would be legitimate for the organisation to continue that relationship through further digital channels. But that's not actually the case – fans have to opt into every channel individually.

The PECR soft opt-in – opting out instead of opting in

Most rights owners, indeed, most businesses, are focussing on GDPR consent as a way to engage with fans and stakeholders and forgetting that's not the only framework that can be used. In addition to the previously referenced 'legitimate interest', there's also the Privacy and Electronic Communications Regulations (PECR) soft opt-in (also referred to as the 'soft spam' or 'b2c opt-out' in parts of the EU), and it's a pretty powerful tool. The PECR have been around a long time but for some reason are not as recognised as the GDPR; yet the soft opt-in is a great opportunity to grow the size of your marketing database.

The soft opt-in states that if you acquire someone's email address in the process of a financial transaction (e.g. online store purchase, ticket sale, stadium tour booking, etc.) you don't have to ask them to opt in; you can instead ask them to opt out. You still need to use clear and concise language, as with

GDPR consent, but the aim is to encourage your fans not to tick – something that might be easier to do than asking them to tick.

However, there is a caveat. While you can continue to send marketing messages – so long as you've provided an opt-out at point of entry (and of course an unsubscribe option in subsequent emails) – they must be in relation to 'similar products and services' to those your customers have already purchased from you.

Now that's the bit of grey I referred to earlier: where laws and regulations are often black or white, what does *similar* mean? I've met lawyers who think that if you sell someone a ticket, you can only sell them more tickets. But that's not 'similar' to me – I see that as very much the same. And I've also met lawyers – ones I tend to side with – who propose if a fan buys a ticket to watch his favourite team, then a replica shirt of that favourite team, a chance to visit the home of that favourite team, or a chance to train under the brand of that favourite team could also be considered similar.

Key points for GDPR awareness

One of the key messages I want to give to anyone who has not yet addressed any element of GDPR compliance is don't panic, but do start moving. To avoid being one of the rights owners handed a data breach fine, or even a complaint, you will need to ensure that you implement a pragmatic approach to ensuring GDPR compliance.

Some of the questions we've discussed still need to be answered to have clarity under the GDPR. What follows will be a snapshot of some additional key articles that rights owners need to be aware of. Note that this list is not exhaustive.

The rights of the data subject

Whether a fan, ticket buyer, shop customer, web visitor, player/athlete, coach, referee, volunteer, member of staff, sponsor, or any other entity whose data you have in any of your systems, each of these individuals has the following right:

- **Information** disclosure – such as the way you use data and how you process it, whether for communication, profiling, or other decision-making.
- **Access** – giving people access to their own data, including confirmation that their information is being processed, and any other supplementary information you may have about them.
- **Correction** – rectifying any information you have about individuals that is wrong or incomplete. In reality, you would want to see this in place, regardless of the GDPR, as inaccurate data is no good to your business.
- **Restriction of processing** – the potential to block you from doing any further processing, although you could retain the existing information you

have. This is an interesting one for me, and it aligns with my mantra that 'no data should be thrown away' because it all provides valuable insight. For example, just because a fan unsubscribes from receiving your emails, it doesn't mean the information you have about them has no further use. Any profiling you've conducted up to that point can still be used in your BI strategy.

Your obligation to report security breaches

The GDPR places an obligation on you to report any breaches that are likely to result in harm to your data subjects. The Swedish Data Protection Authority fined the National Government Service Centre €18,700 for failing to notify affected parties as well as the Data Protection Authority about a personal data breach – the issue was that members of staff could access payroll and other information about their colleagues (EDPB, 2020).

This is the same obligation that applies to a major hack in your security systems. With this in mind, while your IT teams will no doubt have processes in place to deal with issues they encounter, your marketing teams should have the same.

Need for a data protection officer

It's important to assess whether you need a data protection officer (DPO). According to the GDPR, there are three bases under which this would be the case. Do you fit under any of these?

1   Processing is carried out by a public authority.
2   Your processing operations require regular and systematic processing of data subjects on a large scale (note that there is no definition of *large scale* here).
3   Your core activities relate to a large quantity of sensitive data or data relating to criminal convictions or offences.

On this last point, rights owners who are responsible for athlete registration may fall into this category if your records include health and medical information. For this reason, many of you may decide it's prudent to appoint a DPO as a precaution.

Looking after children

Unlike the EU Data Directive, the GDPR applies specific provisions that are intended to enhance the protection of children's personal data. The general ruling is that consent obligations are applicable for a person under the age of 16. In this case, they cannot give consent themselves. Instead, consent much be secured from a person holding parental responsibility. However, it's important to note that each EU member state is permitted to lower that age as long as it's not below 13. The following is a list of the lowest age of consent across the GDPR-relevant territories, as of August 2020:

13 years of age: Belgium, Denmark, Estonia, Finland, Latvia, Malta, Portugal, Sweden, UK.

14 years of age: Austria, Bulgaria, Cyprus, Italy, Lithuania, Spain.

15 years of age: Czech Republic, France.

16 years of age: Croatia, Germany, Greece, Hungary, Iceland, Luxembourg, Netherlands, Poland, Romania, Slovakia, Slovenia.

Second-party data and third-party opt-ins

In Chapter 3 I looked at the difference between first-, second-, and third-party data and gave the following definition for *second-party*: it traditionally comes from customers of your partners (sponsors, ticketing and merchandise agents) who in Europe have ticked the 'third-party opt-in' box. It's your ticketing agents or your sponsors' first-party data, i.e. their customers who have said their data can be shared with you.

On this point, the GDPR is relevant. While your third parties, specifically your sponsors, ticketing and online store providers can assist with the growth of your databases, both from a quantity and quality standpoint, it's important they have ensured the relevant opt-ins are in place in their processes before transferring the applicable data to you. This includes an opt-in for the data to be used by you for communication purposes.

When you work with your third parties to acquire their data (which is classed as second-party data), it's important you do so with full sight of the relevant opt-in. Ensure the processes your partners use are GDPR-compliant, asking for proof if necessary, including the request that when they send you the applicable database, you can see a field that shows a clear opt-in. Without this understanding and proof of provenance, you could leave yourself exposed if your partners have not used the appropriate processes and your data subjects make a complaint.

Case study: AS Roma

It's universally accepted that more sports rights owners generally operate with a leaner office and business staff than most companies of their comparative size; so when it came to implementing new, or improving existing, data-related processes to be able to demonstrate GDPR accountability and compliance, it has been a challenge for the sports industry.

In the first edition of this book, we interviewed Bas Schnater of AZ Alkmar to discuss their approach to learning about and then adopting the GDPR. You can download that case study from www.winnnersfdd.com/winningwithdatafirstedition/chapterninecasestudy.

For this second edition I talked to Paul Rogers, Chief Strategy Officer at AS Roma, a football club founded in 1927 that has consistently played in the top-tier of Italian football (Rogers, 2020). Paul is renown across European football as a leader in the use of digital media to cut through the huge amount of social traffic created by the world's biggest sport, creating content that stands out. This led to *The Drum* to label Roma 'the weirdest football club on social media' and Paddy Power, a betting company that is itself known for its alternative approach to advertising, to claim that 'Roma's media team are on the 'shrooms' (Clarke, 2017).

In my telephone interview with Paul in June 2020, I asked how he combines the club's approach to creative engagement with the dry necessity of data legislation.

> It doesn't naturally fit with the relationship we have with our fans to have to think about tick boxes and policies – our first thought is how to entertain and engage them; not how to make sure we can commercialise their data. On the other hand, we're a sports business, and like everyone else we have to sell tickets, merchandise, and sponsorships, and we want our fans to visit our website, watch our videos, and engage with us on social [media]. So, we have this balance that we have to strike between giving our fans great content, while also making it as easy as possible for them to be able to buy the things they want – whether that's a ticket or a shirt. We believe if we get it right, we can achieve both objectives.

As we discussed earlier in this chapter, rights owners are taking varied approaches to GDPR and data legislation compliance – from doing nothing to adding a DPO (or several of them) to their internal legal teams, so how does AS Roma stay abreast of the legal requirements placed on them by *Garante Privacy*, the Italian Data Protection Authority?

> We decided to appoint the club's lawyers as our DPO. I know some might question that decision, but it made sense for us – as with many clubs our size, we've got quite a complex ownership structure with

several businesses taking care of different areas. Knowing which business owns which data, who can use it, who can't, how we reference the different businesses in our privacy policy – it's all so fragmented we figured we could save ourselves a lot of hassle by working with the people who know us best. When it comes to player contracts, sponsorship deals, and other commercial agreements, we've got lots of internal experience, but navigating the GDPR and all the local derivations of it is a totally different world for us. We knew we were supposed to be data compliant before GDPR, but I think it's safe to say the thought of a €20 million fine really brought home the need to pay more attention to it.

One of the challenges we have with data protection – and I'm sure this applies to all industries not just sports – is that the law is black and white in a world where there's so much grey. This can make it difficult to navigate and understand the correct application to a particular situation. And when there's the risk of not just a fine, but more importantly the reputational damage we referred to earlier, understanding where to draw the line or when we might be able to cross it becomes even more important. I asked Paul how they know when to apply some of the regulations that provide room to manoeuvre in a way that benefits the business while ensuring they don't give the *Garante* any concern should they ever be audited:

I think the way you interpret the rules and how they apply to your business is really important. I can understand the need to protect consumers from aggressive telesales and spammy emails, but we like to think Roma fans want to hear from us, so long as we're giving them content they want and not bombarding them with sales messages. A classic example is the PECR soft opt-in that uses the term *similar products and services*. I've had no end of discussions about what *similar* actually means – I get that if a fan buys a ticket, we can't try and get them to sign up to a telco sponsor's latest mobile package; but if that telco sponsor is offering them the chance to win a VIP experience at the next match, that's something that many fans want to know about.

Our task is understanding how the black and white words that make up the GDPR are applied to our work in the way our fans would want them to be. We're not selling their data; we're not giving it to our sponsors – we're using it to make sure they get the content we believe they want to receive.

The theme of this book has been to impress upon its readers that CRM is not a project or a tech implementation; it's a way of doing business – putting the fans at the centre of our decision-making and communications so they feel valued and want more. By nature, this means an evolution of the way we do things and changes that are either minor incremental tweaks or major shifts in our approach. One of those changes that can be considered quite monumental is the role of our third parties – our ticketing partners, online store providers, and even our mediate partners. We're used to seeking out the strongest provider of the best service who'll ensure the widest distribution, and we (generally) negotiate for the biggest financial gain. But in an era when data has so much value, we should be including it as another key point in our negotiations – who owns it, who can use it, and if it's the rights owners (as it should be) how do they get it?

AS Roma use Vivaticket, established for over 20 years and present in nine countries, to provide their online ticket solution, and EPI SrL to support their merchandise operations, applying their 24 years' experience in both 'click' and 'brick' operations. Paul shared his thoughts on how these important vendors have helped the club and its approach to CRM:

> Getting our ticketing and online store partner on board from day one instead of two or three years into our contract with them would have been ideal – on the other hand we didn't know what we needed to tell them when we first signed our contracts. Our focus was on finding the right suppliers to ensure we could sell tickets and merchandise to as many fans as possible, as efficiently as possible, while making it easy for our fans; making sure the systems worked and were easy to use. With the increased focus we're now putting on opt-ins, and the importance of our SCV, I wish all these companies that want to sell me so-called new and exciting digital platforms that will help improve the fans' experience would also think about this before asking us to sign a contract. That's what I think is missing – an understanding from all these companies trying to sell to us that while it's paramount that we give our fans a great experience, that we make it easy for them, and that our fans feel valued; they need to take the data their interactions create and help me get it into our systems. If they add that to their sales pitch, I'll pay more attention.

And what about their sponsors – arguably the most lucrative area for many rights owners after ticket sales – how do they fit into Roma's CRM ecosystem?

> We've got a lot more to do with our sponsors and partners – we're only just scraping the surface there. Yes, we're sending emails with their logos

and messages, and while that creates some nice brand association, we need to be doing more – getting our fans to their websites so they can start a direct relationship with them. That's when we'll really be able to start ticking the 'direct ROI' box; that's when we'll be able to really talk about using our channels to help grow their businesses.

We also need to consider the customers our sponsors have and how we can use them to find new Roma fans for us. One of our partners recently ran a promotion on their website, targeting Roma fans and using our content, and they asked everyone who entered if they'd like to hear from the club. The numbers were incredible: 25% of their customers said yes, and out of those, 80% were new fans we didn't have in our database. That was just a one-off, so you can imagine how fast our database will grow when we're doing this regularly across all our sponsors.

I ended the interview by asking Paul what single piece of advice he'd give to his fellow sports professionals – with so many lawyers and data specialists eager to help us navigate the GDPR and other legislation, what would he prioritise?

The biggest learning for me was about PECR soft opt-in – which I didn't even know about 18 months ago. Whatever it takes – the time, the discussions, the arguing – look at where you can use the PECR soft opt-in. It really does make a difference. We've now applied it on both our ticket sales and online store, and the difference is incredible. Before we made the change, our general conversion rate for opt-ins was 31%; now the average is 79%, but our unsubscribe rate hasn't changed. We've made it easier for our fans to say yes by taking advantage of the legislation. And as a result, our database has grown faster and will continue to do so.

Key chapter ideas

1 Currently 70% of the world's countries have data privacy legislation in place, so it's important you understand what you need to do to ensure compliance in the way you collect, manage, store, and use your data.

2 The GDPR is the most stringent of all legislation and will be relevant to your organisation if it operates in the EU or is based outside the EU but proactively aims to communicate with individuals who are residents of the EU.

3 The maximum fine under the GDPR is €20 million or 4% of turnover, whichever's the greater. Under the previous EU Data Directive this was just £500,000. Businesses should be aware of their obligations with respect to audits.

4   In addition to GDPR consent and legitimate interest, you can also use the PECR soft opt-in to build your marketing database.
5   If you have not yet started to address GDPR compliance in your organisation, don't panic; but do start to understand what you should do to ensure compliance and make appropriate plans.

References

Bodewits, O. (2020). *Dutch DPA imposed a controversial fine on the royal Dutch tennis association* [online]. Available at: www.engage.hoganlovells.com/knowledgeservices/news/dutch-dpa-imposed-a-controversial-fine-on-the-royal-dutch-tennis-association.

Brand, G. (2015). How the Bosman rule changed football – 20 years on. *Sky Sports* [online]. Available at: www.skysports.com/football/news/11095/10100134/how-the-bosman-rule-changed-football-20-years-on.

Clarke, C. (2017). Why AS Roma revel in being the weirdest football club on social media. *The Drum* [online]. Available at: www.thedrum.com/news/2017/08/31/why-roma-revel-being-the-weirdest-football-club-social-media.

Cottrell, S. (2018). Results of sport sector GDPR readiness survey – data protection report. *LawInSport* [online]. Available at: www.lawinsport.com/announcements/item/sport-sector-gdpr-readiness-survey-2018.

EDPB. (2020). *The Swedish data protection authority issues fine against the national government service centre* [online]. Available at: https://edpb.europa.eu/news/national-news/2020/swedish-data-protection-authority-issues-fine-against-national-government_en.

Greenberg, P. (2001). *CRM at the speed of light.* Berkeley, CA: Osborne.

McCaskill, S. (2019). *La Liga handed $280,000 GDPR fine for 'spying' on fans watching pirated streams* [online]. Available at: www.forbes.com/sites/stevemccaskill/2019/06/12/la-liga-handed-e250000-gdpr-fine-for-spying-on-fans-watching-pirated-streams/#6074e96875d9.

McCormack, M. (1989). *What they don't teach you at Harvard business school.* Toronto: Bantam Books.

Privacy International. (2019). *Cambridge analytica, GDPR – 1 year on – a lot of words and some action* [online]. Available at: https://privacyinternational.org/news-analysis/2857/cambridge-analytica-gdpr-1-year-lot-words-and-some-action.

Rogers, P. (2020). Chief Strategy Officer, interview by phone, 24 June.

United National Conference on Trade and Development. (2020). *Data protection and privacy legislation worldwide* [online]. Available at: https://unctad.org/en/Pages/DTL/STI_and_ICTs/ICT4D-Legislation/eCom-Data-Protection-Laws.aspx.

Chapter 10

Where do we go from here?

I thought long and hard about how best to end this book in a way that would give most value to you, the reader. I realised that if I tried to predict the future that would benefit no one, as I'm no futurologist. Worse than that, I'm a data geek, so the only prophecy that has any value to me is one that's come out the other end of some predictive analytics process. And on top of all that, I'm writing this while the world is still in the grip of a global pandemic caused by the coronavirus.

I received confirmation that my publishers would be supporting a second edition of this book in early March 2020, and I think it's fair to say that while we knew about the coronavirus at that time, we didn't know the extent to which it would come to dominate – and for some poor souls, decimate – our lives. There will be a lot written about the impact this global pandemic has had and will continue to have on our lives – there will be analyses and white papers, films and plays, stories and poems – so I shall leave the dissection of it to better wordsmiths then me. But I couldn't write a book about the challenges and opportunities to use data in the business of sports without including reference to the way we have had to respond to lockdown, to not competing in front of our fans, in some cases not finishing our seasons, and in most cases, the financial losses we've had to bear.

The new COVID-19 normal

In Chapter 3 Dave Callan from Team INEOS shared his participate-at-home initiative with Zwift to ensure their global fan base stayed engaged with his team members. And in Chapter 6 Liam Scully from Lincoln City FC talked about the role of data and automation played to ensure their season ticket refund programme delivered a level of customer service that could not have been replicated through manual processes. Later in Chapter 8 Mic Conetta from Arsenal talked about the impact of lockdown on his approach to business change – regular meetings that motivate, educate, and inspire – but he also provided some additional considerations:

> What we're finding now is that our fans are craving contact from us, so our task is creating and maintaining that in a world where, the natural thing

they want to do – come together and cheer for their team – they can't do that physically. We have to create that environment for them virtually.

You'll read, in our case study at the end of this chapter, how the LA Kings believe that the current situation has helped them fast-track an approach they would have had to tackle at some point anyway – helping fans that can't get to the arena because they live too far away or don't have the time feel like they're just as big a part of the experience as the fans sitting in the stands. The case study also talks about the Kings' approach to data modelling mid-pandemic, and Conetta provides similar insight:

> When it comes to reopening our stadium for fans we have the complexity of looking at how many people we can have in the stadium, how we get them back into the stadium in a safe way, and where we sit them. We have to think about what games they come to because we'll have a reduced capacity, so what does that mean for the pricing on that ticket? Will they be able to sit in the same ticket block and locational price point? And will they be able to sit together if they're in a bubble or will everyone have to be socially distanced? What does that mean for traffic around entering the concourse?
>
> So, all of this is driven by data, everything is being driven by data. But do we have a reference point for this? No. So effectively, we're almost doing a season plan for every single game based on our need to try and accommodate as many people as possible to actually make this work for us.

At the time of writing, Conetta and his team have no sight of how many fans will be allowed into their 60,000-seat stadium, but hopefully it'll be more than the 500 allowed into Belfast's 16,000 capacity Windsor Park in the UK's first trial of a football match in front of a live audience on 31 July 2020. While the trial went well and the Irish Football Association have been praised for their handling of this watershed moment as we slowly come out of lockdown, with just 3% of available seats taken, it's not quite representative of the return to live sports we were hoping for.

Areas of impact

When we look at the business areas impacted by the coronavirus, we can clearly see the role that digital technologies, marketing technologies, and the use of data can have on our futures:

Broadcasting/streaming: Many rights owners by now will have an OTT strategy, or at least have thought about the role of direct-to-consumer streaming, either via intermediaries through a media rights negotiation, not dissimilar to the traditional linear broadcast discussions, or without intermediaries, using their own native platforms. What the lockdown has done for these strategies or these thoughts is to fast-track them – to take whatever timeframe was originally imagined and reduce it significantly. And this isn't unique to sports and broadcasting: a June 2020 article by Mckinsey titled 'Reinventing the organization for speed in the post-COVID-19 era' cited multiple examples of organisations 'getting things done fast, and well. Organizations have removed boundaries and have broken down silos in ways no one thought was possible. They have streamlined decisions and processes, empowered frontline leaders, and suspended slow-moving hierarchies and bureaucracies' (Smet et al., 2020). Formula 1 has seen a tremendous response to their engagement initiatives through Amazon's live-streaming channel, Twitch, leading F1 managing director Ross Brawn to state at the International Automobile Federation's 2020 eConference: 'The thing I've seen that is very striking to me is how, because the real drivers have become involved in these initiatives and these events, how well they've been able to engage with the fans' (Brawn, 2020).

Digital engagement: There are many examples of creative engagement initiatives developed by rights owners throughout lockdown; but rather than talk about them, I want to highlight an approach that did indeed meet the previous criteria– it was creative, engaging, and a new initiative developed specifically as a result of the coronavirus – but I saw it as a rushed execution that did not think about legacy. It did not put enough consideration into the opportunity to secure marketing opt-ins from the hundreds, thousands, or maybe even hundreds of thousands of fans that rushed to participate in the Ironman's Virtual Club.

Most, if not all, rights owners have by now accepted that data is important to us – some may still be trying to figure out what, why, and how – but at it's very basic levels. We all know a marketing opt-in has a value and there should be focus on the quantity and quality of customer data in a marketing automation platform. This is something that must have eluded the developers, as a lot more focus seems to have gone into the short-term creative execution rather than the long-term opportunity because the registration form does not include a marketing opt-in. Indeed, a fan or user goes through further actions post-registration before they're invited to hear from Ironman.

You'll know from Chapter 2, where we discuss the CRM pyramid, and Chapter 3, where we look at the importance of data, that securing consent for marketing is absolutely crucial to progressing CRM or for digital transformation, so I always recommend the opt-in comes early in a registration process, before user fatigue kicks in. So while Ironman was one of the first to launch a creative digital platform that delivered an at-home engagement initiative, if it had added a marketing opt-in tick box to the first page of the registration process, it would have exponentially increased the chances of converting a digital visitor's initial interest into a lifelong passion, their participation in a virtual experience into a financial transaction, and a sofa experience to an at-event one.

Sponsorship: In Chapter 7 I introduced you to the framework we've developed at Winners, 'Changing the Sponsorship Dialogue', and you read the UEFA and Booking.com case study that is now over three years old but still highly relevant. In the MLS case study from Charlie Shin in Chapter 2, you will also have read how they've taken their CRM strategy even further – supporting their sponsors not just with targeted messaging and retargeting programmes, but also providing a data append service.

This type of activity is needed when there's no live sports for sponsors to leverage, indeed a 2020 report stated global spend on sports sponsorship will take a US$17.2 billion hit as a direct result of the coronavirus pandemic (Dixon, 2020). But the general direction of the industry is called out in PwC's 2019 Sports Survey report where they stated:

> In a world where media and sponsorship are converging and rights owners need to have the sophistication of digital advertisers to attract partners, the winners of tomorrow will be the players who are able to build direct fan relationships and develop an intimate understanding of their audience.
>
> (PWC, 2019)

The monetary value of data

Moving on from the global pandemic – because one day we will; the 'new normal' will see live sports back on the agenda and fans back in the stadium – one of the underlying themes of this book is the value of data, and more importantly, the data that a rights owner has acquired from fans, participants, customers, and other stakeholders. You're not necessarily the data owner, but you are the data controller, and you will have received permission from some, or most, of these 'data subjects' to use their data for the purposes you laid out in your opt-in process. I'd like to take that principle one step further and question whether there's a business model that can be created from the existing relationship you have with your customers and your status as holder of their data.

In the same way you might sign a licence with a credit card company to use your logo so that you receive a royalty for every cardholder who signs up, could we turn that principle around and earn money for every fan that opts-in for you to sell their data? Could you then give the company a share of the revenue you make from the sale of that data?

In February 2014, DataCoup launched its service to great fanfare, proposing that individuals 'unlock the value of your personal data' and using their platform to enable DataCoup to sell their personal data and give them a percentage of the proceeds. Early announcements suggested an individual could make $8 per month by signing up to their platform (Tanner, 2014). However, by November 2019, DataCoup had stopped trading. Were they wrong in their supposition or did they have the wrong model? In 2018, Gregory Barber, a Columbia University graduate with a bachelor's degree in computer science and now a journalist who writes about blockchain, Artificial Intelligence (AI), and tech policy, tried to sell his data through a similar business. Barber signed away his Facebook and Strava data, as well as his Apple Health data, and when he checked his account, he'd made the equivalent of €0.03 (Barber, 2018)!

In Chapter 7 I talked about the importance of not handing over your fan data to your sponsors, that the value in your sponsorship was in the association with your brand, that a digital advertising framework may enable rights owners to operate as advertising agencies and make commissions on sponsor ad budgets. The examples cited here suggest that there perhaps isn't an actual market of any sizeable value for data itself – and it is more about how about how that data can be used for other revenue-generating purposes. But, if that were the case – if there isn't an actual market for raw data, just the opportunity to generate revenue from the way you use it – what about the growing business of infonomics, the principle I referred to in Chapter 3, that data can be viewed as a corporate asset? Gartner defines *infonomics* as:

> the emerging discipline of managing and accounting for information with the same or similar rigour and formality as other traditional assets and liabilities (such as financial, physical and intangible assets and human capital). Infonomics posits that information itself meets all the criteria of formal company assets, and, although not yet recognised by generally accepted accounting practices (GAAP), it is increasingly incumbent on organisations to behave as if information were a real asset.
>
> (Gartner, 2020)

If you'd like to understand more about infonomics, I recommend the book *Infonomics: How to Monetize, Manage, and Measure Information as an Asset for Competitive Advantage* by Douglas Laney; but even if you choose not to read any further, know this: industries related to data are growing as data becomes more important. If you've found Chapters 3 and 4 in this book more interesting than 5, 6, 7, or 8, then perhaps a future as a data officer, analyst, or scientist is for you.

Networked stadiums

For some years, the use of Wi-Fi in sports stadiums has been considered a utility in the US. In the same way electricity and water are considered essential to staging a live event, so too is the use of an internet connection for fans to share images, videos, and emotions. However, this side of the pond we've had a different situation, where clubs or venues were looking at the cost to install, as opposed to the long-term cost of not installing. But, are things changing for European sports fans?

In 2014, fans of PSV Eindhoven famously protested against the use of Wi-Fi in the Philips Stadion (The Guardian, 2014), just a week after Manchester United banned fans from taking iPads into Old Trafford in an effort to prevent them from recording and then streaming match footage (Campbell, 2014).

However, a November 2019 report suggested the market for 'smart stadiums' is to grow from $4 billion in 2015 to $22 billion by 2025, with Europe having held the highest share in 2017 (Businesswire, 2019). And certainly, the London Stadium, home of West Ham United and UK Athletics, is leading on Europe's behalf by delivering what is claimed to be 'the fastest free stadium Wi-Fi in the UK, as part of efforts to become Europe's most connected stadium' (The Stadium Business, 2019).

The fan-facing reasons for creating a networked stadium are clear. People expect to have access to the internet, their social accounts, and information on a 24/7 basis, including when they're in a stadium that has to go from a 1% capacity to 99% overnight. However, the upside for rights owners investing in networks can be significant, including increased revenue from the right sales message delivered to fans when a goal or point has been scored. Other direct revenue opportunities include digital signage, managed through stadium Wi-Fi, that advertisers pay so much more for when the ads are personalised, changing in relation to the audience in front of it or the flow of the game/event. There is also scope for partnerships with online betting companies, of much greater value now that they offer fans in-game betting, as well as the option to get their money back before the end of a match.

With more than 50% of purchases now made by card instead of cash, concession stands can provide a much better service thanks to their point-of-sale systems connecting to Wi-Fi (Jones, 2017). There's also the opportunity for increased security when a stadium is networked though the use of facial recognition technology that may help protect fans from threats and, as we discussed in the previous chapter, the use of thermal scanners to check for a high temperature, a sure sign of the coronavirus and other illnesses.

But perhaps one of the most valuable opportunities, now that we know the value of data, is the ability to get contact details from those fans that haven't purchased their tickets online. Friends of the group leader, recipients of gifts or corporate guests, they all tend to end up in a stadium without filling any sort of form; so if they want to tweet the goal, or Facebook their photo, they have to log in to Wi-Fi first. And that's where we can collect their data.

Another opportunity is understanding fan behaviour when they're in the stadium, from knowing their traffic pattern around the concourse (if you also have beacons and other location identifiers) to watching their digital behaviour on your channels. All this data is unavailable to us unless stadium owners provide Wi-Fi. It may be costly, but it's a business win that supports everything I've discussed so far.

The TV rights bubble: digital or bust?

For the over 30 years I've been in the sports industry the same topic has come up for discussion every few years (usually via attention-grabbing headlines): that the market for sports TV rights has imploded, and the bubble has well and truly burst. But, over the last few years – even before the pandemic – that discussion has taken a different path. It's not that the bubble has burst; it's just become a virtual bubble; it's gone digital.

The future of the TV rights market has become one of my favourite topics because there's so much movement, so much speculation, and so much change. From Amazon, Netflix, Facebook, and Twitter buying sports rights to rightsholders themselves delivering OTT services, the options are plentiful, and of course, there are still the traditional linear deals that have been in play since the 1950s.

Let's consider some of the recent deals that have challenged the linear broadcasting industry:

- BT Sport will again provide free coverage of the 2019/2020 men's UEFA Champions League and UEFA Europa League finals through its YouTube channel, having secured 4.8 million digital viewers when it did the same for the 2018/2019 season, a 166% increase on its first attempt at this in 2016 (Impey, 2020).
- DAZN, the OTT streaming service which was widely reported as suffering with financial troubles during the early phase of the coronavirus lockdown, has secured what it claims to be the largest package of major domestic soccer rights ever awarded to a streaming service in Europe. It recently secured the exclusive rights to 106 Bundesliga matches in the 2020/2021 season for broadcasting on Friday nights and Sunday afternoons in Germany, Austria, and Switzerland (Carp, 2020).
- Amazon signed a three-year, $130 million deal in 2018 to stream Thursday night NFL games on its Prime video service and, while I can't find reference to any results, the fact they've now signed an extension for a further three years suggests it worked well for them.
- Google's YouTube signed an exclusive deal with MLB in 2019 to stream 13 games live on YouTube during the second half of the regular baseball season. Figures released suggested an average viewership per game of 1.2 million, including pre- and post-match, with one game seeing a peak of 320,000 concurrent viewers (Dixon, 2019).

In the UK we've also seen the launch of EFL's iFollow service, providing fans outside the UK with a live stream across their three divisions, hosted on their own website, rather than through a third party, at a cost of £110 per season. In the words of Drew Barrand, the former marketing director at the EFL, 'In essence, we're becoming a broadcaster' (Connelly, 2017a).

This mirrors the NFL's GamePass, providing Europeans with multiple options for live or on-demand matches; Ultimate Fighting Championship) (UFC)'s Fight Pass, which can be personalised by the user to follow a specific fighter; and Formula 1's F1 TV, which provides access to live-event streaming for $10 per month.

Many different models are involving third parties, like digital and linear rights being sold to broadcasters, and even non-broadcast media companies getting into the broadcast space. There are also rights owners doing it for themselves, with major success.

But, what's all this got to do with the use of CRM and data? When rights owners move away from linear channels to digital, not only do they give their fans a choice on how, when, and for how long they watch, they collect information about them and their viewing habits. According to BT, not only did their YouTube broadcast of the 2019 Champions League Final increase their viewing figures by 1.8 million, they received data about every viewer who streamed the game. This gave BT invaluable insight that will assist with future marketing planning (Connelly, 2017b). Amazon echoes this sentiment in support of their deal with the NFL. In an interview with Yahoo! Finance, Saurabh Sharma, Amazon's director of ad platforms, talked about how the data they'll generate from NFL viewers will support their advertising sales model, providing brands with behavioural data previously unavailable about fans of the sport (Roberts, 2017). Most importantly for me, if this is the future of the TV sports rights industry (sports fans having full control of their viewing behaviour via a digital platform), then the more rights holders know about their fans, the more direct contact they have with them, the more control they'll have over their broadcasting future.

I'm not a sports media specialist (I've never sold a TV deal), but I consume the coverage of this subject in the same way as anyone who wants to stay abreast of this fast-moving industry. When our clients ask me how they should consider their future in this area, my advice is quite clear: even if you, as a rights holder, think you'll stay with the traditional model of selling or contracting your TV rights to a broadcaster (whether linear, digital, or a combination of both over multiple channels), then by having a rich and deep database of your fans, you'll have far more control over your broadcast negotiations. This approach works, regardless of the scale, as it is relevant for any audience. The principle is that if you can, as a rights owner, go OTT to the fan, and the business model justifies it, broadcasters will want to know about it.

Augmented and virtual reality

Augmented reality (AR) and VR are no longer new in sports, but do they reinvent the fan experience? There's been a lot of discussion, experimentation, delivery, and analysis about the use of these technologies. They're a perfect marriage and they provide delivery of an enhanced or immersive experience in one of the few areas of our lives that we're often absolutely, totally, and irrationally passionate about. With the financial prospect being a share of a $ 571 billion industry by 2025, according to a 2020 report, it's no wonder we want a piece of it (PR Newswire, 2020).

First things first, I'll just remind us all of the difference between the two. AR superimposes digital elements onto a 'real world' situation, most commonly through the lens of a camera on a smartphone. Pokémon Go is perhaps the most well-known of these, with 1 billion downloads as of March 2019 (Dogtiev, 2020).

VR involves the use of headsets to provide an all-encompassing experience where the user is positioned in an artificial environment that feels entirely realistic. Unlike AR, it can't be experienced with just a smartphone but, to help spread its usage, Google has produced a cardboard viewer, and developers are busy making VR apps that can be used to great effect.

Rights holders are already using AR and VR to bolster their offering:

* Over in the US, the Dallas Cowboys launched a 'Pose with the Pro's' AR attraction in the AT&T Stadium that allows fans to take photos of themselves with their favourite players. The unveiling of the interactive 5G-enabled columns at their first game generated over 50 million social media impressions (Draper, 2019).
* The National Collegiate Athletic Association (NCAA) launched a partnership with Intel in 2017 to produce Intel True VR, a headset that carried the March Madness Live app and some NCAA Tournament games and provided a virtual courtside seat experience for users. Although early reports suggest the product (which sold at $2.99 per game or $7.99) was hailed a success, the partnership was not renewed when it expired in 2020.

There's also a suggestion that the use of VR will help restore the fan experience in the post-coronavirus world, if teams continue to play behind closed doors, by enabling people to watch as though they're together when they're remote. And, as we're no longer satisfied with a screen experience, the opportunity for VR to provide us with multiple views across the same, or multiple, platforms will keep the most ardent surfer and stat seeker satisfied.

It's clear that AR and VR are going to play an ever-increasing role in our world, but the point I want to make is that while we might get carried away with the customer experience, we need to remember some fundamentals: using data to design and promote the experience (what we know about our fans, their interests, behaviour, and needs), then using the application itself to collect more data, has to be a KPI. It can't just be about the number of downloads and minutes of usage and will have to support our cross-organisational objectives. Data must be key.

Blockchain and sports data

Blockchain technology was invented by an anonymous person or group of people who use the name *Satoshi Nakamoto*. It's a continuously growing list of records, or 'blocks', which are linked together and secured using cryptography, a method that ensures only those individuals who are supposed to have access to the records can do so. The most well-known use of a blockchain is Bitcoin, the digital currency system with over 42 million wallets set up around the world as of December 2019 (Lielacher, 2020).

There are many other uses of blockchain technology in evidence. For example, Aon, a global insurance brand, is building a platform to speed up insurance operations; BMW is using a blockchain to track materials, components, and parts across its supply chain; and the United Nations has applied the technology to assist in combatting warlords who steal aid using stolen identity cards. Luxury brands LVMH and De Beers use blockchain for traceability and proof of authenticity, and within the financial sector, Mastercard has applied for 116 blockchain-related patents (Castillo, et al). Here in the sports industry, blockchain has been used by ticketing vendors for some time with UEFA first trialling it at the 2018 Super Cup. A crowdfunding concept, SportyCo, provides a micro crowdfunding platform that will use Bitcoin to help athletes with funding (Say, 2020), and there's an ice hockey arena in Denmark, home of Rungsted Ishockey Klub, that's named Bitcoin Arena (Redman, 2017).

Blockchain technology is managed directly in a peer-to-peer network that can't be amended retroactively unless every party in the block is collaborating. To that extent it's considered incorruptible. If this is the case then there's a real opportunity to consider its use for the transfer and storage of data. Consider the range of applications you currently use across the different suppliers that support your business and their role in managing your data for different business units and purposes. With the obligations we're now under with the GDPR and other data legislation, it would make sense that we turn to a technology such as blockchain that can provide us with both the security we need and the ability to involve different parties along the way.

This is of particular interest when it comes to an athlete's performance data, specifically biometrics which are of huge value, not just when it comes to a rights owner's ability to commercialise it, but also for consideration during transfer discussions. The weakness of our data transfer systems has already been exposed by the Fancy Bears, a Russian cyber espionage group supposedly associated with the Russian military intelligence agency. During the 2016 Summer Olympics they hacked into the systems used by both the World Anti-Doping Agency and the United States Anti-Doping Agency and released documents providing highly confidential and sensitive athlete data in an effort to 'create fake news and smear their names in order to divert attention away from their [Russia's] own state-operated doping programme' (Butler, 2016).

Athlete data is one area of focus for BEASY, a US company that has developed plug-and-play applications on blockchain to enable an individual to create, sell, buy, or even limit the use of their own digital content. With governing bodies, leagues, and clubs already grappling with the debate over ownership of athlete data, BEASY is making it easier for individuals to be part of the discussion. This is something that Mike Clohisy, BEASY's president and a sports lawyer, believes will be the next high-profile discussion area in sports: 'The unions are certainly fighting, and they're asking the essential question: if the leagues, the teams and the data companies are sharing the data in a commercial way, why are the players excluded? How can they attempt to gain a slice of the pie?' (Franklin-Wallis, 2020).

In reality, the growth of blockchain in mainstream usage is still incredibly slow. According to a 2020 report of the supply chain industry, only 37% of those companies surveyed have one in development, are piloting a program, or have a live blockchain, although nearly half say they're likely to invest in blockchain over the next two years (APQC, 2020). So, while companies such as BEASY make it easier for the sports industry to use blockchain technology, and the growing discussion around athlete data is providing the perfect use case, it may still be some time before we see greater adoption among the majority of rights owners.

Analytics 3.0

In Chapter 4 I refer to Analytics 1.0, the era of BI, as the appropriate reference for most rights owners. With this in mind, the era of big data, 2.0, could be considered the province of just a small handful of rights owners, along with many e-commerce businesses. But then when it comes to Analytics 3.0, the era of data-enriched offerings, this is where companies such as Google, Netflix, Amazon, Alibaba, and Spotify reside – so, do we ever think there will be a rights owner sitting at this level?

The general definition of 3.0 is the point at which the use of analytics is prevalent across your entire business operation. Data is collected on every device, customer, stakeholder, or action. To achieve this, organisations need the right technological infrastructure, which means a level of computing power that can handle complex calculations. But they also need the business requirement, and I'm not sure the sports industry has that, or if indeed it will ever have that.

The possible caveat to that is the depth to which we can push athlete performance data. Will we ever be able to connect a thought process with an emotion and therefore with a physical action? And, more importantly, if we can do that, will the outcome of analysing that data enable us to influence an athlete's response to the extent that it will make the difference between winning and losing? When you think about Liverpool FC finally finishing the 2019/2020 season as Premier League champions, albeit behind closed doors – thanks to the coronavirus, and that it will have netted them somewhere around £175 million just in prize money, then surely it has to be worth looking at (Ziegler, 2020).

Further, if FC Barcelona's 103 million Facebook followers could actually be converted into records within their own database, with all the rich data that would accompany these fans every time they posted or liked, these fans' actions could be tracked, not just across Barca's digital estate, but across the entire web.

In turn, they could be converted into customers of content, merchandise, or the club's sponsors. In this case Analytics 3.0 may be applicable.

Artificial intelligence, machine learning, and neural networks

AI is, at its most basic, the use of computers to simulate human intelligence to enable them to perform tasks. The most popular and well-known examples of this are Google Home, Siri, and Alexa —Google, Apple, and Amazon's voice-activated digital assistants. But, did you know that AI has been around for as long as computers themselves? In fact, if you read Pamela McCorduck's 2004 book, *Machines Who Think*, you could believe her position that efforts to mechanise human thinking began in ancient history 'with myths, stories and rumours of artificial beings endowed with intelligence or consciousness by master craftsmen' (McCorduck, 2004).

Machine learning is a form of AI that allows computers to learn from data, example, and experience, almost like a human. Rather than following pre-programmed rules, applications powered by machine learning algorithms carry out complex processes by learning from a previous process. Machine learning has also been around far longer than you'd expect, with the term coined in by American pioneer, Arthur Lee Samuel (Samuel, 1959).

Unlike AI and machine learning, neural networks are a more recent phenomenon, a form of machine learning used for pattern recognition and tasks involving prediction. The algorithms are modelled to reflect the way the human brain processes information, and because of this, they have the potential to identify more of the subtle nuances of human thought that traditional algorithms miss.

We've already seen high profile examples of AI. Back in July 2016 the NBA launched a chatbot for Facebook Messenger and, while the early version didn't quite live up to the AI hype, they were one of the first movers with AI in sport (McCormick, 2016). Just a year later, in July 2017, this approach to fan engagement using AI had evolved quite significantly. Bloomberg reported that IBM's AI agent, Watson, was used to power a voice-activated customer service bot called Ask Fred (named after tennis great Fred Perry) at Wimbledon, one of the four Grand Slam tennis tournaments. App users could ask Fred for directions to the nearest merchandise store or the nearest place they could find strawberries. In addition to Fred, IBM also used AI to automatically compile highlights videos and use indicators such as the crowd's reaction, analysing the quantity and sentiment of social media posts, the players' facial expressions, and the importance of a particular play on the outcome of a game (Kahn, 2017). The tennis world has come leaps and bounds since Ask Fred, with the 2019 Roland Garros seeing the debut of the Infosys Tennis Platform which provided fans, both on-site and around the world, with real-time insights and experiences by taking huge tranches of data and using multiple forms of analyses, artificial intelligence, virtual reality, augmented reality, and many other digital applications (Wharton University of Pennsylvania, 2019).

When you consider the incredible power of neural networks to incorporate sentiment analysis, sports and AI is a match made in heaven – fans have an abundance of passion and aren't afraid to show it. The future for the use of AI in the sports industry is vast, and with the global market expected to reach $733.7 billion by 2027 (Grand View Research, 2020), I expect that whatever rights owners are not currently investigating this area, they will be soon. However, creating your AI proposition starts with having data in the first place.

Case study: LA Kings

For this case study I interviewed Aaron LeValley of the Anschutz Entertainment Group (AEG) on 14 May 2020. AEG is one of the world's largest owners of sports teams and events, including the LA Kings, an ice hockey team that has played in the NHL for over 50 years. Aaron joined the Kings in 2009 as a database marketing manager and analyst and is now senior vice president of business operations and strategy, demonstrating the importance of understanding data in a senior management role. Indeed, Thomas Davenport said in his 2006 article 'Competing on Analytics for HBR': 'A companywide embrace of analytics impels changes in culture, processes, behaviour, and skills for many employees. And so, like any major transition, it requires leadership from executives at the very top who have a passion for the quantitative approach' (Davenport, 2006).

Aaron certainly has that passion, along with both the knowledge and the drive to ensure the Kings embrace that cultural change. In this interview he highlighted for us the importance of a) interpreting cues in customer behaviour, b) developing digital products to foster engagement and generate new revenue streams, and c) focussing on growing its local, national, and international customers. I started by asking him at what level of capability he feels they're currently operating:

> From a CRM standpoint, we are independent from the [National Hockey] League (though we work closely with them) and control our own customer data. When I'm asked this type of question I think: 1) How do we compare to other teams in the league? and 2) How do we compare to a typical company in another industry? I think if you were to compare us among the NHL teams, I would say we were at a six or a seven. We do a good job, but I think we can be much better. I think when you compare us and sports to general industry, we're still only about a three.

So where does Aaron feel that the Kings, and other sports rights owners, may be lagging behind other industries – what's the main gap in capability?

We're doing great work integrating data sources, but I think where we need to get better is in our understanding of the 'unknown customer'. We receive information about a person when they buy their tickets, and now with digital ticketing the amount of data we're getting is increasing. But I think we can do a better job of tracking that whole experience – what led them to purchase that ticket; what were the interactions they had before? There are only a handful of teams doing that right now, and it's an area for us to improve. We can also look at what happens after they've purchased that ticket – how we can understand more of what they're doing when they're in our arena and then use those insights to deliver that with personalised offers.

I think where innovative companies (like Amazon) really stick out is when they utilise data to deliver personalised recommendations, allow a better connection with their customers, and deliver more relevant products/recommendations. That's the same thing we have to do, be it selling tickets, selling merchandise, or finding little surprises we can give. Think about it: knowing somebody always buys a beer or some popcorn in the second period and being able to proactively deliver that beer or popcorn to thank them for their support.

So that's my longwinded way of saying that even versus five years ago we're much better, but I think we have so far to catch up. Rather than worrying about getting to Amazon's level, I just want to get to our next level and find what's next. When we do find that next data source, we need to make sure we can use it. We don't want to accumulate data for the sake of having data.

Throughout this book I've tried to reiterate the balance between the importance of technology as an enabler with the need to ensure our strategies are driven by our business needs rather than the software we use, but I wanted to know more about the Kings data warehouse, segmentation, and analytics capabilities:

StellarAlgo provides us with a CDP – really helping us better understand our customers. We have all this data, but we just don't have the manpower to conduct the amount of analyses needed to grow our business. Through their tools, we can provide our sales and marketing teams the ability to build their own customer segments; whether it's a community initiative or an upcoming ticket promotion, this tool puts the power of segmentation at the hands of the marketers, rather than relying on the data administrators.

Now that we've been able to open time for the analytics team, we can utilise the tools to understand how customers are responding across multi-channels (email, direct mail, a call campaign, etc.). This way we understand who's in the segment, how the segment performed – and from that we can start building attribution models.

The last piece we're working on right now is understanding customer journeys. When an individual purchases a (season) ticket, we want to understand what led to that purchase, what types of interactions the customer had (across channels) before they purchased, and what interaction is most likely to occur right before buying a ticket. This is where we're a little short on the data – we're working on aggregating more information on our unknown customers (digital advertising and Google Analytics data, for example), which will help us understand that full journey.

We discussed the customer journey and going from unknown to known in Chapter 7, and Aaron acknowledges the Kings also have a lot of work to do here, but he also goes on to address the point we looked at in Chapter 6, on data-driven marketing: the ability to predict a customer's movement and implement next-best-action marketing.

When we've built that [customer journey] model we're going to try and flip it on its head and say OK, this is where the customer has been interacting; what is the likelihood that this person buys a ticket based on their previous interactions? What is the next best course of action for them? Then we'll know the best way to create a personal relationship – do we need to serve them a digital ad, then send them an email, and then give them a phone call? This is the key – the idea of sports teams cold-calling 100 people just doesn't work anymore. We need to deliver higher quality leads when customers are ready to purchase – and that's what we'll be doing, utilising our technology to deliver the right leads at the right time to our sales team.

We're proud to be iterating on this with StellarAlgo right now – we've finished our initial model, understanding customer behaviours which led to a purchase. Now we're flipping it on its inverse and utilising that data to say now let's identify the next best course of action for the individuals who have not purchased yet. (Not even mentioning the work we want to do with understanding content preferences!)

Aaron raises another interesting point here. As we discussed earlier in this chapter, the outbreak of the coronavirus has been a terrible experience for many, from a personal health, a mental health, and a financial standpoint – but for Aaron and his CRM development it's given them more time to focus on their team's development:

> Our ticketing, reporting, and forecasting models are currently not as they need to be, which gives us a few months to really dive in and identify how we can be better. We have shifted our focus to some of 'want to' projects and find new value within our business. We know many of our prior (lead-scoring) models and tactics may not work as they had pre-pandemic, so we need to be nimble for when we are ready to re-launch our next season.
>
> From a data and analytics perspective, we are positioned to read-and-react, to see how things evolve and decide how data and analytics will help us return. If we have a wave two of lockdown, it's a scary proposition because that would put us out another year from having fans in venues. So, we are preparing for all scenarios and not necessarily committed to what we've done in the past (like a new lead-scoring model launched in September), because it may not matter and the model we create may not be relevant.

Aaron makes a valid point here – over the lockdown period the data points the Kings are collecting are different because there's no on-site data, there's no ticket purchase data, etc. I asked him to expand on this and share the key differences in his approach and his focus at this moment in time:

> A lot of the customer data models that we created pre-COVID-19 may be irrelevant when we do come out of lockdown, so we really have to understand what data we can utilise – just because we have all this information it doesn't mean we should use it.
>
> I think about a friend of mine who was furloughed but wasn't part of the [US government's] stimulus package because he made too much money last year. That's where I think the challenge will be – we have a lot of the data that says, 'this person can definitely buy, or this person bought in the past', but we don't know where their life is at now because of COVID-19. That's where we can add in additional data (digital advertising data, website visits, email behaviour, survey results). We'll need to

look to cues from the customer in the same way online retailers utilise people's behaviour to deliver relevant advertising. When people are looking at our ticketing pages or clicking on our ads, we'll want to know if they really are shopping on the site to look at tickets – we're going to have to focus on consumer behaviour to help us understand who might be ready.

But one thing we're doing more of is 'quick hit' surveys – questions that gather feedback for us so we can understand how our fans are, what content they interested in, and what can make the fan experience better. They also help us understand who may be more 'sales-ready' post-COVID-19, compared to someone who has struggled. We do not have a data source that's going to tell us that, so we need to be combining the behaviours we can track with the direct conversations that our sales and service team are having, and then utilising that information to help us find the best option for that fan, be it tickets, content, or something else.

Aaron's already talked about the need to access different data points because there's so little transactional data available right now, so I asked him about attitudinal data which has always been more difficult to access – you can't watch for it; you have to ask for it. My question was how does he hope to access this post-lockdown, how can he understand attitudes and motivations post-COVID-19, how can he understand the way in which consumers have changed and therefore how those changes will affect the Kings?

We chatted about our surveys – something we can do right now. Step two would normally be conducting focus groups or having meetings at games, but we don't know when we're going to be able to do that again. One thing we instituted with our sales teams is just very simple – it's a red/yellow/green scale for when they make outbound calls. Our conversations are not aggressively focussed on sales; they're focussed on empathy, understanding how our customers are thinking/feeling. We're asking them how they're doing, whether they have been engaging with our content and our community initiatives, etc. With every call we make, it's up to the sales executive to judge where this person's at when it comes to engaging in a sales conversation, and then we use that to factor how they potentially have been affected by COVID-19. We're not doing it by forcing them to tell us if they're feeling fear or feeling this or that; we're just asking our frontline sales team to give us an idea based on the conversation. For example, red would be that they didn't like this call, so don't contact them right now.

That level of information really helps us as we can be smarter in having sales conversations versus relationship-based conversations – the red/yellow/green approach influences our marketing channels and messages so we can sell again at the right time.

With the likelihood of the season starting again in aft November 2020, but ticket sales potentially not being an option for a few months after that, I asked Aaron what other opportunities he's going to have between this interview in May and eight months from now:

We've been working at home for about two months now, and there's has been a lot that we've had to do on a day-to-day basis. When it comes to driving ticketing revenue, we know we won't have the opportunity to do that until probably January 2021, so we must re-evaluate our 'normal'. Building a (lead-scoring) model right now isn't a productive use of time (as discussed earlier). We need to develop a product that we can sell – so we've launched a 'no cash down, no risk' type of season ticket product. If someone is willing to give $50 to guarantee a seat location, that is a great step. Creating a sense of urgency when there really isn't one is tough.

Outside of ticketing, the NHL controls our national broadcast deal, and our local broadcasting deal doesn't expire for a few years; so our ability to create ways to generate revenue without tickets is quite limited. One way might be to find different ways we can engage our partners and activate that within the building; the second could be a digital solution. I don't have an answer for that, but when I think about Pokémon Go and the ability to create small, incremental add-ons (ex: $1.99 for something special), not many in sports have that type of solution right now. We're looking at a way we can create a low-cost product that drives value to fans but that can produce an incremental revenue stream. Think about it – our main revenue streams are sponsorship, broadcasting, and ticketing; but what does that look like if we're facing a long term without fans at our games? Ticketing is pretty much out of the window; when it comes to sponsorship, a lot of companies are facing difficulties as it is – and in broadcasting the deals are already written.

Aaron specifically says that one of the outputs of his work is generating leads for his telesales team, but this principal of a team of people making calls doesn't exist to the same level over here in Europe. So I asked him what percentage of his output is focussed on generating sales leads for telesales versus taking people through the sales process digitally:

> I think this is where we're really starting to drive more to the next-best-action type of model. Our prototypical sales model would have been driving the best lead to the sales team and having them make a call. Well, right now, fewer people are buying over the phone, and fewer people are buying season tickets, so we need to get more hyper-segmented and offer them the right product at the right time. And this is where we'll start to utilise these different channels – more text messaging, more email, even direct mail, digital advertising – so we can aggregate that data to determine the next best action.
>
> We are transitioning to that type of model, and while we are not there yet, I'm of the view that if you're not transitioning you're going to get left behind, because when's the last time you answered a call from a number you didn't know? There are certain demographics that prefer that one-on-one interaction, but younger generations – the future of our industry –don't engage on the phone. We need to find creative ways to introduce them to our team, to grow their fandom, and then the revenue will come. It may be a zero-human-touch type of relationship that gets them there. That doesn't mean that a human touch is not important, but the steps to create the relationship will be digital.

At the end of my case studies I like to ask what advice our industry expert would give to someone who hasn't yet reached their level, but instead I asked Aaron what he would have done differently six months ago had he seen this coming – how could he have better prepared had he been aware that the coronavirus was on our doorstep?

> If I could step back six months, I would be asking myself to consider how we generate revenue if we don't have fans in the building. Teams are losing 50–60% of their revenues, and the minor leagues are struggling. Our sport relies on having people in the building – our industry and our company, AEG, is heavily reliant on large gatherings. While we can find ways to engage our sponsors and generate fan revenue without having games, there's nothing that creates that affinity like the live experience.

So now that Aaron is thinking about revenue generation without fans in his arena, we move on to discuss the future, putting aside COVID-19, to a time when his arena is always full or the reach of the Kings is global, and he has a huge number of people who can't come to the stadium because there are no spare tickets or they live too far away. I challenge Aaron to consider that maybe the legacy of the coronavirus is that it's brought forward his need to think about what he can sell to fans who can't get into his arena – I suggest to him that maybe it's a benefit that has come out of this challenging time. He says:

I think what we're seeing in the US is the leagues are starting to open up to international rights. The [English] Premier League, La Liga, and the main European football leagues have done a great job of growing their international fan base, and I think that's exactly what a lot of US pro teams need to do. We need to expand our reach, and by expanding our reach we're going to grow new opportunities – it's developing that fan in Slovenia (Anze Kopitar, the team's captain is Slovenian) and for the [LA] Galaxy signing Javier 'Chicharito' Hernandez and using that to build a better connection with our Mexican fan base. As we do that, we will be able to identify new brands that are wanting to partner with us because we can reach their target demographics at home and abroad. We need to create a large enough fan base so that when we introduce new products, for example merchandise, we're going to have a bigger launching point. So that is one area where we need to go.

So, going back to your question about seeing this coming six months ago, I'd like to change my answer a little bit. I would say that I would be looking at ways to grow our fanbase and how to grow the ways in which we're engaging with them. I might spend a little bit more to introduce new types of fans and capture more relevant information on those fans so we can communicate with them through this process. Let them know what we're doing, tell them our story, and really grow the relationship from there.

(Source: LeValley, 2020)

Key chapter ideas

1   The global pandemic has set distinct challenges which have impacted how businesses have operated, not least regarding their broadcasting/streaming, digital engagement, and sponsorship.
2   With the threats to how businesses can survive, it is important to acknowledge more than ever that data has a value.
3   The need to gather data leads to more highly networked stadiums, but this needs to be carried out sensitively to avoid a backlash.

4   How TV rights will operate in the future is unclear, but businesses can best prepare by ensuring that their databases are gathering rich data as this may form part of future deal negotiations.
5   Innovations like AR and VR will be increasingly brought into enhancing experiences, but their use must be introduced sensitively, which will rely on a cautious approach and data-driven development.
6   Other future developments like extending the use of AI, machine learning, and neural networks are all areas which have high requirements for data.

References

APQC. (2020). Infographic: Current state of blockchain adoption in 2020. *Supply Chain Management Review* [online]. Available at: www.scmr.com/article/infographic_current_state_of_blockchain_adoption_in_2020.

Barber, G. (2018). *I sold my data for crypto: Here's how much I made* [online]. Available at: www.wired.com/story/i-sold-my-data-for-crypto/.

Brawn, R. (2020). *FIA's first sport and mobility eConference*, 15–18 June.

Businesswire. (2019). *Global smart stadium market report 2019: Market to witness a CAGR of 23.1% between 2018–2025* [online]. Available at: www.businesswire.com/news/home/20190918005613/en/Global-Smart-Stadium-Market-Report-2019-Market.

Butler, N. (2016). *Fancy bears target USADA and British athletes in latest release of hacked documents* [online]. Available at: www.insidethegames.biz/articles/1044097/fancy-bears-target-usada-and-british-athletes-in-latest-release-of-hacked-documents.

Campbell, P. (2014). As Manchester united ban iPads from old Trafford, what else should go? *The Guardian* [online]. Available at: www.theguardian.com/football/blog/2014/aug/12/manchester-united-ban-fans-ipads-tablet-devices-old-trafford.

Carp, S. (2020). *Bundesliga pockets €4.4bn in sky and DAZN domestic TV rights deal* [online]. Available at: www.sportspromedia.com/news/bundesliga-sky-dazn-tv-rights-germany-value.

Connelly, T. (2017a). EFL broadens digital revenue streams with launch of live streaming platform. *The Drum* [online]. Available at: www.thedrum.com/news/2017/05/04/efl-broadens-digital-revenue-streams-with-launch-live-streaming-platform.

Connelly, T. (2017b). BT sport to show free 360 degree VR live stream of champions league final on YouTube. *The Drum* [online]. Available at: www.thedrum.com/news/2017/05/16/bt-sport-show-free-360-degree-vr-live-stream-champions-league-final-youtube.

Davenport, T. H. (2006). Competing on analytics. *Harvard Business Review* [online]. Available at: https://hbr.org/2006/01/competing-on-analytics.

Dixon, E. (2019). *MLB's YouTube live streams average 1.2m views* [online]. Available at: www.sportspromedia.com/news/mlb-youtube-streaming-viewing-figures-baseball.

Dixon, E. (2020). *Study: Sports sponsorship spend to fall US$17.2bn in 2020* [online]. Available at: www.sportspromedia.com/news/sports-sponsorship-rights-spend-2020-study-two-circles-coronavirus.

Dogtiev, A. (2020). Pokémon GO revenue and usage statistics. *Business of Apps* [online]. Available at: www.businessofapps.com/data/pokemon-go-statistics/.

Draper, L. C. (2019). Fans excited to "Pose With The Pros". *Dallas Cowboys* [online]. Available at: https://www.dallascowboys.com/news/fans-excited-to-pose-with-the-pros.

Franklin-Wallis, O. (2020). *There's a big fight brewing over the premier league's player data* [online]. Available at: www.wired.co.uk/article/project-red-card-football-data.

Gartner. (2020). *Gartner glossary* [online]. Available at: www.gartner.com/en/information-technology/glossary/infonomics.

Grand View Research. (2020). *Artificial intelligence market size worth $733.7 billion by 2027* [online]. Available at: www.grandviewresearch.com/press-release/global-artificial-intelligence-ai-market.

The Guardian. (2014). *PSV Eindhoven fans protest against introduction of Wi-Fi at stadium* [online]. Available at: www.theguardian.com/football/2014/aug/18/psv-fans-protest-against-wifi-access.

Impey, S. (2020). *BT sport to air champions league final on YouTube* [online]. Available at: www.sportspromedia.com/news/bt-sport-uefa-2020-champions-league-final-free-streaming-youtube.

Jones, R. (2017). Cash no longer king as contactless payments soar in UK stores. *The Guardian* [online]. Available at: www.theguardian.com/money/2017/jul/12/cash-contactless-payments-uk-stores-cards-british-retail-consortium.

Kahn, J. (2017). Wimbledon to use IBM's Watson AI for highlights, analytics, helping fans. *Bloomberg* [online]. Available at: www.bloomberg.com/news/articles/2017-06-27/wimbledon-to-use-ibm-s-watson-ai-for-highlights-analytics-helping-fans.

LeValley, A. (2020). Senior Vice President, Business Operations and Strategy, interview by telephone, 12 July.

Lielacher, A. (2020). How many people use bitcoin in 2020? *Bitcoin Market Journal* [online]. Available at: www.bitcoinmarketjournal.com/how-many-people-use-bitcoin/.

McCorduck, P. (2004). *Machines who think*. Natick, MA: A.K. Peters.

McCormick, R. (2016). NBA rolls out Facebook Messenger chatbot to give you finals highlights on demand. *The Verge* [online]. Available at: www.theverge.com/2016/6/2/11848874/nba-rolls-out-facebook-messenger-chatbot-to-give-you-finals.

PR Newswire. (2020). *Augmented reality and virtual reality (AR & VR) market size is expected to reach USD 571.42 billion by 2025* [online]. Available at: www.prnewswire.com/news-releases/augmented-reality-and-virtual-reality-ar-vr-market-size-is-expected-to-reach-usd-571-42-billion-by-2025-valuates-reports-301004582.html.

PWC. (2019). Sports industry: Time to refocus? *PwC's Sports Survey 2019* [online]. Available at: www.pwc.ch/en/insights/sport/sports-survey-2019.html.

Redman, J. (2017.) Danish billionaire renames the rungsted capital ice rink to 'bitcoin arena'. *Bitcoin.com* [online]. Available at: https://news.bitcoin.com/danish-billionaire-renames-the-rungsted-capital-ice-rink-to-bitcoin-arena/.

Roberts, D. (2017). Amazon's NFL streaming is all about collecting ad data. *Yahoo* [online]. Available at: www.yahoo.com/amphtml/finance/news/amazon-streaming-nfl-games-collecting-ad-data-110006168.html.

Samuel, A. (1959). Some studies in machine learning using the game of checkers. *IBM Journal of Research and Development*, 3(3), pp. 210–229.

Say, N. (2020). *SportyCo says blockchain will be key to supporting the next generation of sports stars* [online]. Available at: https://coinjournal.net/news/sportyco-says-blockchain-will-be-key-to-supporting-the-next-generation-of-sports-stars/.

Smet, A., Pacthod, D., Relyea, C. and Sternfels, B. (2020). *Ready, set, go: Reinventing the organization for speed in the post-COVID-19 era*. Mckinsey & Company [online]. Available at: www.mckinsey.com/business-functions/organization/our-insights/ready-set-go-reinventing-the-organization-for-speed-in-the-post-covid-19-era.

The Stadium Business. (2019). *London stadium seeks to set new standards with wi-fi project* [online]. Available at: www.thestadiumbusiness.com/2019/11/20/london-stadium-seeks-set-new-standards-wi-fi-project/.

Tanner, A. (2014). *Others take your data for free, this site pays cash* [online]. Available at: www.forbes.com/sites/adamtanner/2014/03/03/others-take-your-data-for-free-this-site-pays-cash/#6403171d7946.

Wharton University of Pennsylvania. (2019). *Serving more than the brand: How Infosys reimagined the tennis experience* [online]. Available at: https://knowledge.wharton.upenn.edu/article/serving-brand-infosys-reimagined-tennis-experience/.

Ziegler, M. (2020). *Liverpool get £175m payout as premier league clubs agree to delay cuts to prize money* [online]. Available at: www.thetimes.co.uk/article/liverpool-get-175m-payout-as-premier-league-clubs-agree-to-delay-cuts-to-prize-money-vkg3h7qf9.

Conclusion

My intention in writing this book was to provide you with a whistle-stop, round-the-world-tour of CRM as part of your business strategy. It can seem quite complex when you're looking at it from the outside, but by providing some key areas in bite-sized chunks I've given you a glimpse at the main areas of consideration for a rights owner operating in the sports industry. We don't have the scale of operation that demands an Amazon-approach to CRM and data, but we do have the same need and intent to service our customers well. We want them to come back for more. If you're a specialist, then I'd like to think I've helped tie together some of the missing pieces for you and helped you understand how your role affects other individuals operating within your businesses. Most of all, I hope I've made the process both interesting and easy to understand.

The key message to take with you is that CRM is not just about software. Even data analysis is not just about data. To implement a data-driven approach, you need five key elements to be aligned within your business: strategy, data, technology, process, and culture – the perfect circle. Without it, your approach will not achieve the same level of success.

I also urge you, if you haven't already done so, to start thinking about how you can achieve your holy grail: an SCV that provides you with a holistic view of all your customers in one database. If you already have an SCV in place, then perhaps you're ready to consider upgrading to incorporate unknown and unstructured data into your environment and look at a CDP or consider the opportunities, particularly in relationship to sponsorship, with a DMP.

The data you have in your organisation about your stakeholders and the way you collect, store, and use it will be the game-changer for the future of your businesses. I can't overstate this. It is unparalleled in its importance to your future. While your number one priority will always be your sport, you need a sustainable infrastructure and business model to ensure its growth and longevity.

Once you have that data, not only will you be empowered to communicate with your fans, customers, participants, and other stakeholders with personalised content that maintains their attention, you'll have the tools to make fact-based decisions that will improve your ROI or ROO. You'll also be able to engage with your fans on a highly personalised level, getting the right message to the right person at the right time. Your partners will also benefit as you provide your sponsors with enhanced leverage opportunities that add another dimension to their activation plans.

The pace of technological change is constantly increasing, and while you're not expected to be an early adopter (your business needs neither require nor support that), you at least need to swim in the same lane. You can only achieve this by embracing ideas and collaborating with your colleagues to implement the technological changes that are right for you. In this digital world we can test, fail, test again, learn, and ultimately, improve.

And if there's one thing that the coronavirus has shown us – if there's one thing that we've learned as a result of the global pandemic – it is that no matter how well we think we know what's happening in our world, our industry, our sports, or our club, we could never have planned for lockdown. We could never have planned for empty stadiums, cancelled leagues, and empty sports fields. To me, this unparalleled level of uncertainty that we've now all experienced only serves to re-enforce the value of data. As someone once said (we think it was E. Williams Deming): In God we trust, all others must bring data.

The future for you, and the future for sports rights owners, is exciting. The future is data.

Index

Note: page numbers in *italic* indicate a figure and page numbers in **bold** indicate a table on the corresponding page.